WEAPONS FREE

WEAPONS FREE

Richard Boswell

Crécy Publishing Limited

Published in 1998 by
Crécy Publishing Limited,
1a Ringway Trading Estate,
Shadowmoss Road,
Manchester M22 5LH

ISBN 0 947554 67 X

Printed and bound by
Redwood Books, Trowbridge

Contents

Acknowledgements

As is customary I would like to start this book with an acknowledgement of thanks to all those who have helped me with the writing of it. However, I would like to stress that I list the following people not because it is customary to do so but because I am genuinely grateful to all those who have offered so much help and support over the last few, sometimes turbulent, years. So, thank you to my parents for always being there for me, to Kate for being the initial driving force behind the book, to Ruth for keeping it rolling and Blanca for being a big part of my life whilst the book was under its long period of construction. Thank you Tim, my long-standing flat mate and founder of the Coffee Club which rekindled so many memories, and Simon and Hugh, naval colleagues who turned out to be true friends when I needed them most. And finally to the Elder family, whose help and support in the face of such adversity has been unbelievable – I thank you dearly. To all those I haven't named, your help has not gone by unnoticed – it has been truly appreciated.

Foreword

As a military commander I was acutely aware that the personnel under my command were not just highly trained and efficient components of a fighting unit but that each was an individual, playing his or her own important role in making the team operate effectively. Never did I feel this more keenly than during Operation Desert Storm when, as Commander British Forces Middle East, I had responsibility for 45,000 men and women.

However much you work to be visible and approachable, it is inevitable that you cannot get to know each individual – what they are thinking, their hopes and fears, what motivates them. Richard Boswell was one of many pilots who ferried me around the Gulf in the aftermath of the hostilities, yet with whom I exchanged no more than a few pleasantries. It was therefore of great interest to read his personal account which chronicles one individual's effort to come to terms with suddenly being at war in the front line – the tension and uncertainties combined with the reflections upon training, comrades and loved ones.

Weapons Free also serves to highlight the Royal Navy's invaluable contribution to Operation Desert Storm, which has perhaps passed by without the recognition it deserved. Richard Boswell's description of the helicopter engagements for which he was justifiably mentioned in *Despatches*, leave no doubt as to the professionalism, commitment and courage of the Royal Navy and Fleet Air Arm when it was needed most in the Gulf War.

General Sir Peter de la Billière, KCB, KBE, DSO, MC*, MSC, DL

Introduction

During the summer of 1996 I had a chance encounter on a train with an old Navy colleague. I had never known David particularly well except that we were both Lynx helicopter pilots involved in the Gulf War. We last met at 12,000 feet above the City of Kuwait during a mock dogfight and seeing him again was a very evocative experience. I had long since left the Navy and my involvement in Operation Desert Storm was a distant memory. But during the few minutes I spent chatting with him my time spent in the Persian Gulf was brought to the forefront of my mind. This encounter prompted me to dig out and read the diaries that I had kept of that period and was the seed from which this book grew.

I wrote it for a number of reasons. Firstly because during the process of transferring the diaries onto computer disk I was encouraged to expand on them by a friend. Secondly because I felt that none of the Gulf War books that I had read dealt with the emotional side of being involved in that particular war. Lastly because during the many hours spent sitting in front of a computer screen transfering my memories into the written word, I became aware that, despite how little I actually think about the experience and perhaps because my life has changed much since that time, those few months when I was involved in the Gulf War are still important to me. This, then, is my story of how I became a Royal Navy helicopter pilot involved in a desert war thousands of miles from home and how I coped with its emotional pressure.

CHAPTER ONE

Joining the Mob

Your destiny is an achievement, not a right.

I lay on the trolley in the operating theatre waiting for the anaesthetist. This was the third operation on my eye and I was anxious about it. If this one went well I could hope for almost near to normal vision which would mean my Commercial Pilot's Licence would be returned. If it didn't go as planned I might lose sight in the eye altogether and that would be my flying career over. So the furthest thing from my mind was the Gulf conflict or my involvement in it – indeed my time in the Navy was becoming a distant memory as I attempted to carve a new life as a 'civvy'. The anaesthetist walked in and looked at my notes.

"Hello Richard, so you're the pilot that's having the eye operation."

He started chatting away to put me at ease before administering the anaesthetic.

"I see you used to be in the Royal Navy," he continued, "I love flying. Back home I was in the airforce for a while as a junior doctor, I used to go flying with the guys as often as possible – I really enjoyed it."

I was feeling drowsy from the pre-med, but attempted to have a conversation as the anaesthetist prepared his drugs.

"Where are you from?" I enquired.

"Oh, I'm from Iraq, I still have a house just outside Baghdad."

As he administered the anaesthetic, I smiled. The last thing I remember thinking before the drug took control was that this really is a crazy mixed up world.

The day that I decided to pursue aviation as a career is still a very vivid memory. I was the princely age of ten sitting in an aunt's back garden that lay directly under the Heathrow approach path. My family had emigrated to Africa some two years previously and this was our first visit back to England. The sheer quantity of aircraft in the sky amazed me. Had I been permanently resident in London I probably would never have noticed the aerial ballet that takes place overhead every day but, being re-exposed to it, I found it fascinating. My father, bored of my constant quizzing as to the identity of the aircraft above, bought me a 'spotter's' book of aeroplanes. By the time we returned to Africa a week later, having read the book numerous times and spent most of the flight back home bothering the crew, I was hooked. I then followed the path that thousands of kids all over the world have taken, spending all of my spare time hanging around the local airfield and hassling people for rides in exchange for helping them refuel or wash their aeroplanes. At the time my family was resident in what was Rhodesia, and a small grass strip just outside of Bulawayo, the city we had made our home, became my weekend residence. It was called *Induna* which means 'meeting place' in *Ndebele,* the local language. For me it was just that, affording me the opportunity to meet a wealth of different people, the majority of whom were aviation enthusiasts. I was fortunate enough to be taken under the proverbial wing of some of the club members which led to weekends and school holidays spent flying around the country in light aircraft and learning the rudimentary flying techniques. By the time I sat my O levels I had no doubt in my mind as to what career I would be following. I had been bitten by the aviation bug and try as I might, it would not go away.

During the run up to my exams I applied to join the national airforce. However, by this time Rhodesia had become Zimbabwe and, quite rightly, priority was being given to the local African population as far as recruitment into any government organisation was concerned. It was at this time that a lot of fear and many unfounded rumours were spreading around the ex-patriot community within Zimbabwe as to how we would be treated and, to my utter horror, my family decided to return to England.

Zimbabwean laws at the time stated that very little money could be taken out of the country so on our return to the UK we were at the mercy of the welfare state. Having been used to a large house with a swimming pool and domestic help, I found it unbelievably difficult to adjust to a family of four sharing a one-bedroom council flat. It was time to leave and start my career as a pilot. Unable to raise the kind of cash required to undertake even a Private Pilot's Licence course, never mind a Commercial Pilot's Licence, I decided that the military was the ideal option and immediately applied to join the Royal Air Force.

At the time I was completely unaware of the thousands of applications that the RAF receive every year and I had no idea about the rigorous selection procedure that the candidates are subjected to. All I knew, or indeed cared, was that I wanted to be a pilot and I believed, in my own mind, that I would make a very good one. It therefore came as something of a shock when, having been invited to the local RAF careers office, I was advised to return to school and re-apply after completing my A levels. Rejected and disillusioned I walked back to the station for the journey home.

I had almost walked past the 'FLY NAVY–JOIN HERE' poster in the Navy careers office window before it caught my eye. From the moment I walked through the door, my application was taken far more seriously and I was treated like an adult. Over the next few months I completed the selection procedure which culminated in a three day AIB (Admiralty Interview Board) in Portsmouth. At the end of the three days I waited with very sweaty hands to be called in front of the board for the last time and receive the results. The captain looked over his horn rimmed spectacles and spoke in an authoritative manner.

"Richard we are afraid that we cannot offer you a position, we suggest that you go back to school and re-apply once you have taken your

A levels."

I got the message. I enrolled at the local sixth form college to start on an A level course but the next two years proved to be very difficult. I had trouble adjusting to the English schooling system compared to the peremptory system I had grown accustomed to in Zimbabwe. I made very few friends and never really settled. Perhaps more importantly, there was no local airfield where I could loiter at weekends. I joined the Air Training Corps which afforded me the opportunity of flying in a Chipmunk from time to time, but I missed the atmosphere that surrounds a flying club and people 'talking aeroplanes'. After the first year of the course I reapplied to the RAF with a view to joining on completion of my exams and, this time, my application was taken far more seriously. I successfully completed the selection procedure and was offered a place at RAF Cranwell to start my officer training the following summer. However the news was not all rosy: the offer was subject to further medical examinations as a very slight abnormality had been discovered on my ECG; I had one or two 'extra heartbeats' that could not be explained.

To me it was obvious: being strapped to this machine with wires glued to my chest, knowing the importance of the outcome, was a fairly large stressor in itself and my heart was beating twenty to the dozen. Extensive tests were carried out, both by RAF and civilian doctors all of which proved inconclusive. Everybody agreed that my heart appeared to look, and function, perfectly normally apart from these 'extra' heartbeats. I was therefore horrified and distraught when I received the letter informing me that it had been agreed that I was unfit for military flying.

They say that bad luck runs in threes and, for me, this has generally proved correct. At the same time that I received this news I learned that I had failed my mock exams and, in addition, the local education authority advised that I was not eligible for a student grant to continue my education at university (due to the fact that I had not been resident in the country for three years prior to the application). I was devastated by the news of not being fit to fly and going to university had always been my contingency plan. I grudgingly started to look around for another option.

It was during a visit to the schools career office that I bumped into the naval officer who had conducted my initial interview some eighteen months before. Recognising me, he quizzed me as to whether I was still interested in pursuing a career in the Navy. I was wise enough not to mention my rejection, on medical grounds, from the RAF and, rather casually, I suggested that I was considering completing a degree before reapplying but was having trouble obtaining a grant. It was the beginning of the boom time in the mid-eighties and all major organisations were waking up to the problem of recruiting people in large numbers. With all the finesse of an accomplished used car salesman, the recruiting officer sold me the apparent solution to all of my problems: I could apply to join the Navy as an Air Engineer. If my application was successful they would send me to their own university to complete a degree in aeronautical engineering, after which I would be in a position to train as a pilot and become a Maintenance Test Pilot – a flying engineer. This appeared to be the answer to all my prayers and, as I was applying to become an engineer, the medical examination would not be nearly as thorough; even if I did not pass the subsequent flying medical, at least I would be able to complete a degree in an aviation related subject.

This time the selection procedure ran more smoothly. I was an old hand at the routine and passed with little problem having learned what I was required to say and when to say it. Yes, I was sure that I wanted to be an engineer, I lied like a cheap Japanese watch. I wanted to fly and saw this, purely and simply, as a back door in. I passed the Board and received a letter informing me that I would be starting my officer training at the Britannia Royal Naval College, Dartmouth on completion of my A levels.

During the train journey to Devon that September it had been easy to spot the other new entrants; we were the fresh faced youths dressed in suits, all looking extremely apprehensive as to what lay ahead. In the forthcoming weeks and months we would be transferred from useless 'civvies' into young naval officers. As we arrived at Totnes station the mingling cadets were efficiently herded onto the waiting queues of military buses to be transported to the college.

I was eighteen years old, had always lived at home, and was unbelievably nervous. The military was a ticket to fly but, having never considered what it would be like to be part of a military organisation, suddenly it was becoming very real. I was so terrified that I could barely speak, the chap sitting next to me on the coach tried to initiate a conservation but soon gave up when he realised that I was barely capable of stringing a coherent sentence together. The buses dropped us off at the parade ground situated at the front of the building and overlooked on three sides by some magnificent turn-of-the-century architecture but I noticed none of this as we were bustled off the coaches and people started shouting at us.

"NAME!" A naval chap in full uniform bellowed in my ear.

"B...B...Boswell, Sir," I eventually managed to mutter.

"I am not a Sir," he boomed back at me, "I work for my living. I am Petty Officer Jones, but you can call me Petty Officer Jones, now move over there. NOW!"

I was young and naive enough to think that he actually meant it when he raised his voice at me. I wanted to be back home with my Mum.

We were divided into five 'Divisions' all of which were named after famous Admirals, the girls making up one small division and the rest of us divided amongst the other four. I was assigned to Cunningham Division and we sorted into groups of four or five people to be assigned 'Sea-Daddies'. These were chaps that had joined the college in the previous entry, some fourteen weeks before, and so were considered old hands by us new boys. They were to be our mentors for the first few days and introduce us to the rigours of life at Dartmouth.

They took us round on a brief tour of the college and arranged for us to collect our uniforms. They showed us how to iron them into perfect squares to fit into our chests-of-drawers and how to polish our shoes into a perfect shine. But, most importantly, they introduced us to the new language that we would be using for the rest of our naval careers – 'Jack-Speak'. Deckheads, bulkheads, stokers, stovies, Killick, Subby: the list just seemed endless. The first twenty-four hours were just a blur of running around not knowing what was happening, ironing brand new clothes that would never be worn and hours spent polishing shoes when, normally, I would have been sleeping.

The accommodation for the new recruits varied between twenty-man dormitories and two-men 'cabins'. I was accommodated in a four-man 'mess deck' and the other three recruits consisted of Andy, a northerner who spoke with a thick accent and sniffed after every sentence, Paul, a recent history graduate who had been in the Royal Naval Reserves whilst at university (and hence knew the ropes a lot better than most), and finally Al Sheri, an Arab from the Saudi Navy, who, along with a number of other Arabs from many different Middle Eastern countries, had come to England to complete his basic officer training. Later in the evening of our first day we were visited by our Divisional Officers (DOs), members of the Dartmouth training staff who were responsible for converting the recruits into something useful to the Navy. We were each assigned a five minute slot for a personal interview with our respective DO.

"Right, what's your name?" Lieutenant Ford opened the conversation in a rather curt manner.

Nick Ford was what is known as a Special Duties Officer, somebody who had joined the Navy as an Ordinary Seaman and worked his way up through the ranks to become an officer.

"Richard Boswell." I replied, trying to appear confident.

"Wrong, you are Midshipman Boswell now, and that's how you should respond, OK?"

This was my first introduction to the rigid social structure that encompasses service life, and something the rebellious streak in me rigorously opposed.

"Yes, Sir." I replied, still feeling like Richard Boswell.

"So you are an Engineer," he commented whilst shuffling through his paperwork. "Are you happy with what your training will entail over the next five years?"

"Yes Sir, I am an Air Engineer and I'm due to start at the Royal Naval Engineering College, Manadon, next year after a year of officer training."

He looked at me in a slightly bemused manner.

"Well you are half right Midshipman Boswell, you will be starting Manadon next year but you will not know what sphere you will specialise in until two thirds of the way through your degree course."

Now it was my turn to look confused.

"But I was informed that I was definitely joining as an Air Engineer."

"You have obviously misunderstood, the Navy has only a very small requirement for Air Engineers, the majority of Manadon graduates complete their training to become Weapons or Marine Engineers, so you had better get used to the idea."

I left the interview feeling very confused about exactly what I had let

My wardrobe ready for inspection.

myself in for.

Later that evening our mess deck was visited by one of the 'Seniors' in the Division. He had joined the Navy as a pilot and was due to graduate from Dartmouth and start his flying training at the end of the term. I discussed my plight with him and, quite by chance, it transpired that he had also applied to join the Royal Air Force but had been rejected on medical grounds. I took a great deal of encouragement from what he had to say.

The following morning, after all of about three hours sleep, we awoke to the first day of our New Entry Period. It began with a tannoy getting us up at 0600 for a period of Early Morning Activities (EMAs). These consisted of an hour's exercise before breakfast and took the form of different activities on different days. On day one it was a five mile run around the hills that surrounded the college. By the end of it, I was reminded of exactly how unfit I was. EMA's were a daily feature of the routine during the first month at Dartmouth.

One of the early lectures that first morning was on the role of the Royal Navy in the modern world. Much emphasis was placed on the fact that we had joined a fighting service and that we could be called upon to fight and kill. I treated the lecture with a certain amount of disdain, the only fighting the Navy had been involved in recently was the Falklands Conflict and a war like that was extremely unlikely to happen again. I was not interested in fighting or being any kind of hero; all I wanted to do was fly.

That lunchtime, whilst waiting in the queue, I struck up a conversation with a guy in the same Division who was standing next to me. I learned that he was a couple of years older than me and, on leaving school, had taken a job in a bank. After a while he had become bored by the routine nine-to-five existence and had joined the Navy as a method of seeking some excitement. Like us all he had never before thought of the consequences of going to war and that one day he might be called upon to fight and kill. However, he was troubled by the thought of it all and wondered if he had made the right decision in seeking a military career. This was not a major issue for me at that time, but Chris and I subsequently became, and stayed, extremely good friends, and in retrospect I realise how poignant that conversation was. However his uncertainty did cause me to question my own career options more deeply, and when Chris had the courage of his convictions to air his doubts with the senior officers at Dartmouth, I followed suit and approached my Divisional Officer with a request to transfer to flying duties.

For some strange reason flying is considered a glamorous job and those recruits who had joined to train as aircrew were looked on with envy by the rest of the cadets. They were organised into consecutively numbered 'flights', groups of *ab initio* aircrew who had joined at the same time. Each flight quickly formed a close knit community which was linked by the common bond of the joy of aviation. The team spirit amongst the flights was very apparent and although they suffered all the rigours of Dartmouth, exactly the same as the rest of the recruits, there was always a far greater sense of enjoyment amongst the flyers. My application to transfer to flying duties was treated with disdain as, it seemed, everybody wanted to be a pilot: I had joined as an Engineer and that, apparently, is how it would have to stay. This reaction from Nick Ford, my DO, angered me, and from then on our relationship was always frosty. Having gained no headway from that avenue I approached the Flight Training Officer (FTO), the officer responsible for overseeing the training of all aircrew at Dartmouth.

During this time the short, sharp, New Entry shock treatment was continuing – the daylight hours filled with practical training on the parade ground and lectures in the classroom; evenings spent cleaning and polishing. Trying to fit a fifteen minute break into the timetable to visit the FTO proved extremely difficult and it was some two weeks before I managed to see him. In the meantime I had not exactly proved to be the perfect recruit: young and naive, I was insecure and lacked the self-confidence and self-assurance that other cadets appeared to have. Part of the reason for this was that I did not want to be an Engineer in the Navy and therefore wondered exactly what I was doing at Dartmouth. Nick Ford and I had formed a relationship of mutual dislike for one another and, as he was directly responsible for assessing my performance, it came as no surprise to learn from him that I was not doing too well on the course in terms of achievement.

When I eventually met the FTO, a Lieutenant Kim Slowe, I achieved more than I had done with my DO. Kim was what is known as a General List (GL) officer who had joined the Navy as a career man, signing up for life as a Seaman Officer, responsible for driving and fighting ships. Some years after joining he had specialised as aircrew and become a helicopter pilot serving with distinction in the Falklands campaign. Normally the GL officers were extremely career minded and all sought to become admirals, hence they behaved with the due amount of decorum. Kim was the exact opposite and rumour had it that he was nicknamed Pig-Pen by his fellow officers on the staff at Dartmouth due to his inability to look smart no matter what he was wearing. He took a slightly more sympathetic line when I aired my case and promised to make some enquiries concerning the possibility of transferring.

Some two weeks passed and I had still not heard any reply from the FTO. My performance continued to be only just satisfactory. One of the key elements of the New Entry period was to assess whether you were truly motivated toward becoming a Naval Officer. I quite blatantly was not, and my reports reflected this. It was becoming a classic Catch-22 situation: I knew that I would have to be well above average to have even a glimmer of hope of being transferred, and yet I had no interest in the Navy outside of wanting to be a pilot and, as a result, was extremely poorly motivated. I returned to see the FTO, hoping that he would have some positive news for me. Not surprisingly he had done nothing since my last visit and so I aired my frustration, and spoke somewhat out of turn as I insisted that I wanted to be considered for flying duties and would leave the Navy if nobody was even prepared to hear my case.

I'm not sure whether my heart-felt plea struck a chord, or he just wanted to get rid of me, but while I waited in the office the FTO phoned the MOD office responsible for appointing aircrew and, after a lengthy discussion, he put the phone down and turned to me.

"They may be prepared to offer you a transfer to flying duties as an Observer providing you successfully pass the Observer grading and the Engineering appointer agrees to release you."

I did not know what to say. I had never considered a career as an Observer, an airborne tactician who sits in the back of a Sea King helicopter and directs the anti-submarine battle.

"I will have to consider this Sir. Is there absolutely no chance of becoming a pilot?"

The FTO looked agitated.

"Look Boswell, I'm surprised that you have been offered the opportunity to transfer at all, now I suggest that you go away and make up your mind as soon as possible and stop messing people around."

With that the meeting ended and I left feeling totally perplexed about what I wanted to do.

The following day seven members of my class and I left the college to undertake a three day practical leadership exercise on Dartmoor (PLX as it is known at Dartmouth). From the very first day we had been indoctrinated with the rationale that, no matter what our specialisations, first and foremost we were Naval Officers and leaders of men. Hence we embarked on a period of training that was designed to teach us the fundamentals of leadership and to hone the natural leadership ability that we were all assessed to possess by virtue of the fact that we had passed the Admiralty Interview Board. Looking at my own performance, and some of those around me, I seriously doubted that particular theory.

The leadership training started with lectures in the classroom and encompassed the theory of good management, introducing us to the principle of 'Action Centred Leadership' – the practicalities of balancing the task, the team and the individual, to produce the desired results in a multitude of different situations. We were also given laminated business cards which, in diagrammatic form, covered the basic principles behind successful leadership and we were expected to keep these in our wallets to provide a quick access guide in the future. Even at the time of issue I had this mental image of a Captain, sailing his ship into a ferocious sea battle and then stopping his vessel in the water, while he casually removed his actioned centred leadership card from his wallet and pondered over what he should do next. I kept the card in my wallet for many years and it always brought a wry smile to my face every time I used it to scrape ice off my car.

The practical aspect of our leadership training started with some very simple tasks, such as building a make-shift bridge out of poles and rope across a garden path. We were taught how to assess the objective of the task and then brief the team accordingly. The scenarios often became comical to me as we spent the first five minutes of the allotted ten briefing the team members on what had to be done and who was going to do it. The following five minutes would then be spent in complete pandemonium as we got in each others way trying to get five people to complete a task which two people could have done in no time at all. There was great emphasis placed on people taking command of the teams and I became tired of the expression, "Take charge of your team Midshipman Boswell."

The practical side of the leadership training culminated in the three day PLX. The theory was simple. In teams, the cadets would walk between different locations situated across Dartmoor in order that they would become increasingly fatigued. At each location they would be allocated tasks to lead so that their ability, as team leaders and players, could be assessed under fairly stressful conditions. Whilst it was nowhere near as physical as the route marches that the new entry Royal Marines had to endure, it had a reputation for being a gruelling experience. I started my PLX in entirely the wrong frame of mind. I had, more or less, decided to reject the offer to become an Observer as I wanted to be a pilot, and accepting the transfer would undoubtedly mean that I would never be completely happy in my work. As the three days passed, and the rain continued to fall, I wondered exactly what I was doing walking over the Dartmoor Tors with a back-pack full of rocks, carrying them as a punishment for arriving two minutes late at a previous checkpoint. At first I took the whole exercise as a bit of joke, but after being reprimanded for not taking the exercise seriously, I began to lose interest and the hills became steeper and the back-pack heavier. My performance was less than satisfactory.

The walk off the moor was a long and lonely one in which I had time to reflect. I knew that I was not meeting the required standard to become a Naval Officer, the reasons were plentiful but there was still no excuse for the poor performance. This left me with a dilemma: if I left the Navy I would not be able to apply to the RAF again as they were convinced that I was medically unfit; if I reapplied to the Navy to join as a pilot I would stand little chance of succeeding given my current performance. Things were beginning to look a little grim.

Shortly after my return to Dartmouth I was greeted by the grinning Lieutenant Ford who informed me that I would be invited to return to the moor the following week to retake the PLX as I had officially failed this part of the leadership training. I was convinced that he was delighted at the news and hoped I would throw in the towel. After three days of being rained upon and with a fine collection of blisters resident on my feet, the last thing that I felt like doing was returning to Dartmoor to do it all again. Leaving the Navy *now* was what I really wanted to do and yet I knew that I would be throwing away my last vague hope of becoming a pilot. As we had just returned from the moor we were given a rare treat – the afternoon off. I used my time to return to the FDO and tell him that I did not want to be an Observer. He was indifferent to the news and dismissed me from his office as soon as I had delivered it.

From that moment my approach towards the Navy changed completely. I knew that I was not going to stay and therefore the pressure of embarking on a career that I did not really want was taken from me. I made the decision to complete the first term – merely as an academic exercise – then resign at the end, safe in the knowledge that I had not failed. I started to enjoy myself a lot more and, the second time around, the PLX was a flying success: I passed with extremely complimentary reports being written on me.

Perhaps one of the most enjoyable aspects of the whole training regime was the parade ground training where we were taught how to march and stand to attention. The parade ground staff were all old and bold Senior Ratings who appeared to have been in the Navy since Nelson's times.

Gas masks and caps were issued.

They never spoke, they always shouted and, after we saw through the hard-man façade, everybody began to look forward to their drill sessions. Two of the greatest characters were Petty Officer Jones, the first person that I had met on my arrival at Dartmouth, and Colour Sergeant Rogers, on detachment from the Royal Marines. The parade ground, situated at the front of the college, was their kingdom and they ruled over it as a pride of lions would rule their domain. Even the Captain of the College gave the parade ground a wide birth and only proceeded onto it when he had to – and with Rogers' or Jones' permission.

Initially we were taught how to march in a straight line and come to a halt in unison. We were all co-ordinated and educated chaps; one might have assumed that trying to teach a group of twenty of us to march in step and stop together would be a relatively easy task. The reality was far removed. There was always at least one person who got it wrong and this would throw the rest of the group into complete disarray. One of the most common problems was 'ticktocking', moving one's left arm in rhythm with one's left leg rather than with the right diagonally opposed. Trying to do this in the privacy of your own home proved very difficult and one looked liked some kind of primitive android. However, as soon as you stepped onto the parade ground, ticktocking became the most natural thing in the world, much to the frustration of the parade ground staff. One particular individual who never really got to grips with the task of marching was Steve Murphy, a small, shambolic Yorkshireman.

Steve quickly assumed cult-hero status among the group for his total lack of co-ordination on parade and his complete ambivalence towards the frustration that he caused the staff.

"MR MURPHY, YOU ARE AN OFFICER, IS THAT CORRECT?" Petty Officer Jones would bawl.

"Aye," Steve would reply in his Northern accent.

"IN THAT CASE I AM NOT ALLOWED TO CALL YOU A FUCK-WIT."

"Er, OK." Steve looked perplexed.

"BUT WOULD YOU AGREE THAT THERE IS NOTHING TO STOP ME THINKING THAT YOU ARE A FUCKWIT?" The Petty Officer continued to boom over the parade ground with his face less than six inches from Steve's.

"That's right PO."

"WELL MR MURPHY, I THINK YOU ARE A FUCKWIT, NOW STOP FUCKING TICKTOCKING"

The rest of the group would dissolve into hysterics at PO Jones's pontifications and it would always draw the same response.

"I NEVER GAVE ANYBODY PERMISSION TO LAUGH," looking some poor individual in the eye as if he had incited the rest of the group to be subversive.

Once we had mastered the fine art of basic drill technique we moved onto sword drill. This proved equally hilarious but this time with more than just a hint of danger, as people who could barely walk in a straight

Enjoying a quiet cup of coffee when it all becomes too much.

line on the parade ground, were let loose with swords. Once again Steve proved to be a constant source of entertainment. On one occasion we were being taught how to move to 'attention' with the sword from the 'at ease' position. As usual Steve had managed to get completely out of phase with everyone else and while we all had our swords resting on our shoulders, Steve was standing at the end of the line blissfully unaware that his sword was held upright. Standing next to him was Chris who, like us all, showed a remarkable ineptitude for sword drill from time to time. Hearing everybody begin to chuckle at Steve's cock-up he looked at Steve and then looked down the line to see everybody with their swords on their shoulders and began to chuckle with the rest of the group. PO Jones marched up to Chris, stood in front of him and smiled. Unfortunately for Chris, his own sword was also held vertical and, as he laughed at Steve's incompetence, with PO Jones standing in front of him, a wry smile on his face, it gradually dawned on him that he had made exactly the same mistake. The expression on his face, as he looked at his own sword and then down the line to the rest of us, was an absolute treat. Chris turned back to PO Jones who, try as he might to look stern, was obviously suppressing the greatest urge he had ever had to collapse in hysterics.

"I guess that you think that I am a Fuckwit as well Petty Officer Jones!" Chris smiled.

Steve was still completely unaware of what was going on and Petty Officer Jones had to leave the parade ground while we all collapsed into fits of uncontrollable laughter.

One of the other tasks that initially seemed tiresome, but soon provided a limitless source of entertainment, was the daily cleaning for rounds. Each day the living accommodation and ablution blocks would be inspected by a member of the Dartmouth staff. We would spend the hour preceding the inspection cleaning and polishing in order to ensure that the place was immaculate. A task that required no mental effort, such as polishing a brass door handle or cleaning a shower unit, was a welcome relief after eight hours of lessons and three hours of physical exercise, especially when you knew that there was at least another four hours revision required during the evening, to prepare for the classes the following day. We would take it in turns to be responsible for organising the cleaning of the Division as a whole and report to the inspecting officer.

The one problem with being in charge of organising the cleaning was the international cadets. A lot of the Middle Eastern guys came from particularly affluent families – some of them were senior members of the Arab Royal Families – and, therefore, refused point blank to become involved in what they believed was beneath them. As the term progressed, and the team spirit began to evolve, the majority of the foreign cadets came round and agreed to help out. There was, however, one particular young Iraqi chap who adamantly refused to help out with the cleaning and, whenever there was any to be done, would mysteriously disappear off the face of the earth. Al-Shamari became a legend for his ability to be rude to everybody and never help out.

On one particular occasion Steve Murphy was in charge of organising the cleaning and, as one might expect, chaos ensued. Steve walked around blissfully unaware that we were due for inspection in a matter of minutes and that the Division was nowhere near ready. I passed him in the corridor and tried to instill some sense of urgency.

"Mate, there's still a bag of shit around the corner which needs to be cleaned away," referring to a bag of rubbish that had been left on the floor by some frustrated cadet, presumably fed up with the endless tidying.

Steve looked completely non-plussed, "It's not that bloody Al-Shamari is it? I've been looking for him all day."

And, with that, he wandered off leaving the rest of us in hysterics again.

After the initial four week New Entry Period the pace slackened off a little and we were even allowed to leave the college on Saturday nights provided that we were back 'onboard' by midnight. Before we had time to realise how quickly time was passing, the end of term was approaching and, having made a significant improvement in my performance, I decided it was time to hand in my resignation, or 'Volret' as it was known, so that I would be a civilian over Christmas and could begin the New Year applying to rejoin as a pilot. I carefully drafted my resignation letter in the formal manner that we had been taught over the previous weeks and months. My relationship with Nick Ford was still frosty and he made no comment when I handed the letter in other than to inform me that I would have to have an interview with the Senior Divisional Officer before I could leave. I duly booked the interview for the following day and it passed without incident; I was referred on to the Commander in Charge of Training, who oversaw all training issues at the college.

Commander 'T', as he was referred to, was a pilot himself and the interview took a very different course to those before.

"I understand your frustration Richard, but remember there is still a chance that you may be selected as an Air Engineer and Test Pilot, while there is no guarantee that you will get re-selected as a pilot if you leave and try and rejoin."

This interview was far less formal than previous ones. I felt as though I could talk and what I had to say would be listened to.

"I realise that, Sir, but I would not be happy as an Engineer. Arriving at the college has made me realise that the only thing that I want to do is fly aeroplanes: the desire to be a Naval Officer is secondary to that, so I am willing to take the chance."

He nodded wisely. I believe that had he been in my position he would have done exactly the same. As I was on my way out of the office he called me back.

"Richard, the next part of the training is three months spent in the West Indies on the aircraft carrier, HMS *Invincible*. If I were you I would resign on completion of that; at least you will get to see some naval flying operations in action, and you will get a three month trip to the West Indies to boot. Rather then spend three months enduring an English winter, I know what I would do."

This was an option that I had not considered before. Commander 'T' continued, "If you like I will hold your Volret letter here until you return at the end of next term and then we can continue this conversation; at least you will have a suntan then."

I had absolutely nothing to lose, "You have sold the idea to me Sir, I will see you back here in three months time."

The decision to stay for an extra three months was made on the spur of the moment and left me with a lot of preparation to do during the final few days of the term. All of my uniform had to be carefully folded and packed and new items, such as tropical uniform, had to be drawn from stores. Everybody else had completed these tasks in previous weeks, so while the remainder of the cadets with whom I had joined began to let their hair down, I was running around preparing for the forthcoming deployment. For a nineteen year old recent school leaver the trip sounded extremely exciting – we were due to visit such exotic places as Barbados, Antigua, Florida and the Bahamas.

After an all too short Christmas break spent at home, I headed for Portsmouth and my first excursion into a naval dockyard. These can be intimidating places at the best of times, and arriving in the dark and walking towards the overbearing silhouette of a 25,000-ton warship in the distance was an eerie and somewhat frightening experience. My emotions were very similar to those that I had experienced when joining Dartmouth some three months previously. The idea behind the Dartmouth Training Ship (DTS) was to give us practical experience of living and working at sea. We were accommodated in ratings' messdecks and ate in the ratings' din-

Four o'clock in the morning and the cleaning continues. Steve Murphy (left) begins to become a legend.

ing halls, in order that we could experience this unique existence before we enjoyed the rather more privileged lifestyle that accompanies life in the Wardroom. On arrival at the ship I was escorted down to my messdeck by another Officer Under Training (OUT) and my first impression was that the ship was enormous – I would never be able to find my way out again. I was shown to my bunkspace and was just amazed at how little space was allocated to each man. There were thirty of us accommodated in a mess-deck that was no bigger than 30 by 20 feet.

We were completely reshuffled from our previous classes and divisions and I was sharing the accommodation with a number of people who, although had also spent the previous months at Dartmouth, I had never met before. The ship spent two days alongside in Portsmouth allowing us to acclimatise with the ship's routine before she actually put to sea. A number of the ship's company had been removed in order to create enough room to accommodate us all, so there were certain tasks that we had to be familiar with in order for the ship to be safe before she left harbour. These tasks included competency in handling the ropes used to secure the ship alongside and the regular cleaning that had to be completed every day. Therefore the first forty-eight hours were extremely intensive and we were all glad when the ship finally set sail.

That euphoria was very short-lived. The ship left the confines of Portsmouth Sound and sailed straight into a storm, which persisted for three days as we set out across the Atlantic. Ninety percent of the new recruits were violently sea-sick and there was a constant queue of people waiting outside the toilets (heads) for their opportunity to say goodbye to their breakfast. I do not hold a particularly fond memory of those few days. After the weather had abated, things began to settle down and the new routines were established. We would spend a week in each department: the first week peeling potatoes in the galley, the next learning to navigate on the bridge, followed by a week standing watches in the engine room and learning about the gas turbines that propelled the ship through the water. Each week introduced us to a new sphere of the ship's routine and, gradually, we adapted to the strange existence that is life onboard a warship. I set out to treat the whole experience as a holiday, courtesy of the Navy, and made no bones about it to anybody, including my new Divisional Officer. He seemed impressed by my frankness and, as a relatively young man himself who was coming to the end of his short service commission of eight years, he was able to relate to my attitude and, somewhat, respected it.

I enjoyed life onboard but, even more, I enjoyed the ship's visits to the West Indian islands. We started off with a three day stop in Barbados. During the time spent alongside we still took our early morning activities at 6 am but these generally consisted of a gentle run along the beach, to shake off the hangovers before the morning lessons began. We would continue with the lessons until lunchtime and, after lunch, a couple of hours was spent working in the respective departments, generally being free to do our own thing by mid-afternoon. We all convened around one of the hotel swimming pools and drank rum punches until it poured out of our ears. We were supposed to be back onboard by midnight but, as this was my holiday and the rule was not rigorously enforced, I gave it a damn good ignoring and partied well into the early hours of the morning. From Barbados we proceeded to Antigua and then onto Granada followed by the Bahamas. The highlight of the trip was a weeks visit to Fort Lauderdale in Florida where we were all to be given four days 'station leave'. This meant that we were not required to return back onboard the ship every night. We all looked forward to it with great anticipation and it lived up to all expectations.

As mentioned earlier Chris and I had become very close friends during the time at Dartmouth and then onboard *Invincible*. Together with two other friends we decided that we would hire a car and drive to Orlando for our four day's station leave. On the day that we arrived the car was waiting for us on the jetty and, as soon as leave was 'piped', Chris and I decided to go for a drive around Fort Lauderdale. Cruising around town, with Madonna's 'Holiday' blasting out of the speakers, we really felt as though we had made it. Even better was the fact that our trip coincided with Spring Break and most of the student population of North America had assembled in Fort Lauderdale. Even as we waited at the traffic lights we were accosted by a group of young female students who appeared to love our accents and insisted we joined them for a party that evening. As an inexperienced nineteen year old I thought that I had died and gone to heaven.

The leave in Orlando and Disney World was a roaring success and a good time was had by all, except for my bank balance! I was glad that I had decided to stay for the deployment and had thoroughly enjoyed every second of it. However, America was our final visit and, following a two week passage back to the UK, our trip would be over and I would soon be a civilian again. As much as I had enjoyed the deployment it had not convinced me that I wanted to stay in the Navy and become an Engineer, in fact the complete opposite was true. My time in the Engineering Department had been fairly boring and mundane, but the week spent with the Fleet Air Arm had been fascinating. The air wing onboard consisted of just three Wessex helicopters but I saw how they were maintained, watched them take-off and land and even got a flight in one to experience the joy of flying from a moving deck. This was my first trip in a helicopter and I was fascinated by it. I was intrigued by the noise and vibration but puzzled as to how the aerodynamics of it all enabled them to sustain controlled flight. More than ever before I wanted to be a pilot.

During the final days of the deployment we were read our end of term reports from our Divisional Officer. I received an extremely complimentary report which was a massive improvement on my first term. For me the whole deployment was a great success and I felt confident that the report would stand me in good stead for when I re-applied. On my return to Dartmouth I visited Commander 'T' again to state that I still wanted to Volret. He had my DTS report in front of him as I entered the office but his reaction surprised me enormously.

"Richard, you appear to have done rather well over the previous three months, are you still intent on becoming a pilot?"

The question hardly needed answering, "Yes Sir, of course."

"With this report I feel that I am now in a position to recommend you for a transfer. I can't promise you anything but I will write to the relevant people and see what I can do for you if you decide to stay!"

This threw me into turmoil. Once again I had mentally prepared myself for leaving, to the extent that most of my personnel items were already packed in my car, but, more importantly, in two days time we were due to sit our final exams which had to be passed in order to graduate from Dartmouth. They covered all of the subjects that we had studied during the previous six months and, although they were not considered particularly difficult, there was a vast amount of information to be committed to memory. The majority of the other cadets had started revising weeks in advance but I had done no work at all, convinced that I would never get to the stage of sitting the exams. I considered continuing with the original plan of leaving and reapplying. However, now that a glimmer of hope with regard to a transfer had been received, I decided to gamble and sit the exams. The big risk was now that, if I failed, I would be forced to leave the Navy, and trying to re-enter, after failing, would be practically impossible. For the next forty-eight hours I worked myself into the ground preparing for the exams. Miraculously I passed them all.

The results were, however, tinged with a certain degree of sadness. For some inexplicable reason Chris failed the exams and was forced to leave. He had become a very close and dear friend during the previous six

Enjoying a rum punch in the Caribbean.

*Dartmouth Training
Ship. Admiring the
view in Florida.*

months and, although he initially doubted his decision to embark on a
military career, he had made an impressive start and appeared to be ideally suited to the role. He was a constant tower of strength to me and kept
me going during my first few months in the Navy. The thought that such
a talent could be wasted, without even the chance of a re-sit, disillusioned
me enormously. I felt like resigning but Chris persuaded me to stay. We
have remained close friends ever since – Chris was subsequently very successful in his chosen career – and I still cannot believe that such a natural leader was allowed to leave in such a manner.

Passing the exams once again left me rushing around preparing to
join a different ship to complete a period of training known as 'Fleet
Time'. All of the Engineers, who were due to start their degree course in
six months time, were to spend the intervening period onboard a warship, but this time living and working as officers. Each cadet was issued
with a 'Task Book' which listed, in detail, all of the tasks that we were

required to carry out as part of our training. Some would be completely menial and mundane such as painting the hangar door, others would be far more involved such as standing a watch on the bridge and learning to navigate by the stars and sun using a sextant and clock.

I was appointed to HMS *Herald*, a hydrographic survey vessel and not, technically, a warship as she carried no weapons except for a Wasp helicopter. The Wasp was of the first generation of helicopters operated by the Royal Navy and looked rather like it had been made by an eleven year old with an out-of-date Meccano set. Its insect-like appearance was squat and ugly. From the moment I joined the ship I spent all the free time that I had in the hangar just talking aeroplanes with the pilot. On occasion I would get the opportunity to fly in the helicopter and relished every opportunity that arose. The ship spent the majority of its time operating off the Shetland Islands and it would conduct its hydrographic survey by sailing up and down in straight lines using its sonar to map the contours of the seabed. Its position was accurately determined using three land based transmitters. The bearings of these transmitters would be precisely calculated by the ship's equipment and a position pinpointed to within one metre. Part of the helicopter's role was to fly onto the islands and position the transmitters. These flights often afforded me the opportunity to sit in the back of the helicopter and witness the flying operations, and this flying on a regular basis reaffirmed my commitment to train as a professional pilot. I would regularly pester the Captain to see whether my transfer had been accepted, and after three months onboard the ship, and nearly a year in the Navy, I received the news that I had been desperately waiting for: my trans-

My first experience of naval flying during DTS.

fer had been approved on condition that I passed a medical examination and the naval pilots' flying-grading procedure.

The first hurdle was obviously the medical and it was something that I could do very little about, except deny that I had ever failed any previous medicals and keep my fingers crossed. Remarkably I passed without any problem; nobody mentioned anything about extra heartbeats or having a partially unserviceable heart. I cursed the RAF doctor who had almost ruined my aviation career two years previously. The flying grading was to be carried out at Plymouth Airport, using a Chipmunk aircraft, and I arrived there for the start of the course feeling immensely excited at the thought of receiving proper pilot training but extremely nervous at the prospect of not making the grade. Having waited almost a year for the chance to prove myself, I wondered how I would react if I failed.

"Richard, if an aircraft looks right then it will fly right."

These were the words uttered to me by some old and bold aviator when, as a child, I sat around the flying club. Seeing the prettiest of little aeroplanes sitting on the grass in front of the makeshift classroom, the words came flooding back. I had never received any formal flying instruction but I just knew this aeroplane would be a dream to fly. A two-seat training aircraft, the Chipmunk was brought into service shortly after the second world war as a replacement basic trainer for the bi-planed Tiger Moth. Designed and built when Spitfires and Hurricanes ruled the skies she just oozed the old-fashioned appeal of aeroplanes that were designed by humans and not computers. She had been in service for some forty years when I conducted my flying grading. Countless military and civilian pilots before me had cut their aviation teeth on this lovely little aeroplane.

The idea behind flying grading was simplicity itself. The student would receive eleven hours of flying instruction; at the end of the eleven hours the student would sit a flying test with a Navy examiner whose job it was to assess the progress made during the course and decide whether the student stood a fair chance of surviving the rigours of an intensive military flying training course. In order to ensure that the student received the best training possible during those eleven hours, some of the most experienced pilots in the country were employed to act as our instructors. To a man they were all over sixty, with the majority having seen action during the Second World War. Walking into the instructors' crew room was rather like entering an old people's home, and yet the moment these senior citizens sat in aircraft the years fell away and they threw them around the sky with the reckless abandon of eighteen year olds, combined with the skill and dexterity of touch that only very senior aviators can ever hope to achieve. In the classroom they taught us how to fly an aircraft straight and level, followed by the basic principles of turning. Catch them in the corridor and, with a bit of gentle persuasion, they would tell you about whole squadrons taking off in formation at night from carriers, shooting down early Russian jets while flying a Sea Fury in Korea or landing at night in a darkened French field to retrieve a downed fellow airman. Stories were recited with such clarity that one could have imagined they happened only yesterday. As they recounted their memories the years would roll off them, and we would listen in awe to stories from times when every day was an adventure and flying very much an unknown science.

The first hour was described as our only free lunch ticket of the course. It was a familiarisation flight and the sole objective was for us to get used to being in the air and in the tandem cockpit. Sitting in the front cockpit for the first time with the instructor behind you, out of sight, felt as though you were alone in a Second World War fighter. Built before electric engine starters were the norm, the old Gypsy Major engine was cranked over using the explosive charge from a cartridge, and fired by pulling a wire trigger in the cockpit. It would then cough and splutter for a second until all the cylinders, fired up then purr with the confidence of an engine half its age. After the 'thumbs up' from the instructor to the ground crew, to indicate that the aeroplane was serviceable, the chocks would be removed and the aircraft would taxi away like a drunken sailor returning back onboard, weaving from side to side so that the pilot could see around the engine that pointed skywards and obscured his view.

My first instructor was Mike Sparrow. A man well into his sixties but with the youth and enthusiasm that put us young whippersnappers to shame. He regularly ran marathons and had a dynamic and invigorating approach to life. Like all the instructors, his whole working career had been devoted to flying and, by his own admission, he had been fortunate enough to have been part of the Air Force during the golden

At sea on HMS Herald. *Working with the Wasp helicopter.*

years when jet aircraft came to the forefront of aviation technology – before the time when computers and ergonomics alleviated the need for basic stick and rudder skills, and a sense of humour. Mister Sparrow – we always referred to our instructors as Mister as a mark of respect towards both their age and experience – took me aside for a quick brief before getting airborne.

"Have you flown before Richard?"

"Only as an interested passenger."

"Excellent, you will not have any bad habits to unlearn. Is there anything that you would like to see specifically?"

"I wouldn't mind having a look at some aerobatics."

"Excellent, a man after my own heart. Let's go flying."

I had no idea at that stage that Mike was one of the most experienced and respected aerobatic pilots in the country. Fifteen minutes later, as we rolled off the top of what I now know was a perfectly executed loop, and I viewed the Devon countryside through the top of the canopy, I realised exactly how privileged we, as students, were to fly with such talented and experienced pilots. But the flight was over in twenty minutes and so ended the first and last time that I was afforded the opportunity to sit back and enjoy the ride. Each successive time we were expected to take an increasingly active part in the conduct of the flight. Nights were spent in our rooms rehearsing what we were supposed to be saying on the radio; any period during the day when we were not flying we would become proficient hangar pilots, sitting in the aircraft on the ground trying to drum into our brains what appeared to be an unimaginable number of check items that had to be recalled from memory. The first lessons concentrated on how the flying controls functioned and what secondary effects they had on the aircraft. We learned to apply rudder in a turn to offset the secondary yawing effects. Once mastered we progressed onto the principles behind climbing and descending the aircraft; the importance of selecting the correct power and trimming was also instilled into us. For each basic flying skill a story would be recounted as to why the principle was so important: maybe it had saved a life whilst flying at thirty feet over the desert in a Vampire during the Suez crisis; maybe the principle related to insurgence operations in Borneo. Whatever it was it made us sit up and listen and take heed of what was being said. It added a degree of realism and importance to what we were learning. Above all, I was flying and no matter how much work was needed to ensure that the required progress was made, it was an immense amount of fun.

From climbing and descending we progressed to stalling and spinning where we began to acquire a true feel for the aircraft. After this we moved into the circuit, which combined all the basic skills we had learned earlier into one neat package. It was the middle of summer and the weather was warm and wonderful. Those of us not flying would sit on the grass in front of our classroom that looked over the airfield and watch the little Chipmunks droning around the circuit with our compatriots wrestling at the controls.

The instructor would initially demonstrate the circuit. At the end of the runway he would complete the take-off checks and smoothly open up the throttle. As the power increased, the gyroscopic effects of the propeller would try and steer the aircraft off to the side of the runway. He would gently apply opposite rudder to keep the aircraft perfectly straight and, as the speed increased through thirty knots, ease the stick forward so that the tail wheel was lifted and enabled the pilot to see over the nose of the aircraft. As the speed increased further the stick would be gently eased back and the aircraft would lift slowly into the air. Once established in the climb, at exactly the right speed, the after take-off checks would be carried out. Just as they were completed the aircraft would be at exactly the right height to turn cross wind. The turn would be perfectly executed laying off the correct amount of drift to ensure that the aircraft tracked away at right angles to the runway. At 1,000 feet above the runway the aircraft was turned to parallel the runway 'downwind' and levelled at ninety knots in one graceful and co-ordinated movement. A call on the radio 'nine-zero-four downwind to roll', to ensure that the controller and other aircraft in the circuit knew exactly where he was and what he was doing, followed by the downwind checks to ensure that the aircraft was correctly set up for the landing. These checks would all be carried out in plenty of time which would allow the instructor to point out a ground feature that would aid circuit planning. At the end of the downwind leg the throttle would be closed in one smooth movement to set 1,500 rpm on the tacho. The airspeed would be reduced to seventy knots and then the aircraft turned onto 'base leg' with the flaps extended. At 700 feet the aircraft would be turned again, this time onto 'finals', rolling out and exactly lined up with the centre line of the runway when the final stage of flap was taken. Without the power being touched the aircraft would fly down the glide slope and centre line towards the runway with the controls barely being moved. As the aircraft flew over the end of the runway, at fifteen feet, the throttle would be gently closed and the stick eased back. The aircraft would then settle gently onto the runway so smoothly that it was difficult to know whether it had actually landed or not. It all looked, and indeed sounded, so simple.

Then it was my turn. I sat in the cockpit at the end of the runway, my mind blank, the take-off checks, which I had learned to regurgitate in my sleep, escaping me. I mumbled into the microphone as I desperately tried to recall the five simple checks. Eventually, after a gentle prompt from the instructor, I stumbled my way through the list and opened up the throttle. The aircraft lurched to the side of the runway determined to gallop straight across the grass and into the fence. I responded by pushing the opposite rudder pedal to try and return the aircraft to the centre of the runway. With the ferocity of a Rottweiller attacking a trespasser, it snapped around and headed straight towards the control tower, heading at right angles across the runway. Suddenly the rudder pedals moved of their own accord and the aircraft returned to the centre line; the aircraft was behaving itself again as the instructor had taken control. The moment he handed it back, like a horse that senses an inexperienced rider, the pretty little aeroplane started misbehaving with the vengeance of a demon. Before I knew it we were heading towards the side of the runway again. As I fought to keep the aircraft on course a desperate glance inside the cockpit revealed that the airspeed was accelerating to forty knots and well past the speed to lift the tail wheel. I eased the stick forward just as I had been shown and the tail of the aircraft leapt into the air as if I had placed an explosive charge under it, threatening to smash the propeller into the concrete runway. Once again the instructor intervened and managed to avert the impending disaster.

Already I was perspiring profusely and felt like I had just run a marathon. The aircraft had yet to leave the ground. Things could only get easier once we were airborne. As the side of the runway was looming ominously close I decided that now was a good time to ease the aircraft gracefully into the air. I gently pulled back on the stick and the Chipmunk leapt off the ground with its nose rotated towards the sun, pushing me back into the seat. I frantically pushed forward on the stick and the nose pivoted back down again, the aircraft certain to smash back into the runway. I pulled back on the stick again and the aircraft gradually pulled its way into the sky. As I struggled to find the correct climbing attitude, the after take-off checks completely forgotten, another glance in the cockpit revealed that we were climbing to 700 feet and I had forgotten to turn. To my relief the instructor took control and positioned the aircraft downwind for me before we lost sight of the airfield. This gave me the opportunity to try and catch up and recompose myself. He returned the aircraft back into my control and I gingerly placed my hands and feet on the controls but moved nothing. I had fooled it, the aircraft had not realised that I was piloting and for a few seconds it sat there as obedient as when the instructor had been in control. However this peaceful bliss was shortlived, for as soon as I attempted to carry out the downwind checks the aircraft realised that I was back in charge and attempted to roll inverted and throw itself at the ground. I fought with the controls, trying to remember the checks at the same time. This led to complete brain overload with the result that I achieved none of the tasks that I was attempting. I heard the instructor transmit on the radio on my behalf as I wrestled the aircraft to the end of the downwind leg.

Now it was time for me to play with the throttle, as if there were not enough levers and controls to juggle. I pulled the cold metal lever back and the rpm needle cantered around the gauge, generally heading downwards. At the same time we pitched, nose down, the climbing and descending lesson long forgotten. The aircraft was now falling out of the sky and I was already plummeting through 700 feet when I should still have been maintaining 1,000 feet. The speed was increasing to 100 knots when it should have been decreasing and the demon in the machine had returned. I reapplied some power and raised the nose to try and recover the situation. My flying overalls were drenched with perspiration and I was fervently wishing that it was December and not July. Carving a random path through the air the aircraft eventually ended up pointing towards the runway with the throttle being pumped

backwards and forwards in an attempt to achieve the correct height and speed. The aircraft would start to descend and so I would pull the nose up to try and stop the descent; it would then begin to climb with the result that the speed would wash off rapidly. I applied full power to stop it stalling and before I knew it we were high and fast. I would close the throttle again to try and regain the flight path and the cycle would start again. Then, by some miracle, we were over the runway. I closed the throttle and the aircraft descended; landing firmly on the main wheels, before I had time to celebrate it had bounced back into the air entirely of its own accord. It was obviously thoroughly enjoying the opportunity of publicly embarrassing me and was not yet ready to start behaving itself. After a further two bounces the aircraft eventually struck the ground and stayed. Now I was back into the routine of trying to keep the aircraft on the runway, my feet a blur as the rudder pedals travelled from full movement in one direction to full movement in the other in the blink of an eyelid. I fumbled around inside the cockpit trying to locate the brake handle, not daring to take my eyes off the runway and give the aircraft the opportunity to head towards the control tower while I was not looking. After what seemed an eternity my hand fell upon the lever and I pulled it. The aircraft lurched forward onto the main wheels and once again attempted to smash its propeller into the runway, before the tail crashed back down onto the ground as the aircraft came to a shuddering halt.

   "OK Richard, I have control," Mr Sparrow spoke rather calmly over the intercom. I looked down at my hands, they were still grasping the flying controls with a vice-like grip. I tried to relax them and took two

Flying Grading in the venerable Chipmunk.

enormous breaths to try and calm down.

"I'm really sorry," I stuttered nervously. It was all I could think of saying, hardly appropriate when I had spent the last five minutes hell bent on killing the instructor. This must mean the end of my flying career.

"Hey, for a first attempt that wasn't bad at all – nice to see you trying to correct back to the datums. Try relaxing on the controls, the lighter you hold them the more stable the aircraft will be. Let's go and have another go!"

And off we went again. When the sortie eventually ended I wanted to get out and kiss the ground. Surely flying could not possibly be this difficult?

With each flight things became a little easier and gradually the aeroplane grew bored of throwing itself around the skies with me chasing after it and began to behave itself. However what I did discover was that they all loved running around on the ground and all had an aversion to the centre line of the runway. No matter how you fought with the controls, all of the aircraft would make a determined effort to run into the lights at the side of the runway. I tried everything I could think of and even resorted to talking nicely to the aircraft when they were in the hangar, selling my soul to the god of straight landings but all to no avail. Like all the other students on the course each take-off and landing was an action packed adventure ride during which we would visit all four corners of the airfield.

Halfway through the course I changed instructors and Mr Brown became my new mentor. A man of immeasurable age, there were only two things we knew about him: he had flown Spitfires during the Second World War, and he was reputed to eat small children for breakfast. He did not know how to speak, he only growled. Had I been a Luftwaffe pilot I would have been very scared of him; as a young student pilot I was terrified. This added a whole new dimension to flying the circuit, for the instructor and aeroplane would now go into a quiet corner before a flight and collaborate as to how best they could ensure that my ineptitude was magnified a hundredfold. Mr Brown was a perfectionist and his attention to detail improved my flying immeasurably.

From the circuit, we progressed onto aerobatic flying. Where the Chipmunk was a devil in the circuit she was a complete angel during aerobatics and her perfectly harmonised and balanced controls meant that even with my inexperience in the air I was able to execute the basic manoeuvres with a degree of confidence. They did, however, lack a little style and polish. I quickly acquired a great fondness for flying at unusual attitudes. Not only did I really enjoy this particular facet of aviation but it boosted my confidence being able to fly the aircraft around a loop or stall turn. Flying aerobatics greatly increased my feel for the aircraft with the result that flying the circuit became a little less fraught, although landing was still a nightmare.

All too soon the eleven hours were complete and it was time to sit the test. There were twelve of us on the course and, statistically, that meant that one of us would fail. I was one of the last to fly with the examiner, by which time one member of the course had already failed the test. I tried to console myself with the thought that statistics were now on my side, but knowing that a colleague had not made the grade only made me realise that being given the right to continue onto flying training proper was no God given right. When my turn eventually arrived I passed, but only just, the trip did not go at all well, but I think my enthusiasm won through and I was allowed to continue.

Shortly after completing the flying grading I was informed by letter that my transfer to flying duties had been approved. That was the good news. The bad news was that I lost a year's seniority due to the year of extra training that I had just completed as an Engineer. Additionally, I was required to return to Dartmouth for another term of training. All of this was totally irrelevant to me as I had finally succeeded in fulfilling the most difficult part of my ambition: I was to train as a pilot.

It was a strange feeling returning to Dartmouth, as an Officer Under Training again, although this time the circumstances were very different. My mental attitude was very positive and I was there because I wanted to be there. The three very enjoyable months passed in no time at all and I graduated with a first-class pass.

CHAPTER TWO

Flights of Fancy

*Any advice is good advice, with the provision the provider allows
you to ignore it.*

On the first Monday back at work after Christmas leave I breezed into
the squadron and greeted my fellow aviators who were sitting round
drinking coffee and shooting the breeze. When one of them muttered
something about my loudness so early in the morning, I responded with
my usual disregard for protocol.

"Hello Shagnasty you miserable git, I see you didn't get a new sense
of humour for Christmas then!"

I had been on the squadron for almost a year now and had earned a
reputation for being slightly boisterous, verging on a loud mouth. I
loved the atmosphere, the slightest perceived chink in anybody's armour
resulting in merciless banter inflicted upon the hapless individual only
until a sign of weakness was detected in someone else; then everybody
would switch their attack. A quick wit and a sharp sense of humour were
essential. I couldn't stand a quiet office and feeling confident in my abilities as an officer and aviator I revelled in the light hearted entertainment the banter provided.

I felt relaxed and at ease although, by comparison to some aviators, I
was a new boy to both the squadron and the flying game. I had been in
the service for five years and my career up to this point had appeared to
be one of permanent training. I had followed a long and convoluted path,
but as a front-line pilot on an active squadron I finally felt that I had
achieved my original objective and took a great deal of pride from it.

Around me were people from every different walk of life, all with different tales to tell about how and why they ended up as helicopter aircrew on a naval squadron. A few had been around for longer than they
cared to remember and had served throughout the world, a small
minority were veterans of previous conflicts, but most were relative newcomers, like myself, none of whom believed that we would ever become
involved in a shooting game.

My days at Dartmouth were now irrelevant to me. As I entered the
briefing room for morning 'Shareholders', Nick caught up with me. Nick
was my Observer, the other half of the two-man team that made up a
Lynx helicopter crew; 'Shareholders' was the name given to the daily
briefing which every aviator would attend. During the morning brief we

would receive a thorough weather forecast for the day's flying followed by a quick reminder of any 'Notice to Airmen' that might affect our flying that day. Finally the squadron Engineering Officer would stand up and explain why all the aircraft were unserviceable and we could not go flying anyway.

The name 'Shareholders' originated in the golden days of naval aviation when the Fleet Air Arm really was a force to be reckoned with, and the Navy was making the transition from propeller driven machines to the far more capable jet powered aircraft. With angled decks, catapult launches and jet flight from a deck still in its infancy, the attrition rate for my predecessors had been incredibly high. Rather than ponder on the seriousness of this situation the young aviators turned it to their advantage. They would form syndicates and take out life insurance policies. If one of them was unlucky enough to come to a premature end the rest of the syndicate would share the pay out on the insurance policy between them. These 'Shareholders' would be announced at the morning brief. It was a morbid way of relieving the grief felt for a lost colleague but, by all accounts, it worked very well.

The period of daily deaths had long since passed by the time my naval flying started and, for us, it was a rarity to have a problem, let alone a death on the squadron. They did, however, happen from time to time and Nick, as one of the most experienced Observers in the fleet, had seen active service in the Falklands Conflict and possessed the ability to be completely pragmatic in his approach to aviation and the dangers involved. A giant of a man with a thick beard, he was the caricature of the old and bold helicopter aviator. With over 3,000 Lynx flying hours to his name, he was known, if not necessarily liked, throughout the Fleet Air Arm. He took no shit. A devoted Chelsea supporter – when he was not at sea he travelled to all of their games – he had twice been court-martialled for associated incidents. We were an unlikely combination: me, the slightly built, fit young pilot, Nick, the burly and worldly-wise Observer. In the six months we had been crewed-up together I had grown to like and respect Nick. We had forged a working relationship whereby I had learned an awful lot from him and, despite my inexperience, he had every confidence in my piloting ability. This mutual respect was to stand us in good stead over the next six months. I liked Nick as a person and for me one of his most redeeming features was that he was his own man and had refused to be moulded into the 'typical' naval officer that so many others had become.

Nick's confidence in my basic stick and rudder skills was to me the ultimate compliment. My passage through flying training had been a roller-coaster of achievements and failures and, on more than one occasion, it looked as though I would fall by the wayside and become another failed pilot statistic. Now I would fly at 100 feet over the sea at night and land on a heaving postage stamp of a deck, throughout which Nick would never doubt my ability to get us both back safely.

"Dickie, the plan's changed. I haven't got your phone number so I couldn't tell you yesterday, but the ship has already sailed. We depart to join her just south of the Needles at 1000. We'll brief after Shareholders."

I was shocked. For the first time in a long while I was lost for words. We could not sailing already, we were not due to sail until the following Monday and I had the forthcoming weekend all planned. I was going to take Jill away, our last opportunity to spend some time together for six months and my surprise present to her before I left.

The decision for HMS *Manchester* – the ship I was serving on as the helicopter pilot – to depart from Portsmouth earlier than planned and join a task group preparing for the Gulf, had been made two days earlier. Jill was the girl I was madly in love with and whom I had been dating for almost four years. On the same day that we had decided to buy a house together, Saddam Hussein invaded Kuwait. Like the majority of people of the time, I knew very little about Kuwait, or the vital role it played in world oil supplies.

Over the next few months we went through the tortuous process of buying a house whilst Saddam dug his troops into the Kuwait desert. By the Christmas of 1990 the house purchase was complete and we were ecstatically happy. There was but one thing spoiling our complete happiness, and that was the ship's schedule. Since the previous summer HMS *Manchester* had been programmed to sail to the Persian Gulf in mid-January as part of the Armilla Patrol. The Royal Navy had been involved in the Gulf for ten years, enforcing various blockades and monitoring shipping traffic.

After the invasion of Kuwait there was some confusion as to what would happen to our programme; we knew that we would be going and had completed all of the training for it, but what we didn't know was when and for how long. Unlike the Falklands Conflict, nobody wanted to go out to the Gulf. Nobody knew how things would develop but we were all convinced that Saddam had the capability and the mental attitude to use biological and chemical weapons. No sane person had any desire to become involved in that type of warfare and I had seen television pictures of the Kurds in Eastern Iraq after a chemical attack. Over the Christmas period the ship was put on twenty-four hours notice to sail and we realised that it could leave at any time should the situation in the region deteriorate.

Christmas itself was fabulous and we spent it with Pat, Jill's mother, receiving all the house warming presents from our respective families. However, we all kept one eye glued to the television screen, monitoring the developing situation in the Middle East. It looked as if things were going to blow over as Saddam made muttered promises about withdrawing his troops. On the morning I returned to work after the Christmas break, I was convinced that the ship would sail the following week, giving me one last weekend with Jill before departing on the long deployment.

The morning brief finished – I hadn't listened to a word of it – Nick rejoined me. "Its a simple transit to the ship, and we'll spend the next couple of days working up in the areas before *Manchester* joins the *Ark Royal*. Beyond the fact that we are going to the Gulf, I'm not sure what the plans are."

I guess he could sense that I was feeling distraught. It was bad enough leaving for my first long deployment, even worse knowing that I was sailing to a war zone.

"I'll sort all the brief out for the trip. You go and make some phone calls and say your goodbyes."

I retain a vivid memory of standing in the phone box on the squadron base and physically crying when I couldn't get hold of Jill. It was one of the most difficult tasks, leaving a message with one of her work colleagues, saying simply that I was leaving early and I would see her again in July, six months down the road. That is what I hoped but I suddenly realised that there was no certainty that I would.

Jill and I had met in Yorkshire, four years previously when I was a young student pilot. The first stage of flying training for all Navy pilots was conducted under the auspices of the RAF at an Army airfield in Yorkshire. As students we were accommodated at the nearby RAF station, Linton-on-Ouse, where the *ab initio* Air Force pilots carried out their basic training. As I drove into the airfield on the first day I knew that I was going to have a good time here. It had the feel of an RAF Second World War airfield with an abundance of fresh faced aviators cutting their flying teeth and enjoying every second of it. As it was one of three bases where the RAF students carried out their basic flying training, the majority of residents were in light blue uniform as opposed to our darker variety. This created a healthy atmosphere of competitive spirit, working hard and playing even harder.

Everyone at Linton was there because they wanted to be, they wanted to fly and it was an unbelievable atmosphere to work in. The first six weeks were confined to the classroom for a period of intensive ground school. Here we learnt about air traffic procedures and basic aerodynamics, about meteorology and the technical aspects of aircraft, but above all about flying and all that it entailed. At the end of the ground school there was a series of exams in all of the subjects covered. I studied hard and achieved top marks in these exams but the late nights, with our heads in our books, did not stop us from enjoying ourselves socially.

One of the first pieces of worthwhile advice I received, while still undergoing basic training at Dartmouth, was from a senior officer who still lived life to the full. He looked over the course of fresh new recruits and, with a mixture of nostalgia and envy, spoke from the heart.

"Gentlemen you are in a very privileged position. Hundreds of thousands of young men have applied to be in your position and you are about to embark on the most enjoyable and important two years of your life. During the course of flying training you will be expected to work harder than most of you will have been called upon to work before but, along with that, you will undoubtedly have the time of your life. While you do not need telling that if you do not do the work you will be removed from the course, I implore you to work hard and, by promoting the team spirit, you will all stand a healthy chance of passing."

He then stood in quiet introspective thought for thirty seconds.

"What I'm saying guys is that you must not get too bogged down in too much work and no play. While an evening out with the Swedish netball

My first formation trip. Big fun.

team the night before your final handling test may not be the best idea in the world, when the opportunity arises, party your pants off. Navy life means that you never know when the next opportunity will arise!"

It was about the only piece of advice that we all took to heart.

I joined a course that had been together since their basic training a year previously. While there was no tribal bond that excluded me from this close knit group, I naturally formed a close alliance with Bruce Morrison, another Midshipman, who I had befriended at Dartmouth and who was also an 'outsider' to the group. Bruce was in his late twenties, married with a child, and had been in the Navy for almost ten years.

The aircraft that we were to fly was the Bulldog. This was designed as a replacement to the veritable Chipmunk, two seater trainer, but it lacked the appeal of its predecessor. Having said that it was a handsome aircraft in its own right. Sitting next to the instructor, rather than in front of him, the seats were racked back and the large perspex encased cockpit gave it a modern and purposeful feel. The 200hp engine delivered significantly more power than the Chipmunk and it could be conducted through a sequence of aerobatics without losing too much height.

It had been almost six months since I had completed the Chipmunk course and, taking to the skies again, it was hard to believe that I had undertaken the course at all. Fortunately the policy was to assume that students had retained nothing and start from the very beginning again. The assumption proved entirely correct and, for me, the first trip was again a pleasure ride. Of forty minutes duration, the object was just to get us airborne and have a look at some of the local landmarks. Half of the instructors were RAF and the remaining fifty percent Navy. For my first trip I flew with a very experienced Navy instructor who came from a helicopter background but flew the little Bulldog with an abundance of natural ease, and confidence befitting a man of his experience. Some years later I watched a Navy Jetstream aircraft displaying at RNAS Portland during a Sea Cadets Open Day. The aircraft flew in over the harbour and pulled up steeply into a wingover to the right. It appeared to enter too low and slow to safely complete the manoeuvre. As the aircraft, built as a civilian transport aircraft and not a military display aircraft, exited the semi-aerobatic manoeuvre it became obvious that it was too low to execute a safe recovery. As I watched the aircraft plummet towards the water, the pilots tried to raise the nose to avoid the impact but, without enough airspeed, it cart-wheeled into the harbour killing both crew members. I learnt, later on that day, that one of them was the instructor that taught me the basics on the Bulldog.

He was not the first colleague that had died in an aviation accident, however it was the first time that I had actually witnessed an aircraft crash, and the fact that I knew the pilot made it all the more disturbing. In a moment of quiet reflection I pondered on the fallability of man. Flying, military flying in particular, has always had a degree of danger associated with it. At the time of the accident I considered myself a relatively proficient and experienced pilot and yet here was a more experienced and competent aviator than I making, what appeared, to be the most fundamental of errors – a man at whose skill and knowledge I had marvelled a few years before and a man who I had tried to emulate. I took some solace from the fact that, like most aviators, I am sure that he would have wanted to go that way if his time was to be up prematurely. He was a born again Christian and a deeply religious man. Although I never really got to know him as a friend, the fact that I had held him in such high esteem as an instructor all those years ago, while I was an inexperienced student pilot, meant that his death had a profound effect on me. Rather than turning away from flying I found myself accepting the fact that flying is dangerous and that, although flight safety is always first and foremost in any pilot's mind, sometimes it is all to no avail.

The elementary flying course initially followed exactly the same pattern as the flying grading on the Chipmunk; from effect of controls to straight and level, to climbing and descending, to circuit work. This time there was an added pressure to the flying: within twelve flying hours we were to go solo. The Bulldog was slightly more complex than the distinguished Chipmunk and, with a variable pitch propeller, it had one more lever and a couple of extra dials to worry about. But, more importantly, it had a tricycle undercarriage with a wheel at the front of the aircraft rather than the rear. This made it infinitely more easy to control on the runway and, hence, very popular with the students.

After ten hours flying my first solo flight was drawing near. Around a third of the course had already completed their first solo trip, but they tended to be the people who had flown other types before. After being taught normal circuits we progressed onto glide circuits, simulating an engine failure and gliding the aircraft back to the runway. Once that was mastered we moved to flapless circuits where the loss of flaps, that slowed the aircraft for landing, was simulated. We had to demonstrate a proficiency in all the different types of circuit before being allowed to attempt a circuit on our own. The final requirement was to conduct three circuits in succession without the instructor needing to intervene. The landings did not need to be perfect, just safe.

After completing the third circuit the instructor took control of the aircraft and taxied it back to the squadron building. He quizzed me on some basic emergency procedures then, shaking my hand, he wished me luck and jumped out of the aeroplane to make his way up to the Air Traffic Control tower to witness my first solo flight. I felt lonely and, as much as I had been looking forward to this moment, the cockpit seemed to possess a hostile feel about it without the comforting factor of an instructor, sitting next to me, to take control if all went wrong. There was another strange phenomenon that happened as soon as the instructor left the cockpit – my brain emptied itself of everything that I had learned since starting the course. I taxied the aircraft out to the runway, struggling to remember what I was supposed to be saying on the radio.

For first solo flights the Air Traffic Controllers have to ensure that there are no other aircraft in the circuit. Taxiing onto the runway I felt rather like a rookie actor taking to the stage for the first time, knowing that all eyes were on him; but here a good performance was far more critical. With the pre take-off checks all but forgotten, I opened the throttle and started to accelerate down the runway. At the required speed I pulled back on the stick and the aircraft departed from the safety of the ground. The first thing that struck me was how quickly the aircraft climbed without the added weight of the instructor. The procedure was to climb to 500 feet and then turn to the left, parallel to the runway in the opposite direction to that from which you had taken off, and continue the climb to 1,000 feet above the airfield.

Rather like my first attempt at a circuit in the Chipmunk, by the time that I had settled down and caught up with the aircraft I was almost at 1,000 feet and I hadn't even thought about turning the aircraft. I took a deep breath and tried to compose myself to sort the aircraft out. I turned 'downwind' and looked out at the runway to confirm that I was the correct distance from it and then it dawned on me. Here I was flying this aircraft on my own and the thrill was enormous. I allowed myself the pleasure of sitting back for a few seconds to enjoy the moment. This was what I had been dreaming of, and battling for, over the last two years and I was enjoying every second of it. The moment, however, was short lived and I had to take charge of the aeroplane to bring it in for a landing. I made the call on the radio and tried to remember the landing checks but my mind had gone blank, the drill which I had been able to recite in my sleep had escaped me. I looked around the cockpit hoping to see something that would jog my memory.

'Hangar Pilot'. Learning the checks on the Bulldog.

As my eyes wandered aimlessly around the cockpit panic started to rise through my body and it took at least three deep breaths and countless' Hail Mary's before my eyes settled on the Rpm lever and the rhythm returned.

Rpm max, mixture fully rich, induction air cold...

Fuel booster pump on, flaps to inter, harness locked and tight.

From that moment on I never forgot them again. Even today they are permanently ingrained into my long term memory.

With the checks complete my immediate future looked slightly more assured. At the end of the downwind leg the power was reduced and the aircraft turned and descended towards the runway. I kept the threshold a fixed distance up the windscreen, as I had been instructed, and the aircraft tracked towards the runway as if it knew which way to go. With a satisfying squeak the aircraft settled gently onto the tarmac as I flared it over the threshold. The world's biggest smile broke over my face and it just would not go away. I taxied the aircraft back to the apron and shut the engine down.

My instructor strode over to the aircraft and shook me firmly by the hand. No matter what aircraft people fly, whether they fly for pleasure or professionally, they will never forget their first solo flight. It is a wonderful feeling indeed, looking back at the aircraft, safe in the knowledge that your skill, judgement and coordination has caused it to slip the bonds of earth and descend back in contact with it. We were not allowed to fly for the rest of the day. The euphoria of completing the first solo tends to distract the mind and experience has shown that subsequent sorties on the same day achieve very little.

After the first solo, the training in the circuit continued and, having proved that we were safe as pilots, the idea was to put some polish on our performance. More solo flying followed but now we would spend a whole hour flying around the airfield on our own. The atmosphere on the course was brilliant and I would not have missed it for the world. All fifteen of us were fulfilling our ambitions and we all worked hard to try and do well. This also meant that we played very hard. Weekends would begin with Happy Hour in the Officer's Mess where large quantities of beer would be consumed amid much banter between the Air Force and Navy students. This friendly rivalry produced a brilliant feeling within the mess. After Happy Hour we would all take a taxi into nearby York and continue the jollifications at the King's Arms, the popular hang-out for the local student nurse population that attracted the young bachelors like bees around the proverbial honey pot. As a bachelor aged twenty I felt that I had made it in life and was exactly where I wanted to be.

The atmosphere at Linton was exciting and vibrant for a number of reasons. The fact that there were both Navy and Air Force there helped, but I believe the principle reason was simply that there were in excess of three hundred young men (it was before girls were permitted to join the military as pilots) who had been given the opportunity of fulfilling life-long ambitions. We were all undergoing basic training so the aeroplanes that we were flying were designed as trainers and we were taught basic flying skills. There were no tactical weapons skills or learning how to use weapons of mass destruction, all of which could be fairly sobering: we were just being taught stick and rudder skills. Each day was an adventure as we would learn a new skill to add to our repertoire, be it a new aerobatic manoeuvre or learning how to cope with a new emergency. As my confidence in my ability to fly an aeroplane increased, so did my general confidence. I believe that this was true for most of the student pilots. Consequently we were a group of self-assured, content young men. Working hard and playing hard simply became a way of life, as it had done for generations of young pilots before us.

From the circuit we progressed onto basic aerobatic skills. Once we had completed our first 'check ride' after going solo, we were allowed to carry out solo aerobatics. From the moment the first loop was demonstrated to me in the Chipmunk, I fell in love with aerobatic flying and the humble little Bulldog proved to be a great trainer. Often described as 'overbuilt', it was incredibly well constructed and just begged to be thrown around the sky. With its bigger engine one was able to carry out a series of manoeuvres without, if handled correctly, losing any height – a feat impossible in the slightly underpowered Chipmunk. Once basic loops, rolls and stall turns were mastered, the art was then to link them all together, ensuring that height was maintained and that the aeroplane was kept on the display line. To achieve this pick a line feature, be it a straight length of road or river, and attempt to keep the aircraft parallel to it. As the nose of the aircraft is pulled up at the start of a loop, tilt your head backwards. As the nose goes through the vertical, look for the inverted horizon. As it comes into view, ensure that the wings are still parallel with it and continue straining your neck backwards to look for the feature on the ground so that the aircraft can be steered to fly parallel to it. Keeping the nose of the aircraft coming up, the aim is to level the aircraft at the same height and speed as it enters the manoeuvre. A quick check to ensure that the sky above the aircraft is still clear and pull the nose smartly up until the aircraft is pointing vertically upwards. Look left and right to make sure that the wings bisect the horizon and glance into the cockpit. As the speed reduces through sixty knots, apply full right rudder and look back out at the horizon again. As the nose of the aircraft cuts the horizon, close the throttle and keep looking out as the other wing cuts the horizon. Apply rudder in the opposite direction to keep the wing on the horizon and now look out of the front of the aircraft to ensure that it is pointing vertically down. The speed starts to build quickly now so snap the nose of the aircraft back to the horizon and open up the throttle again. Ensure that the area around the aircraft is still clear and pull the nose smartly up to where the spinner on the propeller cuts the horizon. Now check forward on the controls to hold it there, move the stick to the left and the aircraft starts to roll in that direction. As it does, apply top rudder to keep the nose up. Keep rolling the aircraft as the secondary effect of the rudder tries to stop it rolling, now the aircraft is approaching the inverted position and the stick is being pushed forward to keep the nose of the aircraft above the horizon and keep the aircraft level. The rudder has been taken off now and as you hang in your straps, pulling negative 'g', the space around your head fills with dust and grass cuttings that have gathered in the cockpit. Look out to ensure that the aircraft is still paralleling the road and keep it rolling at the same rate. The forward pressure has now been taken off and top rudder applied as the aircraft goes through ninety degrees to the horizon. As the aircraft rolls level again, slowly take the rudder off and keep the aircraft pointing straight. The speed has bled off slightly now, so pull it up into a sixty degree climb and bank it steeply into a wingover. This changes the direction of flight and allows you to have a good look to ensure that no other aircraft has penetrated your little piece of sky. The speed has now rebuilt enabling the aircraft to be pulled up sharply into a loop again. This time, as the aircraft goes through the inverted position at the top of the loop, you check forward and hold the aircraft there. Now you carry out the second half of the slow roll. Completing it, the speed is slow and the controls are sloppy and unresponsive. You dive to build the speed again and a large grin breaks out over your face. What a thrill!

From there we moved onto instrument flying, the basic skill of flying an aeroplane without reference to the horizon. Following this phase, solo flights through cloud were allowed. This meant that we could climb up to the blue sky above the clouds and practice our aerobatic skills. I felt like I was now becoming a real pilot. Approximately a quarter of the flying hours we flew were conducted solo. This was designed to build confidence in the newly acquired flying skills although, for me, it did produce one or two fairly exciting moments. There were strict rules concerning exactly what we were allowed to do during these solo trips and dogfighting was strictly prohibited. Of course as soon as the programme was published for the day our practice was to check whether anyone else would be flying solo at the same time. If this was the case a rendezvous would be arranged and, rather than spending the hour practising steep turns as briefed, the two pilots would spend the time chasing each other around the skies. The risks with this activity were great indeed for not only was it extremely dangerous to have two aircraft piloted by novices in such close proximity to one another, but if caught by the instructors you faced instant withdrawal from the flying course and a premature end to a career. That did not stop any of us doing it, it merely added to the excitement. With hindsight I guess that the instructors knew exactly what was going on; they probably did exactly the same when they were students. As dangerous as it was, we really believed it improved your basic handling skills.

Topcliffe, the airfield where the flying training was conducted, was situated some sixteen miles north of Linton-on-Ouse, our home. This meant a fairly lengthy bus journey every day through country roads to get to our place of work. Each day one member of the course would be nominated as duty student – one of his responsibilities was to get up early and drive to Topcliffe to set up the morning brief for when the rest of the staff and students arrived. In order to enable the 'duty stude' to get up to the airfield before everybody else, a staff Metro was provided. Boys being boys we quickly established a routine whereby two students

We enter the local raft race. Our submarine eventually sank!

would take the Metro up first thing in the morning: the duty student to drive and a companion to time him. Fifteen and a half minutes was the record established by the senior course for the journey door to door, and we all attempted to beat it. Driving at these kind of speeds around narrow Yorkshire country roads was a particularly invigorating way to start the day and called for far more skill, judgement and coordination than flying the Bulldog ever did.

The morning brief would always start with a time check, ensuring that we all had our watches synchronised to the nearest second, not that it really mattered. However, as a course we managed to demonstrate a remarkable amount of ineptitude when it came to telling the time. Every day the 'duty stude' was guaranteed to get the time check wrong, sometimes just by a few seconds, sometimes by days! Somehow it was self-perpetuating. Each time someone got a time check wrong the senior pilot would became extremely agitated and the whole course would receive a large bollocking. This would put even more pressure on the student for the next day who, by then, would be so nervous that he would get it wrong as well.

The issue began to get out of hand and, at one stage, the squadron boss threatened to ground us all until we learned how to give a proper time check. It was a small thing but it was my first insight into how, sometimes, the relative importance of things can get distorted as a result of service life.

Halfway through the course, after forty flying hours, another check flight had to be taken. By the time we had all taken this test our numbers had dwindled from nineteen to fifteen. One guy failed to go solo and was removed from the course, another failed his spinning and aerobatics check and a further two failed at this intermediate stage. Once again it was a very emotional experience seeing these guys being chopped. Because the course, as a whole, was always in trouble the team spirit was extremely high and, although I had only been with them for four months whilst the rest had been together for almost two years, we were a very close knit group of which I felt an integral part. Seeing a close friend and colleague suffer the torment of being removed from flying training was not a pleasant experience. However, this was also my first insight into how quickly you forget people in the service environment. At the time these people were the closest and dearest friends that I had; now I can't even remember their names.

The second half of the course was devoted to more applied flying and, as a result, was far more enjoyable than the first half. Now low level navigation skills were introduced followed by in-flight diversions and, finally, we were taught how to fly in formation. By this stage we were in the midst of a wonderfully hot summer, and afternoons would be spent playing volleyball on the lawn in front of the hangar as we waited to go flying. Evenings were enjoyed relaxing in the sun supping a pint of beer as we discussed what we would be doing the following day.

Bruce and I forged a strong friendship during our time at Linton. In terms of natural piloting ability I probably had the edge over him, although in terms of all round ability he was streets ahead of me. Having been in the Navy for ten years he knew exactly what was important and what could be ignored, hence he maximised the use of his time and, although he had come to flying rather late in his career, was doing very well on the course. With both of us continuing to avoid the dreaded axe that could come down and chop any one of us at any time, during the second half of the course we found more time to enjoy ourselves. Bruce was the master of funny naval anecdotes, and although of slight build he had a reputation for enjoying a pint or two. Suitably oiled he would hold audience with the rest of the course and recite tales from his previous naval experience. They were made even more hilarious knowing that Bruce never fabricated for the sake of poetic licence. If he recited a story, you could be damn sure that it was the exact truth.

On one particular evening quite by chance, he and I stumbled across a barrel of Theakston's Old Peculiar left in a marquee a few days after the summer ball. Assuming that the barrel had been opened and that the beer would only be thrown out, unless it was drunk, we felt up to the challenge. Pulling a pint and passing it to me Bruce shook his head and sighed.

"I vowed that I would never drink Old Peculiar again after the last time."

Pulling up a chair I knew that I would be in for another Brucie classic.

"Go on mate, give us the brief."

"Well, it was nothing particularly exciting but I had just been promoted to Chief Petty Officer when the ship visited Norway." Bruce's soft Scottish accent only added authenticity to the story. "Someone in the mess knew of a bar that sold Theakston's, apparently the only place in the whole of Norway to sell it. Having just been promoted and with my paper's in for promotion to officer, I was determined not to go out and get pissed. Anyway, on the final night, after spending the whole visit on board behaving myself, I was persuaded to go there . Not wanting to end up in trouble I decided to limit myself to only three pints. Unfortunately I had forgotten just how strong Old Peculiar is, and, well you know how it is with the stuff, one pint is too many and ten not enough. Before I knew what was happening I was well into my Billy Connelly impression. The next thing I knew I had been adopted by two blonde Norwegian women. They were just brilliant and I remember one of them telling me that in Norway, in the summer, they go fishing and shagging: in the winter it's the same except there's no fishing!"

I was already in stitches at the way in which he recited the story. He was just so matter of fact and blasé about it all.

"The next thing I knew I was invited back to their place for a drop of whisky. Well I had to accept – it was far too expensive to drink whisky in the bar. I was pretty pissed by this stage but I remember catching a taxi to some obscure place in town. The only thing I remember about the journey was that it seemed a long way. Anyway, I was intrigued by what was going to happen next. We were sitting around in the lounge talking about what things turned us on. Isn't it amazing how all Scandinavians speak such good English? Quite by chance I glanced at my watch only to notice that it was seven-thirty in the morning and the ship was due to sail at eight. Now ordinarily I would have stayed with the Norwegian birds but, having my commission resting on it, I thought I better make an effort to get back to the ship. I made my excuses and left but, unfortunately, I had no idea where I was or, more importantly, where the ship was. After leaving the apartment I wandered around for about ten minutes until I eventually struck upon the idea of climbing a hill to see whether I could see the dockyard. The plan worked unbelievably well and, from the vantage point, I could see the dockyard and the ship below me. Unfortunately I could also see that she was preparing to sail and that the fo'c's'le party had already begun to slacken the ropes. I ran down to the dockyard as fast as possible but, realising that I wasn't going to make it, came up with plan B. The gangway was already in the process of being removed so I figured that if I took a run at it, I would probably be able to jump onto the ship. I took a *long* run at it but unfortunately I was running towards the fo'c's'le which was the first part of the ship to move away from the pier. By the time I arrived at the edge, the ship was already a good six feet away from the side. Without taking a break in my stride I decided to jump the gap. I'm not quite sure who was more surprised at my decision, me or my Divisional Officer who was in charge of the fo'c's'le party and at whose feet I arrived in a snotty heap."

By this stage I was in hysterics, the icing on the cake was when he added the epilogue.

"I was really gutted."

"Why, did you get trooped?"

"No, my DO thought that I was a bit of a hero with my long jump so I got off scot-free: I was gutted that I had left two Norwegian babes just gagging for it – had I not been pissed on Theakston's Old Peculiar I would have made the right decision and stayed with them!"

For me that's what the Navy was all about: flying aeroplanes and getting pissed whilst getting paid for it. What more could I have asked for?

All too soon the end of the course was drawing near and we found ourselves preparing for the Final Handling Test (FHT). This was the last flight of the course and everything rested on it. Lasting an hour and a half, the test could encompass any phase of the flying course. A good pass was required in order to graduate from the Elementary Flying squadron and, as preparation for the final test, each student had two sorties with his regular instructor in order to brush up on any sphere which both instructor and student thought necessary. The test itself was conducted by either the squadron boss or a senior pilot. I was as nervous as the next man before the test, but in the end had nothing to worry about; the flight went extremely smoothly and involved a short low-level navigation trip followed by some aerobatics, during which the boss feigned a heart attack so that an impromptu diversion was made to the nearest airport. Fortunately both the weather and luck remained on my side throughout the flight; it was a glorious summer's day and my instructor had given me a diversion from exactly the same spot the flight before.

Unfortunately the FHT did not go as smoothly for everyone on the

ROYAL NAVY ELEMENTARY FLYING TRAINING SQUADRON

The 'survivors' graduate. (Front row, second from right.)

course and another fell on the imaginary sword, the final tally: nineteen starters, fourteen completed. With the FHT completed, all that remained was for log books to be signed and a few loose ends to be tied up. During the last few days at Topcliffe, each of us was invited to an interview with the squadron boss who gave us an appraisal of our over-all performance on the course. During this interview I was informed that my performance had warranted selection to train as a Sea Harrier pilot. This meant transferring on to a Royal Air Force course and remaining in Yorkshire for another year – I could not have been happier. Three of us were selected as potential Sea Harrier pilots while the remainder of the course were posted down to Cornwall to start their basic helicopter training.

For the three of us it meant four weeks leave before starting the Jet Provost course, based at Linton-on-Ouse, but this time flying from Linton as well. I was twenty years old with four weeks leave and some money in my pocket which I wanted to burn. Two immensely enjoyable but expensive holidays followed, one to Monte Carlo and the second to Washington. Obviously a good time was had by all: then it was back to work to start the next course.

It was back to basics again and I joined a course that was fresh out of RAF Cranwell, the Air Force equivalent of Dartmouth, but, to these guys, I was an old hand. We started with a three week aviation medicine course, an Air Force run course which went into great detail on matters such as high altitude aviation physiology and which involved numerous runs in the decompression chamber. From the moment I met the new members of the course I knew that I was going to enjoy being part of the team. Again they were a close knit community that had been together, as a group, for over a year, but although we wore a different uniform and came from a different background, all three of us were immediately accepted and new friendships quickly formed. It transpired that these were some of the few military friendships that stood the test of time. I found a number of characters within the course that I could instantly relate to, those that had a passion for flying but a healthy degree of scepticism towards the system and what it attempted to turn you into. More than that, they had a sense of fun. Within the first few days of the course we had smuggled a semi-inflated, blow-up doll into the decompression chamber which trebled in size and eventually burst when the chamber was rapidly decompressed from 25,000 to 40,000 feet. Watching this wrinkled old lady of a doll inflate into a sex goddess and then an obese piece of roly-poly plastic before exploding, all in the blink of an eyelid, was humorous in the extreme. We received the first of many bollockings for not taking the course seriously. The remainder of the three weeks contained the usual boring mundane classroom trivia, interspersed with copious amounts of insane drinking. Perhaps one of the more enlightening experiences was the ejection seat simulator. Strapped to the seat with a steel ladder behind you, it propelled you into the air and thirty feet up the ladder with an acceleration that left your eyes unable to focus and your back stiff for days. It was put into perspective when we were told that the rig only had a third of the charge of the actual seat. It crossed my mind that I would think long and hard about pulling the ejection seat handle for real.

With the aviation medicine course complete, we nursed our hangovers back to Linton and started another six weeks of ground school. This was tedious in the extreme and involved a lot of self-study rather than the old fashion 'chalk and talk' which I had become accustomed to. We all found sanctuary in the Friday evening piss-ups during Happy Hour and then onto the night life in York. It was during this period that I met, and fell head over heels in love with a student nurse completing her training in York. Jill redefined my definition of attractive but, with it, she was relaxed, confident and self-assured. Even though it took me a long time to pluck up the courage to ask her out, from the moment I first saw her I was transformed. For the next eight months I gradually started concentrating more on Jill and less and less on the flying training. The course itself was a lot of fun and I was now flying the Jet Provost Mark 3, a vintage jet of very limited performance but a jet none the less. The first part of the course was back to basics – again. Effect of controls, climbing and descending, turning. I had no problem with this and breezed through it, spending more hours in the bar during the week, and all of my weekends with Jill. For the first time in my life I had genuinely fallen in love and it was a wonderful experience. Those early days at Linton on the Jet Provost course will always remain fixed in my memory as some of my happiest. For me a military life was about flying, drinking and being in love, and there was nothing to suggest that it would ever be any different.

One particular event epitomises my frame of mind at the time and remains prominent in my memory.

The RAF was holding a leadership training day at Cranwell and each training squadron was invited to send a team down to participate in the event. The drinking team, of which I considered myself a founder member, volunteered, as we all assumed it would be a good laugh. Unfortunately the whole day was a little boring and unimaginative, back to the old, "Can you build a bridge out of the four bits a wood and a length a bailing twine?". If that proved decisive leadership skills then perhaps the country should be permanently led by West Country farmers. One of the final tasks was based around survival skills, during which we

were given a live rabbit and asked to kill, skin and then cook it. When given a rabbit a year earlier to kill and eat, it was during a properly run and organised survival course, designed to teach the basic skills necessary to survive behind enemy lines. Now we were being asked to kill a rabbit for fun. An executive decision was taken which exercised far more leadership and management skills than any of the exercises, which we had been asked to participate in, could produce. We decided to steal the rabbit and scarper. Clutching the poor, petrified creature we ran back to the bus and asked the driver to take us back to Linton as quickly as possible. The driver look perplexed, until he saw that we were being pursued by a number of snotty-nosed RAF officers, and then obliged. We guess we lost

...and getting vertigo.

the leadership contest, but we did end up with a squadron mascot.

The first problem we encountered was choosing a name for the newest squadron recruit. Eventually we decided on 'Effel', it came from the initials F and L as we reasoned that the rabbit was 'fucking lucky' not to have had his head pulled off like all of his compatriots. The next and most pressing problem was what were we going to do with him. One of the married guys on the course agreed to take him home for the night and the following morning, in between flying sorties, we set about building him a hutch. Effel quickly settled into the routine of squadron life. During the day he would be allowed to wander around the squadron building and at night he would be placed in his hutch outside. He was a remarkably good judge of how your sortie had gone. If you had just experienced the nightmare trip from hell and were not exactly feeling benevolent to all man-or rabbit-kind, Effel would steer well clear of you. However if you had just experienced one of those trips where everything had fallen into place and you had finished it with one of those perfect landings, when you barely know that the aircraft has touched the ground, then Effel would be the first one to greet you on your return to the squadron. He would sit, looking as content as the owner of the lap that he was perched upon, as we drank our coffee and mused over how easy all this flying lark was. Effel was a real star.

From the Jet Provost 3, which we had been flying for six months, we progressed onto the Jet Provost 5, a faster and more sophisticated version of the same aircraft. Now I could no longer fall back on my previous experience, we were learning new and more complicated flying manoeuvres each day, and yet I spent more and more time with Jill, and less and less concentrating on the flying course. Eventually the inevitable happened. Due to my lack of progress, it was deemed that I was not of the required standard to fly fast jets and I was removed from the course. The reason was indisputable; I had not put in the required amount of work. As Navy students we were expected to do better than the rest as we would be graduated onto Sea Harriers, a single-seat fighter, flown from a moving deck. We would not have the luxury of a Navigator or 10,000 feet of concrete runway to return to at the end of a night flight.

Dave and I celebrate our first jet solo.

But perhaps it was more than that: not only had I not reached the required standard, I had not shown the commitment. There were other members of the course who were in the same boat and I often wonder if I was made an example to the rest; either way I was officially chopped.

To say I was devastated does not even touch upon how I felt. To me my world had ended and it was the first time I had experienced failure. I immediately contested the decision. The Naval Staff at Linton were surprised at my failure – the golden boy had fallen, how could this be so? I apportioned blame to everyone except myself, true there had been a slight clash of personalities between myself and my new young inexperienced instructor, but that did not detract from the fact that I had not put in enough work. I was interviewed by the Senior Naval Officer.

"Richard, we are surprised by what the squadron says about you. You have two choices: if you think that you have been hard done by then we can make a representation to the squadron in an attempt to get you reinstated on the course – obviously nothing is guaranteed; alternatively we have a place for you on a Navy helicopter course starting on Monday."

I knew that the squadron would never entertain the idea of reinstating me on the course and so, that afternoon, I packed my bags and drove down to Cornwall to start my helicopter flying career.

The drive to Cornwall took almost six hours, but it was a period of quiet reflection in which I thought a lot about my predicament. It had been preceded by an evening spent with Jill which had put things back into perspective. I did not know how to tell her I had failed; she was the most important thing in my life and I felt that I had let both of us down. I drove to the Nurses' Home and picked her up. The look on my face probably said it all and words, somehow, seemed irrelevant. We simply got in the car and I drove, not really knowing where I was going. I guess she must have heard from the other guys on the course and so knew exactly what had occurred. She held my hand as I drove.

I took the car up onto the Yorkshire Moors and parked by the side of the road which overlooked the Dales. It was a beautiful, early summer evening, cool and clear.

"It's not the end of the world Richard. You still have me and you will still be flying."

But it *was* the end of the world and I did not know how to cope with failure; I was too young and naive to realise that I would be a better person for it. She talked about Dave. Dave and I had become very close friends over the preceding eight months. He had struggled on the course right from the very beginning. During the period when I was breezing, Dave had battled; but he had never let it get him down. He wanted to be a helicopter pilot and his sole aim was to make it to the point where he would be streamed into the helicopter pipeline, about half way through the course. He had been chopped about two weeks before the selection point, had taken it on the chin and was extremely pragmatic about it. We all knew that deep down he was cut to pieces but he never let it show and was an inspiration to all of us.

Jill reflected upon the fact that Dave would have given his right arm to be in my position, having failed one flying course and being given the opportunity to start another. She was right of course. Just before I joined the Navy I had attended an air show at Biggin Hill, and I had almost forgotten that the display, which impressed me most, was that by the Navy Lynx. On completion of the display the aircraft landed and I watched the two-man crew unbuckle and disembark from the helicopter. As they left, they removed their helmets and hung them up in the cockpit. I watched them laughing and joking with one another and was envious that they seemed to have the best job in the world. They were flying the most capable helicopter in production and they seemed to be having the time of their life doing so. Perhaps flying helicopters would not be such a bad thing after all. As the daylight faded so did my aspirations of becoming a fast-jet pilot. I was going to be a Lynx helicopter pilot, this time I would not squander the opportunity. Even though she had known that it might mean moving 300 miles away, Jill had helped me to put the whole matter into perspective. That evening strengthened the bond between us.

CHAPTER THREE

Going Rotary

There is no such thing as a good time, unless you have experienced the bad.

Standing in a phone booth trying in vain to contact Jill, my love of flying was the furthest thing from my mind. I often joked that the greatest compliment I ever paid Jill was telling her I loved her almost as much as flying, but my passion for flying seemed irrelevant now.

I was feeling so emotional but not able to show it for fear of losing face with the rest of the guys in the squadron – it was unbearable. I wasn't sure if it was the thought of spending six months away or the prospect of going to war which upset me the most; either way I just wanted to be able to speak to Jill, then leave the squadron.

We strapped into the helicopter and started her up. The rest of the team that made up the nine man unit responsible for flying and maintaining the helicopter had travelled to the ship the night before, and they would be ready to receive us when we landed onboard.

"Three-six-zero you are clear to taxi, Runway 22, QFE 1011."

I read back the information, not really taking any notice of it, and lifted the helicopter into the hover. The Lynx was a wonderful aircraft to fly, even in the hover, the flight regime that required the most power, there was still bags of it to spare – and I felt extremely at home in it; with 600 hours to my name, 300 on Lynx, I was now confident. I tried to mentally cheer myself up: Boswell you love flying, this deployment is going to be a breeze.

Ten miles from the ship, one of the Central Warning Panel captions illuminated, indicating a loss of oil pressure in one of the engines. The oil pressure gauges sat untroubled, safely within limits. "Bollocks," I muttered. This wasn't a real crisis (even if one of the engines failed we could still fly quite safely on the other engine), it was more of an irritation: not having seen the ship since the beginning of the previous October, I wanted to join her via a very punchy fly-by.

Nick was on the radio requesting a priority landing. This involved the ship turning into wind to give us the best relative wind over the deck and some of the crew dressing in fire-proof clothing to drag us out of the wreckage, should we crash on deck. Not the best way to arrive and start a long deployment.

From the moment I first sat in a helicopter I was intrigued by them. The first I was to train on was the sporty little Gazelle, single-turbine,

training and communications helicopter. The course was eight months
and eighty flying hours long. As always it started with a lengthy period
in the classroom. I arrived late for the course, missing the first two weeks
due to the fact that it had already begun at the time I was removed from
fixed-wing training. This necessitated a lot of hard work to catch up with
the rest of the students. With the ground school complete it was back to
the basics again, effects of controls, straight and level, climbing and
descending. Although the techniques are very different to that of a fixed-
wing aircraft, it was not until the hovering phase of the course that the
fun and games really started.

The big difference between a helicopter and a fixed-wing aircraft is
that the helicopter has no inherent stability. If you remove your hands
and feet from the flying controls, in an aeroplane, the wings and tail are
designed to keep it flying in a straight line. This is not so in a helicopter
and it really becomes apparent when it is in the hover.

"Right Dickie," my instructor began with the aircraft in a perfectly stable hover and the controls barely moving, "I will start by giving you control of the yaw pedals. What I want you to do is keep the nose of the
aircraft pointing towards that tree on the other side of the airfield. Just
use small control movements to keep it pointing straight if it starts to
wander off. Follow me through on the yaw pedals."

I placed my feet on the pedals, feeling my legs start to tense up.
Merrick, my new instructor, a young and extremely competent pilot, vis-
ibly moved his feet off the controls. For a second nothing happened and
the perfect hover was maintained. A slight gust of wind gently moved the
nose ten degrees away from the tree; I pushed the appropriate pedal to
bring it back. The nose swung through the tree and ended up pointing
thirty degrees off in the opposite direction.

"You don't need quite so much control movement as that, keep looking at the tree and just feel the controls rather than push them."

I tried again, within a few minutes I could keep the nose of the helicopter pointing within five degrees of the tree.

"That's great Dickie, this time I am going to give you control of the
collective. By using the backdrop technique I want you to maintain the
helicopter in the five-foot hover."

The collective controls how the helicopter climbs and descends and
the lever is situated by the side of the seat, rather like the hand-brake in
a car. Raising the lever collectively increases the pitch angle on all three
blades at once. This increases the amount of lift that the rotor blades
generate and the helicopter will start to climb vertically. The back drop
technique is used to help inexperienced pilots maintain a constant
height over the ground. By merely looking at the grass in front of the
helicopter it is extremely difficult to differentiate between five and seven
feet. The theory goes as follows: you start by picking a marker on the
nose of the aircraft (the tree); now you choose a second marker behind it
(a fence post perhaps); when the aircraft is in a five-foot hover the top of
the fence post may just be hidden behind the first branch on the tree; if
the helicopter starts to climb, the top of the post will become visible

Learning to hover.
(Gazelle of 705 Sqn.)

underneath the branch; if the helicopter starts to descend the top of the post will become visible above the branch. Using this technique small fluctuations in the aircraft's height can be quickly assessed and therefore corrected. That's the theory anyway.

"All right Dickie, follow me through on the collective; you have control of the collective."

We bumbled up and down for a while until the aircraft settled around a median position with the top of the post making the odd appearance above and below the branch. We moved onto the cyclic control.

The cyclic is the control column that is situated in front of the pilot. By moving the cyclic to the left the helicopter will move to the left, push it to the right, the helicopter moves right. It also moves backwards and forwards, pull the cyclic back we move backwards, push it forwards and the helicopter starts to transition into forward flight. With Merrick looking after the yaw pedals and collective I attempted to keep the helicopter over the same spot. This was probably the hardest control to master. If the helicopter starts to move away from the spot, you move the cyclic in the opposite direction to return it to its original spot. Once the helicopter returns to the spot you then return the cyclic to the central position. However life is never that easy, and the momentum of the aircraft carries it past the spot and out the other side, necessitating a movement of the cyclic in the opposite direction. All too soon a horrendous oscillatory motion is set up by the pilot with the aircraft bucking wildly out of control and the instructor having to take charge again.

"I have control," Merrick spoke in a calm self-assured manner, seconds before the helicopter tried to disappear off the side of the airport. As soon as he said this I removed my hand from the cyclic and the aircraft stopped moving immediately, sitting obediently over one spot.

"Try and relax on the controls a little Dickie. Remember you hardly need to move them."

We continued for another few minutes and eventually I started to master the art. Merrick must have seen the smug 'look at me I'm a helicopter pilot' smile creeping over my face.

"That's fine, how about having a go at all three together?"

What could be difficult about this? The helicopter was sitting in a perfect hover when Merrick handed control to me, and there it stayed, for about five seconds. Then it started to drift slowly to the right. Remembering what I had been taught, I moved the cyclic to the left. The aircraft started to move back to the spot, but because I had tilted the rotor disc it started to descend as well. Still thinking that I had it hacked, and remembering how to correct for height, I pulled in a little collective; sure enough the rate of descent was arrested, however the nose swung around to the left. By increasing the power the torque had increased and, according to Newton's Second Law, the body of the helicopter moved in the opposite direction to the rotors. Things were beginning to get away from me now. The helicopter had moved way past the original spot and was pointing sixty degrees away from the original heading. I displaced the cyclic in the opposite direction and put in a boot full of yaw pedal to try and get it back. The helicopter leaped across the field, swung

Formation flying in a Gazelle.

through ninety degrees and plummeted towards the ground.

"I have control," muttered Merrick.

I prised my vice-like grip off the stick and lever and looked down at my white knuckles; I felt my heart pounding in my chest and sweat on my brow. As soon as I had passed it back to Merrick the aircraft re-established itself in the stable hover condition.

"Try and relax a little Dickie, you're a bit tense and that is leading to overcontrolling."

*Over*controlling, he must be joking – the helicopter had been *out* of control. Nobody had told me that moving one cocked up the others.

As the hovering phase continued I gradually became more proficient and discovered the technique behind the black art. As the helicopter moved away from the datums, the secret was to stop it going any further, rather than try and correct it back to the original position. So if the aircraft started moving to the left, you had to stop the movement and worry not where you ended up. This meant smaller control movements which minimised the secondary effects. As confidence and skill built I was able to assess the movement away from the datums, very quickly, and I could soon detect it almost before it had occurred and maintain the hover over the same piece of ground, at the same height and pointing in the same direction. As the course progressed I started to look forward to my first solo flight in a helicopter.

Watching your colleagues trying to hover-taxi the aircraft back into the apron became the most popular spectator sport. With the helicopter out in the open area of the centre of the airfield, the hover always looked pretty stable. However, as it approached the confines of the apron with other helicopters parked in close proximity, you could tell that the student was starting to tense up on the controls and the movement of the helicopter would become increasingly erratic. Painted on the ground were large white circles known as spots, the idea being that if the helicopter landed in the centre of the spot there would be adequate clearance from the helicopters parked in adjacent spots. As the helicopter arrived in the apron, a marshaller, standing adjacent to the intended landing spot, would direct the pilot towards it. It was quite hilarious watching your mates trying to steer the machine in the right direction and avoid all of the others parked around it. Once the helicopter was over the correct spot the marshaller would signal for the helicopter to land: unfortunately this was not as easy as it may seem. As the helicopter descended vertically towards the ground a cushion of air would form underneath it due to the downwash of the rotor blades. Descending into the cushion of air, two things happened sequentially: first the helicopter would stop descending, due to the high pressure air beneath it; next the helicopter would effectively fall off the cushion and, if left to its own devices, crash into the ground. We would sit around in groups and watch the helicopters stagger towards the spot and then, after establishing themselves in a reasonably stable hover, start descending towards the ground. As the ground cushion built the rate of descent would diminish and the helicopter would start to wobble. The student would then tense on the controls and exaggerate the problem. By now the skids of the helicopter would be inches away from the ground. Due to the risk that they might strike it, the instructor would take control and we would see the helicopter re-established in a solid five-foot hover. The student would then take control and the whole process would start over again. Sometimes the helicopters would bob up and down dozens of times in succession with the students desperately trying to take charge of the machine and drive it firmly but smoothly through the ground cushion.

It was a great source of entertainment, watching other people's cock-ups but, sitting in the cockpit yourself, as you approached the apron, was a living hell. Handling the helicopter was a breeze out in the open, but trying to maintain the same level of competence, knowing that there were things to hit and that all your mates were watching you, proved almost impossible. The problem was self-perpetuating in that after the first time I messed up the landing, I would start to worry about the next time I approached the ground; because I was worried I would start to tense up on the controls; being tense I would replace my usual relaxed fingers and thumb grip on the cyclic with a clenched fist around the top of the stick. This would make all control inputs very erratic, just what you did not need with other helicopters parked in close proximity.

Perhaps the bravest men on the airfield were the marshallers. Watching the Gazelles weave across the apron, they would be standing twenty feet in front of you, at the edge of the spot, as the helicopter danced over the concrete in a vain attempt to make contact with it in a controlled manner. As the helicopter leapt towards them they would casually wave it backwards, with total faith that the instructor would be able to regain control should it all start to escalate into a crisis situation. In the cockpit, with my eyes glued to the marshallers wands, I tried to respond to his commands. As the helicopter descended into its own ground cushion it would start to wobble: to lower the collective quickly and force the helicopter through it would result in an excessively heavy landing with possible damage to Her Majesty's property; trying to gently ease the machine towards the ground and it would start to move laterally. Landing sideways onto one of the skids could result in the aircraft toppling over and smashing itself onto the concrete. Landing with the aircraft moving backwards would result in the tail of the helicopter striking the ground. This happened so often that replaceable frangible farings were fitted to the tail boom of the helicopter to facilitate easy repairs should a tail strike occur.

Due to the aerodynamics of the helicopter, they all hover with one side lower than the other. This meant that the lower skid came into contact with the ground first. Once this part of the helicopter was safely on terra firma, the technique was to slowly lower the collective until the other skid gently rested upon the ground. In practice, as soon as the first skid contacted the ground, the aircraft would try and pivot around it and move in any direction that it wanted to. It was not until both skids were firmly on the ground with all the weight of the helicopter on them that you could afford to relax. The thought of ever being allowed to fly one solo seemed an impossibility.

Despite the distance between us, my relationship with Jill flourished. The weekend would start at five o'clock on Friday evening and while the rest of the student population would congregate in the bar for Happy Hour, I would drive from Cornwall to York, typically arriving in the small hours of the morning. Waking at around midday on Saturday I would then spend the next twenty-four hours in Jill's company before setting off at midday on Sunday, to arrive back at Culdrose in time for me to get a decent night's sleep in preparation for the following day's flying. Somehow the physical distance between us only brought us closer together. Again the attrition rate was high in terms of people not making the grade and being removed from the course. However, this time I was determined to put in the required amount of work and I found a pleasure in helicopter flying that I never came near to achieving when flying jets. There was not the sheer excitement factor of flying a jet, but in terms of pure hand and foot flying skills, it was very demanding and extremely enjoyable. Although I had never had an abundance of natural flying skills I seemed to cope better flying helicopters and found it extremely rewarding.

With the first solo flight completed we moved onto more advanced helicopter flying techniques: auto-rotations, engine-off landings, landing on sloping ground, low level navigation, instrument flying, landing in confined areas and winching. With each new skill mastered, my confidence increased dramatically. It was never easy and there was little time to spend socialising as the flying was extremely intense. Returning to the Officers' Mess, after a day in which I had completed three training sorties, I would be physically and mentally exhausted. For me, perhaps the most intensive part of the course was learning to fly the helicopter with sole reference to the instruments. With no inherent stability, instrument flying in a helicopter, to the novice pilot, was a living nightmare. On my very first instructional sortie during the instrument phase, Merrick offered me an extra strong mint just before we took off. Placing the mint in my mouth I completed the checks and launched into the air. With a screen inserted around the cockpit so that you could not see out, I started trying to fly the machine with sole reference to the instruments. I was instantly overloaded, trying to look at all of the instruments and keep the aircraft flying in a straight line, so much so that I did not possess enough spare capacity to suck the mint. Stuck in my mouth, it started to burn a hole in my tongue as I battled with the helicopter. It took an eternity to dissolve leaving me in agony for the remainder of the trip. I was never able to enjoy an extra strong mint again!

The true versatility of the helicopter as a means of transport was illustrated to me near the end of the course. We were required to plan and fly a navigational exercise that took us well out of the usual operating area and into new, unexplored territory. The exercise was to take the whole day and we had pretty much a free hand as to where we wanted to go. As Merrick's family owned a farm in the Midlands, we decided that we would plan our trip to enable us to stop there for lunch.

Landing in the farm yard and popping in for a bite to eat really high-lighted what great toys helicopters are. From there we flew over London via specially designated helicopter routes. It was a glorious day, and flying along the Thames at 1,000 feet, looking down on the Houses of Parliament and St Paul's Cathedral, was a real thrill. The thought that such a wonderfully pleasant means of transport could ever be used as a weapon of war never once entered my mind. Flying was simply wonderful and enjoyable.

The Gazelle is a fast, manoeuvrable and versatile helicopter, and I enjoyed every second flying it. After six months, and eighty hours flying, the course was finished and it was time to complete the 'dream sheet', cit-ing what we would like to fly operationally. There were three choices: Sea King Mark 3, in an anti-submarine role; Sea King Mark 4, in a comman-do support role; or Lynx, the multi-role attack helicopter. I was desper-ate to fly the Lynx because it looked good and was very impressive at air displays. Our preference counted for little in the decision-making process concerning our flying destinies. The first, and most important, criteria was how many pilots of each type the Navy needed. Generally 60% of the course would go on to fly ASW Sea Kings, 30% onto Commando Sea Kings and the remaining 10% would be selected to fly the Lynx. Normally between ten and fifteen students successfully completed the course so there were normally one or two Lynx slots on offer. As the Lynx is a sin-gle pilot helicopter flying off very small decks, only the better students

The Gazelle course comes to an end...

...and prizes are awarded. We all receive our 'wings'.

were selected to fly, but I was extremely lucky that, from our course of twelve, three Lynx slots were made available. It was deemed that I was of suitable ability to guarantee one of the places.

The successful completion of the course heralded an important milestone in my flying career. Although we could not be considered military pilots, as we knew how to fly a helicopter but not fight in one, we were awarded our pilot's wings. With the wings sewn onto our sleeves we suddenly had some credence and warranted some respect. Many people want to become military pilots, few are selected, fewer still reach this stage; for me certainly the path had been extremely torrid, so it was a proud moment when I received my wings in front of Jill and my parents.

As I was completing the final throws of the basic helicopter course, Jill was completing her final nursing exams. She finished her nursing training and, to my complete delight, started working in the West Country so that we could be closer together. I was posted to Portland in Dorset to fly the Navy Lynx; a two crew, single pilot, multi-role naval attack helicopter, operating from frigates and destroyers.

CHAPTER FOUR

Goodbye Blighty

*The biggest difference between men and mice is that mice
know when to squeak.*

As HMS *Manchester* cut through the water she looked purposeful and
menacing. I had never noticed her in this light before and, as a Type 42
naval destroyer, she possessed the elegant lines of a thoroughbred.
Designed, principally, to locate and destroy enemy aircraft using radar
and missiles, she was crowned with a large rotating antenna and a threatening missile launcher sat on the fo'c's'le.

The atmosphere on the ship was odd, very odd. *Manchester* was usually a very happy ship but, bar the usual pleasantries, nobody was really
speaking to one another. Even the ship's Supply Officer, a fully trained
barrister who always had something witty to say, greeted us fairly solemnly on arrival. As the Flight Deck Officer he was responsible for mar-
shalling us over the deck, and so was the first person we met onboard.

I left the helicopter in the hands of the maintainers – we carried a
team of seven engineers, specialising in different fields – to sort out a
technical problem, and solemnly made my way down to my cabin. As an

*My first view of the
'Mighty Manch'...*

officer I was fortunate to have a cabin to myself but, as I sat in the six foot by eight foot room, I suddenly felt very lonely and, perhaps more importantly, I felt very scared.

Over the preceding five years I had trained as a pilot. For eight months I had been a fully qualified Lynx helicopter pilot. Now I was the only pilot onboard a warship, that was sailing towards a war that had the potential to develop into the first conflict in which all the evil weapons of mass destruction could, and probably would, be used by both sides. I was now trained to use these weapons.

We were on our way to join up with a task force led by HMS *Ark Royal* and the plan was to spend a week exercising in territorial waters, before transitioning to the eastern Mediterranean to assist with the eviction of Saddam Hussein from Kuwait. I had never kept a diary before, but my emotions were running so high that I decided I would. The reason was simple. Should I die, I wanted people to know what was going through my mind in the last weeks and months of my life. I survived and the diaries are now a record of my involvement in the conflict. But more than that they are a portrayal of my emotions, with the gradual dawning that my aerial mount was no longer an airborne sports car, but a deadly weapon with which I might have to kill people.

Monday 7 January 1991 – Portsmouth Exercise Areas

Today saw me plucked from the relative tranquility of domestic bliss and placed in a ship preparing for war. I woke up this morning looking forward to the forthcoming weekend, my last in England for six months, but by eight o'clock I realised that the weekend was not going to happen.

The news hit me extremely hard, much harder than I had anticipated, and in a flood of tears I desperately tried to contact Jill but with no joy. This broke my heart. I managed to say a tearful farewell to Pat who promised to drive down and see Jill the next day, which put my mind at rest no end.

The farewells to the guys in the squadron were brief and unemotional – it was new to me this going away lark – but they had all done it before and deep down they knew exactly what I was going through.

The flight to the ship in itself was fairly eventful, we were forced to make a priority landing because of a faulty oil pressure switch. The atmosphere onboard was very strange indeed. Everyone was trying to hide it but the fear of what might be lying ahead, coupled with the anguish of leaving loved ones, struck a chord deep down. It hurts very much indeed. I love Jill and miss her already.

I drafted Jill a letter this evening, it was so hard to express my feelings towards her without making the letter really sad. I keep trying to convince myself that six months is not a long time but deep down I know it is. Sometimes I am worried about the length of time we will be spending away, at other times I worry about the threat of war, all the time I worry and long to be back with Jill. I hope that I am not a coward.

Tuesday 8 January – Portland Exercise Areas

A long and tiring day with much planned but nothing actually achieved. We were due to fly twice today but the inclement weather ensured that both sorties were cancelled.

It truly has been a day of mixed emotions for me. Sometimes when I am laughing and joking with some of the lads, the trip ahead doesn't seem too daunting at all, but most of the time I am still concerned. It seems funny how the emphasis has changed, from being concerned about the time spent away from Jill, to being concerned about sailing into a potential war zone. Although it seems less and less likely with each hour that passes, I am still hopeful that a peaceful settlement can be reached, for the sake of both sides.

This afternoon it emerged that we will have to disembark to Portland to have the engineers look at Yellow Veil. This may give me the chance to quickly pop home and say my goodbyes to Jill. My initial reaction was that this would be too upsetting for both of us, but the more I think about it, the more I want to see her again before I go. It would also give me a chance to make sure things are OK with the house and confirm that Pat has actually arrived.

Overall I am a lot happier today but I fear that this is a false sense of happiness brought about by the knowledge that I may be able to say goodbye properly tomorrow. I hope the rest of the deployment goes quicker than these last two days have.

The following day things had settled down a little and some of the usual banter was beginning to return; however, there was an air of seriousness that was impossible to escape. We had planned to fly a Yellow Veil training sortie but the English mid-winter weather was awful; it was blowing a 'hooly' which ensured that the deck was moving out of limits for flying operations. Yellow Veil is an electronic jammer fitted to the side of the helicopter. The jammer's primary role is to decoy missiles fired at the ship. But a fault was discovered during the course of preparing it for

...and my first landing on her.

flight. It was deemed imperative that it was working before we continued en-route into a hostile environment.

Nick and I had spent many hours practising with the equipment and making sure that we were both completely happy with its operation. The technique was fairly long and convoluted. If a hostile raid was suspected inbound we would launch from the ship and position ourselves in the vicinity. Once airborne we would ascertain the frequency of the missile's associated radar and then attempt to jam it. If it was an older type of missile, its radar picture would become confused and it would lose lock, enabling the ship to safely sail away. A more modern missile would automatically switch to 'home on jam' mode whereby it would track towards the jammer. In this case our role was to entice the missile towards the helicopter rather than the ship. This role was successfully carried out during the Falklands Conflict. It was understood that the Chinese Silkworm missiles, which the Iraqis had in their armament, would climb towards the jammer. In this case we would have to wait until we could actually see the missile thundering towards us and then dive away at the last moment, leaving the missile to pass safely behind us. This was the theory: it had never been tested for real.

With no-one onboard with the necessary expertise to repair it, we had to return to Portland to have it fixed or replaced. With the weather prohibiting a launch, we had to wait until the following day. On landing back at Portland, I immediately jumped into my car and drove back to the house. Jill was at work but her mother was there, so we had a great chat. I needed to pick up a few bits and pieces that I wanted to take with me but had to return quickly to Portland to re-embark. Fortunately it emerged that the ship was going to have to come alongside to sort out some of its own technical problems, which afforded me the opportunity of seeing Jill that evening.

It was somewhat ironic that the news about peace talks breaking down, came out just before I met Jill for the final time. At this stage Saddam Hussein had made it clear that he had no intention of withdrawing his troops, and the Allies realised they had no choice but to offer an ultimatum to him: either withdraw by the 16 January or risk taking on the full might of the Allied forces currently assembling around Kuwait. All the same, I had a brilliant evening with Jill. I tried to appear nonchalant about the prospect of being involved in the war and I think that I managed to convince her that I wasn't the least bit worried. In fact I was very scared about the prospects: the Iraqis had a huge armed force, weren't exactly renowned for their fair tactics when it came to throwing chemical weapons around, and the rumour was that their treatment of prisoners could be barbaric.

Wednesday 9 January – Portland Exercise Areas

Today was a good day as I had the chance to say goodbye to Jill. I love her more with every second that ticks by, and now that I have had the chance to say goodbye properly I feel better prepared to face whatever trials lie ahead.

The day started with a disembarkation back to Portland to fix the Yellow Veil, secure speech and HF radio. This gave me the opportunity to dash into town and buy the necessary domestic items to see me through the trip and partake of a much needed haircut.

I then spent a few hours at the house sorting out my gear with Pat. I am just so glad that she is down at the house at the moment. Her support and under-standing this afternoon was fantastic and just what I needed at the time.

The night out with Jill went far better than expected; we laughed, joked and enjoyed each others company just like we always do. There was no hint of tears until the last few minutes before we had to separate.

I am now forcing myself to look ahead and face each new challenge as it aris-es. I think in my heart of hearts, after the peace talks broke down today, that there will be a war. I truly hope that it is short, decisive and as painless as any war can be. I know that the guys on the other side do not want to kill us, just as much as we do not want to kill them, yet it must be so. My thoughts and prayers go out to the soldiers in the desert on the frontline. I am so grateful that I am not in their position, it must be awful for their families.

I have said my goodbyes today and they hurt a lot. Now I just want to get out there and do what has to be done, facing each new day and problem as it aris-es. Perhaps the time will go quickly and I will soon be back home for good.

Thursday 10 January – Portland Exercise Areas

I am now getting used to the ship's routine and concentrating more on the job in hand than on my personal feelings and emotions which, in many ways, is good news.

We flew twice today, a Yellow Veil training sortie and then a period of night flying. I find that while I am busy I am happy and this appears to be reason-ably true for the whole ship's company. It is only when I have a few seconds to myself that all the worries and anxieties come flooding back.

I am now looking forward to leaving UK waters and actually getting on our way: it was incredibly frustrating flying around Weymouth Bay tonight and being able to see the lights of our village in the distance. I wrote a letter to Jill this afternoon, but I found it so difficult to know what to say. I had no real fur-ther news and I didn't want to upset her by talking about the wonderful night we had together and me going away.

Overall it was a fairly indifferent kind of day, getting on with things and trying to concentrate one hundred percent on work. Staying busy appears to be the way to get through the deployment and I'm sure that in the weeks and months that lie ahead we will be kept very busy indeed.

Having joined the ship eight months previously I was well acquaint-ed with it, the Captain and most of the rest of the ship's company. However, this was my first long deployment. The previous trips on *Manchester* and indeed *York*, another Type 42 destroyer which I had completed my training on, had all been relatively short exercises last-ing a maximum of six weeks. Knowing that friends, family and loved ones will not be seen again for over half a year is difficult to relate to. In that time babies will become small children, pregnant wives will become mothers. Therefore these early days of a long deployment are always difficult. Everyone onboard has a vital role to play in the complicated infrastructure that makes up a modern warship's company. It appeared that during these first few days each and every man threw himself into his job, almost to justify his reason for being onboard. Some members of the ship's company had been in the Navy for twenty-odd years; it was strange to me that they appeared to be as unsettled as the new boys such as myself. I do not know whether this was due to the fact that leaving home for long periods of time never gets any easier, or quite simply that like me, they wondered what the next few weeks, months, maybe even years held in store. Everybody had their own theory as to what our immediate future held and, as the days went by, people began to talk about it.

Friday 11 January – Portland Exercise Areas

The day began very badly indeed when I overslept and woke up to 'Action Stations' being piped. A very rude awakening. The day did improve, however, mainly because once again I was kept busy, and so consequently time went extremely quickly. The morning was spent practising boarding party operations, good 'steely stuff'. I'm sure that no matter what happens we will have to do it for real very shortly.

I had my anthrax jab today which, apart from making my arm extremely sore and grounding me for twenty-four hours, also brought home the harsh reality that we could very well be going in to a war in which some very nasty weapons would be used.

The papers today were full of headlines about war being imminent and comparing the size of the two armies facing one another across the desert. I have also read with dismay that a number of countries are threatening to join in or even change sides and join the Iraqi forces. The amount of speculation going on is unbelievable, everyone has their own little theory about what may happen, but the truth remains that nobody knows what really lies ahead and I believe that most of the time people are just trying to convince themselves that everything is going to be OK.

"HANDS TO ACTION STATIONS, HANDS TO ACTION STATIONS, HANDS TO ACTION STATIONS."

I awoke with a start to the main broadcast. Shit, I should've been up half an hour ago. I threw on my flying coveralls and raced down to the hangar. Bad start to the day. The ship practised going to action stations fairly regularly. During the procedure all the weapons and equipment are fully manned ready for an imminent enemy attack. My role was to man the helicopter ready for an immediate launch with the jammer on the side of the helicopter. I reasoned that I had the best job. If the ship was hit, at least I would have the option of taking off, providing the helicopter was not damaged.

Before joining *Manchester* I had spent six months on HMS *York*, understudying another pilot to gain an idea of helicopter operations from sea. As it turned out, the pilot who was to be my mentor was Kim Slowe, Pig-

Pen, my old Flight Training Officer from the Dartmouth days. He   *Dawn patrol.*
remembered me bending his ear, wanting to transfer and seemed suitably
impressed that I had achieved my goal. Professionally I found him impossible to work with. He was perhaps the world's most disorganised man
and epitomised the 'shag' naval aviator. He was, however, an extremely
competent pilot and socially he was a real star. I found it difficult to imagine that he was the same person that I had tried, so unsuccessfully, to
negotiate with fours years previously. Despite the difference in age and
experience we became friends. He was a veteran of many conflicts around
the world, including the Falklands, and over a few beers he would tell stories of how his ship had been hit by an Exocet missile during the conflict.
He was test flying a newly reassembled Wessex helicopter at the time and
spent the rest of the day winching his colleagues out of the icy cold water,
as the ship first became engulfed in smoke and subsequently sank. If
Manchester was hit, I wanted to be airborne when it happened.

As soon as the ship was stood down from Action Stations we went
straight into the flying serial, the aim being to practise boarding party
operations. Like the Yellow Veil training, boarding party operations
were something that we practised fairly regularly. As the Navy had
been involved in the Gulf for many years and had been called upon to
stop and search many ships, there was a wealth of experience on the subject and a fairly straightforward but effective system had been devised.

Each ship on patrol in the Gulf carried onboard a detachment of
Royal Marines. The boarding entailed landing the stick of marines onto

The busy office.

the other ship as quickly as possible, to ascertain what cargo it was carrying. The method we used was to hover over a relatively unobstructed part of the ship, Nick would then throw a ninety foot rope out of the back, one end of which was attached to the helicopter. The marines would then slide down the rope onto the deck, rather like firemen sliding down a pole. Using this method, we could land the team of six marines in less than thirty seconds. It was excellent fun from the pilot's point of view. You did not want to be hanging round over the deck for too long in case the crew decide to start shooting at you, therefore you would come roaring in low over the sea, flare vigorously to slow the helicopter down and position it over the right spot, give the nod to the observer to dispatch the rope and marines, and exercise an equally expeditious departure to clear the area as soon as possible. For Nick, in the back, it was not quite so enjoyable as he was left to haul in the ninety feet of thick rope which took quite some effort.

When I met the detachment of marines for the first time I was shocked. I had expected to see a group of trained killers with daggers in their mouths. I was greeted by a motley crew, some of whom looked as though they would get out of breath running for the loo. It transpired that, due to the number of ships requiring a marine detachment, and the lack of marines available, our group was made up from many different specialisations – one chap had been an Admiral's driver for the last three years and hadn't even seen a weapon in that time. To their complete credit, under the stern guidance of their Colour Sergeant, they worked extremely hard at becoming an effective fighting unit and achieved it in a very short space of time. I admired their courage and stamina. By the time we reached the Gulf they were a group of trained killers (although I never did catch them wandering around with daggers in their mouths).

The afternoon that followed was fairly unpleasant. I hate injections at the best of times. The anthrax jab was designed to build up the body's immune system should biological weapons be used. We received a number of different jabs as immunisation against a number of nasty chemical weapons. Nobody questioned the validity of the injection programme; as far as we were concerned, if it was going to deteriorate into chemical warfare, we wanted all the protection we could get. There has subsequently been a great deal of research into whether the vaccinations that were given may have caused significant long-term harm to some people.

I sat talking to Nick during the afternoon, as my arm slowly started to swell up. We were playing 'Uckers', a naval version of ludo, of which Nick was the supreme champion of the known universe. "Do you think they will actually start using biological weapons?" I tried to look unconcerned.

"I really don't know," he replied. He looked as nonchalant as me, but I guess he must have been just as worried, despite his experience in the Falklands.

The ships forming the task group were still acting independently. The intention was for *Manchester* to stay in and around the Portland Exercise areas, testing all of the equipment before leaving to join the rest of the group. This is common practice for all ships prior to leaving for a long deployment and it seemed all the more relevant this time. Remaining around Portland made for a bizarre existence; of working up for war but still being able to see home in the distance. It made me ponder over how strange it must have been for the Second World War pilots during the Battle of Britain, fighting ferocious aerial battles over the English countryside and then landing, popping down the local pub for a pint of ale and wondering if the next day you might not make it back. Practising for war in sight of home was bad enough; fighting a war over the top of it must have been very strange.

Saturday 12 January – Portland Exercise Areas

A day to relax, not really much to do today. Nothing planned and not a lot achieved. I was unfit to fly for most of the day and because of the jab, none was programmed.

The morning revolved around paperwork but I failed to make much of an impression on it, my heart really wasn't in it. The afternoon was spent relaxing, chatting with the guys on the flight and watching the worst video in the world, but at least it killed a couple of hours.

I find that increasingly I am blocking my thoughts against what may lie ahead so consequently I am not getting anxious about it at all. The ship has definitely settled down and all the initial 'war excitement' has gone. People are just getting on with their jobs as if it were any other exercise, although there is a definite 'willingness to learn' atmosphere in the air. People rarely need to be told the same thing twice on matters that concern the fighting effectiveness of the ship. July seemed a very long way off today.

Sunday 13 January – Portland Exercise Areas

Another long, quiet day, in which the continued bad weather precluded flying, so the battle to keep on top of the secondary duties continued. Most of the day was spent with my Entertainments Officer's hat on, trying to sort out the 'entertainment package' for the rest of the deployment.

I was going to write another letter to Jill today but when I sat down and thought about it, I found that, apart from continued war preparations, I had no real news to tell. The main highlight onboard the ship today was the successful launch of three Sea Dart anti-aircraft missiles, which proved that all the systems worked, should we need to use them in anger.

We had a team of Nuclear, Biological and Chemical (NBC) warfare instructors on board today and we received an extensive lecture concerning flying in a chemical environment. This once again re-opened all the worries about what may lie ahead.

Overall though, not a totally unpleasant day but I am looking forward to going flying and doing the job that I am paid to do. I hope that it amounts to flying – not killing.

From the moment I joined the Navy, I found the whole experience of going to sea very strange; being cocooned in a metal box led to an odd existence that had good points and bad. Being able to fly on a regular basis and leave the confines of the ship made our life far more tolerable than most. During peacetime, being the ship's helicopter pilot was an enviable position. I had the best job on the ship, got paid more to do it, and everyone wanted to be my friend in exchange for a helicopter flight. Having said that there were parts of naval life at sea that I found intolerable; some of the antiquated customs and traditions that were held in such high regard within the service only led to a degradation in quality of life. As much as I enjoyed flying helicopters, I identified very early on that I did not want to spend my entire life in the Navy.

These quiet days onboard were even more peculiar than the busy days, when the whole ship was involved in naval evolutions. As in any career, after a busy week you feel like you need a rest and a break from the routine. Onboard, you may have a day off from your primary responsibility but you can't escape from seeing the same people in the same environment and the same pile of paperwork on your desk demanding attention. You cannot visit the pub for a quiet drink or take a stroll in the park – simple pleasures, but ones that even after a relatively short time at sea, I really missed. I would always take books to read and language courses to learn but the atmosphere was so devoid of creativity that I seldom pushed myself intellectually while onboard. This situation was made even more frustrating by being able to see the coast of Dorset.

During quiet periods such as these I spent many an hour just talking to the rest of the ship's company. A peculiar bond is built between the aircrew and the rest of the flight, mainly because you are their seniors in terms of rank, but you are completely reliant on them to keep your aeroplane flying. I found it very odd that some members of the ship's company were significantly better educated than me and yet, because I had entered the Navy as an officer, I now found myself senior to them and effectively in a different social class. There is a vast social void in all three services between officers and other ranks, but somehow the void did not seem so large on HMS *Manchester* at the time. Probably because she was a very happy ship, captained by one of the best leaders and managers I had ever met.

Each officer onboard the ship was allocated some secondary duties in addition to his primary task. I had two, both of which proved extremely time consuming and took up far more of my time than flying the helicopter actually did. As the Meteorological Officer I was responsible for receiving weather maps, interpreting them and making an informed forecast. As Entertainment's Officer, my remit was to organise the showing and swapping of the reel-to-reel films and videos that were held

Before we are taught how to fly a frontline helicopter we learn how to survive in a chemical environment.

onboard. Reel-to-reel films were shown at various locations around the ship on different evenings and the videos on closed circuit TV, with a television situated in each mess deck. Every time we came within contact of another Royal Navy ship I would attempt to organise the exchange of films and videos; on a six month deployment you require a healthy turnover to keep the men entertained, especially when it is one of the few leisure pursuits open to them. I spent the morning trying to catalogue the films we had onboard and arrange for a transfer to swap the rubbish at the earliest possible opportunity.

During the afternoon both Nick and I listened very intently to the NBC training. We were not being taught anything new, however this time we actually wanted to listen and learn. The NBC instructors were there to refresh our memories on the correct procedures for flying and fighting in a chemical environment. This training has always been taken very seriously by the Navy, but even more so during this period. Based on the way that he had treated the Kurds in eastern Iraq, we assumed Saddam wouldn't be afraid to do the same to us.

"The suits have a charcoal lining which absorb the chemicals and protect the skin," the instructor reminded us; "the dressing and undressing procedures must be followed at all times to ensure that you are not contaminated."

The NBC suits, in which we would have to fly if the situation dictated, were very hot and uncomfortable, even in the middle of an English winter. I was not looking forward to the prospect of having to fly in them in the Persian Gulf where is was not uncommon for the temperature to reach 40°C. Over the head a rubber bag, with a face mask sewn in, was worn. Into the mask clean, filtered air was blown. A four foot length of tubing connected the oxygen mask in the rubber bag to the filtration unit. The unit was shopping bag size, fitted with an electric motor that whined all the time whilst it was sucking in the air for filtration. It was known as the 'whistling handbag' and was carried around at all times when out of the gas-tight citadel of the ship. When we were flying it sat behind the seat. If we ditched, the procedure was to disconnect the tube from the whistling handbag to enable evacuation of the aircraft. Unfortunately, this also allowed water to flow in and fill up the rubber bag, making breathing somewhat impossible. The technique was to lift the tube above the water and blow out hard, rather like clearing a snorkel. Nick and I had practised this drill in the pool before leaving Portland, it was difficult and nobody had any suggestions as to what might happen when we started breathing the unfiltered air.

The method of getting dressed and undressed in and out of the clothing was an extremely convoluted and tortuous process, but designed in such a way that chemicals were not taken back into the gas-tight citadel of the inner ship. It involved using gas-tight chambers to move from the inner citadel to the outside world, placing extra bits of clothing on as you moved from one stage to another. The method of getting back into the ship took some twenty minutes as each item was cut off so that nobody had to handle it. Life in a chemical environment would surely be very unpleasant. Nick suggested that we find a hole in the programme and practise some of the procedures again. He got my full support.

The culmination of the work-up period was the Sea Dart firing. The missile is the principle weapon onboard the ship and is designed as a long range anti-aircraft missile. The ship's primary role is to position itself 'up threat' and use its long range radar and missile systems to deter any potential air attack on the rest of the fleet. It was obviously vitally important then, to test the missile system before we left UK waters. With each missile costing, at the time, some £750,000 each, it was an expensive but necessary exercise. Watching the missiles launch was very impressive – I had never seen a live missile firing before. A jet at 30,000 feet would tow a target some distance behind it the fire control radar for the missile would lock onto the target and turn the launcher to the correct bearing. The missile would then fire, accelerating to 600 miles an hour in the time it took it to leave the launcher. It looked and indeed was menacing: "If it flies, it dies" was the slogan that accompanied the pictures on the promotional literature. I was inclined to believe that it was true and took reassurance from the fact that it would be looking after us. I had but two concerns, firstly the fact that the Weapons Engineering Officer was looking so delighted when it worked, (it was as though he didn't expect it to work every time), secondly I wondered what we might have to face in return.

Monday 14 January – En route Bay of Biscay

Today has been a long and tiring day but one that has gone relatively quickly. I have flown a total of 4H hours today but it seemed a lot more. It started in the morning with some boarding operations which lasted until around eleven o'clock. We then had to fly the Captain to Ark Royal *which killed another pair of hours. The remainder of the day was taken up with further NBC training which included some dressing and undressing drills. I truly hope that we do not have to fly with the NBC suits on for real. I believe the chances of survival are pretty slim.*

This evening we flew a two hour night flying sortie which was not the most enjoyable flying in the world. It was an extremely dark night and the wind was by no means ideal. This meant the whole serial was fairly sporting and a night flying beer in the bar afterwards was most welcome.

A busy and enjoyable day in which the time passed very quickly. I thought about Jill a lot and wished I could be with her, at least for her birthday.

Tuesday 15 January – Bay of Biscay

I woke up this morning to the most magnificent day – flat calm seas, clear blue skies and unlimited visibility. There has been a definite increase in the temperature and the atmosphere onboard has improved with the weather. People seem generally happier and all of a sudden the world seems a far nicer place just because the sun is shining.

Most of the morning was spent planning a long transit to Gibraltar (over 230 miles) to pick up two computer experts and bring them back to the ship. In the end, thanks to all the preparations, the flight went very well indeed and it was great to spend an hour on dry land.

I managed to pick up some papers for the ship's company whilst on the Rock. After we returned, and had time to sit down and read them, I became quite depressed with the sudden realisation that we are not just sailing into a potential war zone but into a potential World War III. This fear lasted for a couple of hours until, on reflection, I realised that all the news stories are merely media hype and nobody knows what the next few weeks will bring.

During the evening we had a Wardroom film evening which was thoroughly enjoyable and cheered me up no end. I then wrote a few letters and as we are due to spend the day in Gibraltar tomorrow, hopefully we will receive some mail.

Why I thought about Jill's birthday I do not know, as it was still some weeks way. Perhaps it was the fact that in the four years that we had been seeing one another, I had never been around for Jill's birthday. Service commitments had always ensured that we could not celebrate it together and this year was definitely not going to be an exception – there was no guarantee that I would even still be alive by then. I tried to put such morbid thoughts out of my mind and continued with the flying.

Seeing sunshine the following morning, after such a long miserable spell, cheered everybody up. With the blue skies and being able to see for miles, I felt as though I could have been on a cruise in the Pacific. However today's task was to fly to Gibraltar and collect some stores.

We were still over 230 miles from Gibraltar, a long transit over water in a helicopter. The thought of having to ditch hundreds of miles away from any help tends to concentrate the mind somewhat and the reason we spent such a long time planning the sortie. I chased around the ship organising diplomatic clearance for Spanish airspace and filing a flight plan.

Nick was glad that we had the opportunity to visit Gib as he had some goodies to give to a mate of his who was stationed on the Rock. I was glad as it was an opportunity to leave the ship and experience a change of scenery. With an hour stop planned, I had time to catch some RAF transport to the local shopping arcade and buy all the papers I could lay my hands on. The quest for knowledge as to what's happening in the outside world is always intense when onboard ship. During this period it was even greater; we all wanted to know what we were sailing into. Over the previous few days we had only had the World Service to rely on. With a ship's company in excess of three hundred, I had to make sure that there were enough to go round.

I did not have time to read the papers while on Gibraltar and it was only when we had returned back to the ship that I opened them. I was shocked. They were all full of stories about the might of the Iraqi military. I had no idea that they were such a military superpower. Sure, I had looked at the capabilities of their Navy; it was a small but efficient unit. I had no idea their Army and Air Force was so vast. There was a lot of speculation about which side other countries in the Middle East would support; it was all very scary. The Wardroom was very quiet as everyone assimilated this information.

To cheer the officers up it was decided to hold a film night. The

Wardroom film nights became a popular part of the week for most of the officers and a great method of escapism. It was always a very civilised affair with the Captain invited down to join us. The furniture was rearranged to turn the area into a makeshift cinema, the seats at the front reserved for the more senior officers with the Officers Under Training (OUTs), responsible for running the projector. To make the evening complete we would have ice-cream at the changeover of reels. The other ranks would have film showings at different locations around the ship, although they did not get ice-cream.

CHAPTER FIVE

A Walk in the Park

The skill of survival is self-belief, self-belief is sought but rarely found.

Wednesday 16 January – Gibraltar

Well it has just happened. A few minutes ago we learned that the United Nations commenced hostilities in Iraq. This means that I am now on a warship sailing to war – there is no more time for peace talks – now the guns will be loaded and people will be shooting to kill. It is all very unreal. I cannot get it out of my mind that as I write this there are aircraft airborne, with real humans flying them, heading towards Iraq and some of them will not be coming home.

The reaction when the news was passed was very strange. The First Lieutenant walked into the Wardroom just as I was walking out on my way to bed. As the door closed behind me I overheard him announce "Gentlemen, we are now at war!".

I rushed back into the Wardroom to be met by a brief silence followed by the laughing and giggling that had been going on before the announcement was made, except this time we were joking about going to war.

What will happen now, still nobody knows. I could write about it until the cows come home but I need some time to think.

What my diaries do not mention is that, prior to the news breaking that hostilities had commenced, the ship came along side in Gibraltar for six hours, which was to prove the last time the rest of the crew would set foot on dry land for almost two months. During the course of the visit a local school donated six budgies as 'sniffer birds' in the event of chemical weapons being used. It was meant half in jest but, at the back of everyone's mind, we all thought it was a good idea. The budgies were to become an important part of the ship's character and the ship became famous for them. The whole joke escalated out of control and became absurd; they had their own watch bill drawn up for them as to when they would take turns on the bridge as the 'on watch sniffer'. The birds, in their cages, were divided amongst the mess decks and some of the sailors became extremely attached to them during the course of the next six months, to the point where there was almost a mutiny when the birds were given back to the school, on our return visit to Gibraltar homeward bound.

During the time that the ship spent alongside, those of us that were not involved in the refuelling and storing went into town on a 'postcard run'. This would normally involve buying the worst postcards possible and then finding a bar in which to sit down and write them as you got pleasantly drunk. As the ship was only stopping for six hours before sailing again, nobody drank and we found a coffee shop in which to write them instead; the whole experience was very odd.

The ship had actually sailed from Gibraltar when the signal, concerning the commencement of hostilities, arrived onboard. It was fairly late in the evening and some of the members of the Wardroom had gone to bed while the rest of us sat around shooting the breeze about nothing in particular. There was a knock on the door. (Other members of the ship's company were required to knock on the door and wait for it to be answered, they were not allowed into the Wardroom). Somebody stood up and answered it. It was one of the Radio Operators clutching a signal for the First Lieutenant, who left to read the signal outside, while the rest of us continued our discussion about nothing in particular. I was feeling tired and, with a busy flying schedule for the following day, decided I would have an early night. As I left the Wardroom I passed the First Lieutenant bustling back in and, with the door closing behind him he made an announcement.

I burst back into the room and was greeted by a stunned silence. We had all been expecting it but not quite this soon. The First Lieutenant left to discuss the news with the Captain and, when the door closed behind him, the Weapons Engineering Officer, a likeable man in his early forties, ripped the night cover off the budgie's cage and shouted,

"Wake up, you're needed already!"

It was an entirely spontaneous and hilariously funny action. Everyone in the Wardroom fell about laughing. I giggled until my lungs hurt and the poor budgie, on his first night in the Wardroom, just looked confused. The First Lieutenant returned a few minutes later and, on seeing a whole room full of grown adults giggling like school children, tried to restore some decorum.

"Listen, I'm being serious."

It was to no avail as we just laughed and laughed. It took at least ten minutes for people to stop giggling and wander off to their cabins to contemplate the implications of the announcement.

For the second time that evening I left the Wardroom to go to bed. Once I had sat down on my own and thought about the implications of it – by this time it was about midnight – I was genuinely very scared. Hence the rather curt entry in my dairy. The diaries were intended to inform family and friends how I was feeling in the last few weeks of my life, in the event that I did not survive the deployment. When I tried to write, for the first time I actually realised that this was becoming a possibility. I had to come to terms with it myself and therefore could not really write anything in the diary. It was a moment I did not want to share with anybody.

Thursday 17 January – Mediterranean
The day started with spirits extremely high as the first news reports came pouring in: no aircraft lost, Iraqi Army and Air Force almost wiped out. This

war was going to be over before it had began, and certainly long before we arrived on the scene.

As the day progressed the truth began to emerge and the initial euphoria was replaced with anxiety and fear. It now appears that the raids were moderately successful but nowhere near as effective as first reports were suggesting. Aircraft have been lost including at least one Tornado. My heart really goes out to those poor bastards, who, if they are still alive, will be wandering around in the desert behind enemy lines.

As one might expect, the ship was extremely busy today, continuing its work up to war. As a consequence we spent most of the time strapped into the aircraft. The day ended with a long period of night flying using the darkened operations procedure which, quite frankly, I think is plenty dangerous enough, without some bastard shooting at you as well.

The day ended at around two o'clock in the morning and I went to bed feeling tired, knackered and very concerned for the future.

It transpired that my fears were correct and the poor bastards that had been shot down were wandering behind enemy lines, soon to be captured, tortured and put on display in front of the world's media. I never knew any of this until much later, but what I did know was that given the choice I would opt for returning to base and a warm bed rather than enemy capture, and with some justification. The Navy has always taken survival and resistance to interrogation training very seriously, far more so than the Air Force. The first course that all prospective aviators undertook after graduating from Dartmouth was the month's Aviation Physiology, First Aid and Survival Training held at Seafield Park in Lee-on-Solent. The first week was devoted to aviation physiology where we learnt how the body coped with life in the air and some of the design faults that made life as an aviator precarious at times. By the end of the first week we all wondered why we wanted to be pilots so much. The next week consisted of an intensive first aid course, the final part being a large exercise of a simulated air crash in which we had to administer first aid to the victims. At the end of this exercise becoming a bank clerk seemed like a far better option. For the next five days we returned to the classroom and were taught, in detail, the finer points of survival, escape and evasion. Following the theory in the classroom, the practical part began, the part that we had been dreading – nine days in the New Forest learning how to survive for real.

We knew that the exercise would start on the Friday so, on the Thursday night, we held a big party in the Officer's Mess. A good time was had by all and copious amounts of alcohol were consumed. As always this seemed like a tremendously good idea at the time, we jested that starting the course with a hangover would be a great way of simulating ejection shock. The following morning, woken early, we were made to run around the sports fields for half an hour and then strip searched to ensure that we were not attempting to carry any money or food with us; having a hangover did not seem like quite such a good idea. After being searched we were issued with a few bits of equipment that would become our worldly possessions for the next week and a half. I looked down despairingly at what we had to live with: a parachute that would serve as a tent and sleeping bag; a small survival kit consisting of some windproof matches and some glucose sweets; a waterproof jacket – given as a concession as the weather was so cold – and a few wooden sticks so that we could construct a backpack from the aforementioned materials. Just to make the course completely realistic we were given a pair of flying overalls and flying boots to wear in the forest. In addition to the waterproof jacket, as protection against the forecast extreme cold, we were given the option to wear a jumper if we wanted to do so. We all did as it was bloody cold!

The course started with a two-hour drive to the middle of the New Forest. We were sitting in the back of a five-ton lorry with canvas sides and even before we had travelled a mile I began to feel very cold as the wind whistled around the inside – a very practical example of the wind-chill effect about which we had learned the previous week. Military five-ton lorries are not renowned for their soft suspension and creature comforts and, after being rattled about and frozen half to death in the back of one for two hours, it was rather like bashing your head against a brick wall – it was great when it finally ended.

We gradually emerged from the lorry and huddled together against the chilling January wind; already we were fatigued, cold and regretting the excesses of the previous evening. As always we were not allowed to

'Action Lynx'. Getting airborne in a hurry.

wallow in self pity for long. A curt word, shouted rather than spoken by one of the instructors got us moving down the track towards the first rendezvous that would be our home for the night. By now it was dark and, as we walked nosily down the track, we stumbled across a rabbit staring blindly at the headlights of the lorry as it left us behind. A quick thinking member of the group shone a torch into its eyes to hold its attention while the rest of us circled the fluffy, rather cute looking bunny. We had formed a tight cordon around the animal before it realised that an ambush was being set. Startled and frightened it tried to make a break from the carnivore *homo sapiens* who was determined not to go hungry on the first night of the survival course. As the rabbit bolted we jumped back, treating it like a man-eating lion rather than prospective supper. The rabbit ran harmlessly into the forest leaving us feeling rather sheepish and not like trained killers at all.

After a two-hour walk we arrived. The grid reference we were given put us by the side of a small lake and, floating majestically in the centre, illuminated by a brilliant moon, a twenty-man life-raft waited for us. By the lakeside lay a number of survival suits that were ready for donning and the message was simple; we were being treated to a short swim followed by the luxury of a night in a dingy. There were two small problems with the plan. The first that the water next to the bank had already begun to freeze, which made us all less inclined to dive in. The second made itself apparent as soon as the first brave individual entered the water en route to the life-raft. The suits were dry suits that covered the whole body, just leaving the hands and head exposed, with rubber seals to prevent water pouring in where these protruded. I had seen them during my time onboard *Herald* and *Invincible*. They were known as 'Once Only Suits' and I now discovered why. They were only meant to be used once and then discarded, but these had obviously been used on many occasions. As we entered the icy water the suits began to fill up and, as I swam to the life-raft, I could feel the water level rising inside mine, sensation at the extremities of my limbs gradually subsiding as the cold took effect.

The night that followed was cold, damp and miserable. Despite being incredibly tired we were all too cold to sleep and, as we had now gone in excess of twelve hours without, food became the only topic of conversation.

"I fancy beef stroganoff now, made with fresh cream and lots of paprika to keep you warm," a voice announced to nobody in particular.

"No, what you need to keep you warm is a Burger King Spicy Bean Burger, they would be ideal in this situation," somebody else replied equally hopefully. I would have settled for either.

The following morning we were woken by voices from the bank. The loudness of the shouting indicated that it was the survival course staff returning to move us on, rather than a friendly passer-by offering us breakfast. This could only mean one thing – an early morning swim. I had never really warmed up from the swim eight hours previously and therefore, calculated that getting cold and wet again would not make the least bit of difference. I was the first student to take the plunge into the icy water – but I was wrong. Overnight the temperature of the water had fallen still further and, as I entered, it flooded into the suit taking my breath away. For a moment I felt incapacitated and almost panicked. It was only a fifty yard swim to the bank and I tried to compose myself to make the distance. Shortly my cold feet touched the bottom and I had never felt so relieved. The ice around the edge had reformed and I broke through it with vengeance en route to dry land. We had been on the course for less than twenty-four hours out of the forecast ten days, and already I was cold, tired and pissed off. For the first time I asked myself whether any of this was really necessary. All I wanted to do was fly an aeroplane. The next guy stumbled onto the bank and shook himself like a dog emerging from a pond. He looked down at his blue finger tips and shook his head. "I want my Mum," he mumbled, half in jest, but I couldn't help but think that there was an element of truth in the comment, and it applied to all of us.

From here we were broken up into teams of three and sent on cross-country navigational exercises in different directions. Although it was still bitterly cold, the sun began to shine and, walking along, we began to dry out a little so things did not seem so bad again. In total we walked for about eight hours and, by the end of the day, we were feeling the effects of having no food. Inevitably, we all began to get a little irritable. That evening, after we had built a tent and sleeping bag out of the parachutes as taught the previous week, I sat around and talked with my two team-mates. Like me, Fraser had left school at eighteen and had joined the Navy wanting to fly and, like me, he had received some slightly misleading information. Fraser had joined as a General List Seaman rather than a specialist aviator and spent the next three years trying to transfer. He had not succeeded, but was eventually allowed to train as a pilot after three years, instead of the usual five that seaman officers have to complete before they are allowed to specialise. He was the guy who had fantasised about beef stroganoff and the fantasy had still not abated.

"A nice hot plate full of stroganoff and a pint of Guinness is what I need right now."

Fat-Boy Fraser was half a stone overweight and I was beginning to realise why. I tried to steer the conversation away from food and started talking to Jerry, the third member of the team.

"What made you join the Navy Jerry?"

I wish I had not asked the question. He launched into his life history from the time he was about five minutes old. Jerry had a reputation for being a very nice guy, but just a little bit too keen and enthusiastic in everything that he did, to the point of becoming a complete pain in the butt. Having said that he had a heart of gold and, as discovered throughout the course, he would go out of his way to help you. Despite this fact and on more than one occasion, as Jerry launched into one of the world's most boring stories, I wondered if he might be more useful in a casserole. Failing to turn the conversation from either the merits of using UHT cream in stroganoff, or Jerry's formative years between the ages of fourteen and nineteen, I decided to try and close my ears to the conversation and sleep. Notwithstanding the arctic conditions, I managed a couple of hours, my body demanding some rest. The third day of the exercise started with another early morning, pre sun-up, break the ice off the make-shift tent, call from the staff. We were now instructed to operate as individuals and given separate routes to follow, all ending up at the same location at the end of the day. I walked off into the distance using my map and compass, feeling slightly apprehensive at the prospect of getting completely lost in the middle of the New Forest. By now we had gone in excess of forty-eight hours without food and the hunger was beginning to abate. I was not sure whether this was due to the fact that my body was acclimatising to life without calories, or simply because I did not have to listen to Fraser talking about food anymore.

I walked for most of the day and gradually found my way around the intended route. Fatigue and lack of stamina were increasingly becoming important factors. The right mental attitude was now required to keep the legs moving and to remain motivated towards completing the task. Walking alone it was all to easy to stop and rest on a frequent basis, the route was designed such that you had to keep moving to complete it in daylight hours. The sun had begun to set by the time I arrived at the rendezvous position, but thankfully I was not the last to arrive. After a quick chat I decided to erect my 'pup tent' before all light was lost.

The principle behind the pup tent was simplicity itself. The parachute was repeatedly folded along the seams until you were left all of the parachute material folded into a layered triangle shape. The top layer was then lifted and secured to a tree whilst the remaining layers, underneath, became the bag in which you slept. The tent took less than ten minutes to erect and I had just taken my shoes off and was in the process of crawling in, when a member of staff arrived on the scene, and told us to dismantle our tents as we were going on a solo night navigation exercise. I have never been afraid of the dark, but the thought of blundering around a forest in the thick of night seemed rather scary. On top of this I had walked in excess of sixty miles over the previous two days, all with an empty fuel tank and I did not want to walk any more. Unfortunately we had no choice in the matter, and half an hour later I found myself stumbling around the countryside trying to feel my way through the forest.

After walking around for half of the night I eventually, and quite literally, bumped into another member of the course. It was such a relief meeting him that it took my mind off the Beast of Dartmoor, which I had convinced myself was taking a vacation in Hampshire and which I was bound to meet around the next corner. We talked for a while and decided that we would travel together for the remainder of the night, working on the theory that, although we were not supposed to, it was far too dark and cold for any of the staff to be out to catch us. A while later we stumbled across another individual who joined the party, and by the time we had reached the next RV we were a group of five. It was a great advantage travelling as a group, as we offered each other encouragement to keep our legs moving through the periods of intense tiredness.

As the sun rose the following morning we reached our destination. By now four days had elapsed, almost entirely spent on the move and without anything to eat. Initially I had kept myself motivated by repeatedly telling myself that this was an exercise and it would all be over soon. This was the last hurdle before I started flying training proper. By the time the night exercise ended it no longer seemed to matter that it was only an exercise. The fact that I was lost exhausted and hungry was not an exercise, it was very real. Morale and stamina were very low indeed. We now entered the static stage of the course, the object of which was to teach us how to survive if we found ourselves in an inhospitable country, but without the threat of immediate capture.

We reformed into our groups of three and the first objective was to build a 'basha'. These are more permanent structures and are built from logs and bracken into a lean-to design. The basha took most of the morning to construct but, had we been asked to build it at the start of the course, it could have taken less than an hour. Once complete we manufactured snares and traps from materials procured around the new base camp. Sitting in the classroom the theory behind a fairly intricate spring loaded rabbit trap had seemed relatively easy. Trying to construct one while barely able to walk and with hands so cold that they would hardly function became somewhat more difficult.

The afternoon ended with a treat. The instructors returned to inspect our new accommodation and snares. By way of a reward for our hard efforts we were presented with the surprise. From the back of the Land Rover one of the instructors pulled a large cardboard box. In the back, huddled nervously were five rabbits, brought straight from the pet shop. The rabbits were distributed, one per group of three. The instructor demonstrated how to kill them cleanly and effectively. Held upside-down by the tail, the rabbit was laid across the hip and, in one movement its head was pulled down and twisted, breaking the spinal cord and killing it instantly. Our group looked around at each other: who was going to carry out the deed? After four days without food there was no way that we were going to let this rabbit escape. I picked it up, laid it across my hip and killed it in one movement as instructed – sentimentality had no place on a survival course; we were tired and hungry and far removed from the content, if hung-over, group that had started the course. Once dead, the rabbit was skinned and drawn and placed in a pot of boiling water to simmer for an hour. I had eaten rabbit before but never had any food ever tasted so good. A third of a rabbit would not usually be considered a banquet, but in our eyes, at that moment in time, it was a feast fit for a king.

After the meal, as the sun began to set, we settled down for our first good night's sleep since the course had begun. With the basha to sleep in we had three parachutes to use as sleeping bags. We elected to use one as a ground sheet, make a large sleeping bag for the three of us to share body heat in from the second, and use the third as a duvet to spread over us. We threw our boots off, put our dignity aside and snuggled down into the sleeping bag. No sooner had we started to get comfortable when, predictably, we were woken by the staff and taken on a two mile run through rivers and swamps. By the time we returned to the basha we were cold and exhausted. Some of the guys had been violently ill due to the exercise so soon after eating. The thought of losing the calories so soon after gaining them prevented me from even thinking about being sick. That night I slept soundly for a full twelve hours.

The following morning there was no early call and we were allowed to wake of our own accord. The temperature was still subzero and lying huddled up in the parachutes no one saw any good reason for making any effort to arise. Eventually the dreaded staff arrived and we threw ourselves out of the basha for fear of being taken on another forced march. The day was spent building smoke lamps to be used in the event of spotting a search and rescue aircraft and generally honing our survival skills by surviving. It was midway through the course and I believe the day was deliberately low key to give us chance to recuperate before the more arduous part of the course began.

Day six started early. Even before sun-up we were woken by the distant sound of a Land Rover approaching. This could only mean one thing – the staff arriving. By the time they appeared we were up and ready to move. Leaving behind the basha that had become home, we progressed onto the next stage of the course. We reformed as a group and were given two hours to complete an eight mile trek to the next rendezvous. Ordinarily this would have been the proverbial 'walk in the park' but in a weakened state every step was a complete effort. The batteries were now very low indeed. Each day I had woken feeling exhausted, convinced that I had reached the limit that the body could sustain without any food. Each day I would push through the pain barrier and then fall asleep, convinced that I couldn't take any more the following day.

Finishing the eight mile jaunt we were greeted by the staff yet again. This time they played the final psychological joke on us. As we arrived the largest member of the group was taken away. Not surprisingly this was Fraser (although he had lost weight like the rest of us, he had more to lose). He arrived back a few minutes later with his leg in a mock splint. The new scenario was that he had fallen and broken his leg. We had to construct a stretcher out of flora and fauna that surrounded the area and carry him back to the site that had previously been our base camp, the site we had just left. We had all convinced ourselves that we could not go any further. The prospect of re-covering the same ground, this time carrying a stretcher, filled the mind with the possibility of new, as yet untouched pain barriers that we would have to go through. It had now been almost a week without any real food, but with almost non-stop activity. I doubted in my own mind whether I would be able to make the march.

As I assisted with constructing the make-shift stretcher every bone in my body hurt. For the first time since the course started I considered quitting. This course was all nonsense. All I wanted to do was fly aeroplanes. I could quit now and apply to join British Airways as a trainee airline pilot – rumour had it that they would be recruiting soon. I would not have to continue with all of this irrelevant warlike nonsense, playing at soldiers, and, more importantly, I would not have to complete this agonising stretcher march. In the end I plumped for the easy decision and elected to continue. Having said that, if anybody else had quit in front of me, I would have been right behind them.

There were nine people on the course. With Fraser as the casualty, eight people remained to carry the stretcher. After a short discussion we elected to utilise the following system: six people would carry the stretcher with two resting; when it all became too much for a member of the carrying party he would rotate with one of the 'resters'. Using this method we intended to keep moving for the eight miles. The only way to do this was to do it quickly.

The stretcher was now complete. Fraser lay upon it and we gathered around and lifted. Initially it did not feel as heavy as anticipated. We adjusted the stretcher to take the weight on our make-shift back packs. As if to ridicule us one of the staff members started his stopwatch and informed us that the course record was one hour forty-eight minutes. As if I cared.

The first hundred yards were not too bad, then Fraser started to get heavy; by the time we had completed another hundred yards he had become very heavy. The weight started to bear down on your shoulders and initially became uncomfortable, but within a couple of minutes the discomfort had turned to pain. We started to manoeuvre the stretcher around on our shoulders to try and find the position that induced the least amount of pain. It proved elusive. One of the resters carried out the map reading – getting lost and walking twelve miles instead of the predicted eight would have been too much for any of us to handle, hence the weight of responsibility for the two non-carriers fell as heavy on their shoulders as the weight of the stretcher on the carriers'. We had covered about half a mile at what felt like a blistering pace when the pain on the shoulders became unbearable – all the bearers agreed. The only saving grace was that the pain was so intense that it stopped us thinking about our tired legs. A group decision was taken as we walked. We would stop, rotate the carriers around and try carrying the stretcher in our hands as opposed to on our shoulders.

We all rotated around one. This meant that next time we rotated it would be my time to rest. Words could not describe how much I was looking forward to that. We stopped for just long enough to change positions. Once again, for the first few seconds, having the weight off the shoulder was just bliss. However, no sooner had the pain in the shoulder started to abate than the weight on the arms started to tell and the pain returned, only in a different position. For the next hour I have no real recollection of what happened. It hurt a lot and I closed my mind to it. Just put one foot in front of the other and keep moving. Ignore the pain. If you ignore it for long enough it goes away. Don't think about the walk, don't think about the stretcher, in fact don't think about anything. Almost in a trance-like state we continued, the pace still far quicker than the outward journey when we had not been carrying a stretcher. One foot in front of the other, just keep going. After taking my turn to rest, I elected not to have another rest period. To rest meant to navigate. To navigate meant to have an active mind. To have an active mind meant thinking about how tired you were, knowing that you still had another five hell-like miles to complete. Knowing that a wrong turn would induce untold misery in the group, once again I elected for the easy option – just carry and forget.

"Only another mile to go."

It was the first time that I had really taken notice of what the navigator had said. It brought me out of my trance. My entire body hurt and I wanted to go back to my zombie existence.

"What's the time?" I enquired.

"Who gives a fuck!" another zombie from the other side of the stretcher replied.

"No, seriously, how long have we been carrying this stretcher for?"

The navigator looked at his watch.

"One hour and thirty nine minutes."

Somebody else realised what I was getting at, but the pace was slowing, there was no way any of us could go any faster.

"Boswell, we would have to run to break the record from here."

There was no way any of us could run with the stretcher on a shoulder in the condition we were in. Nobody said anything but somehow the pace quickened. We all started taking bigger steps, with only a mile to go the end was in sight.

"It would be a great fuck-off pill to the staff if we did break the record," somebody else replied from behind me. And then we were running. The stretcher was bouncing around on our shoulders, bruising the flesh every time it landed. Fraser was holding onto the sides, realising that it was a long way down, or perhaps he realised that if he fell and we stopped, we would never start again. He started offering words of encouragement, pushing us on. But they were words that we did not need. We were running as fast as we possibly could, the ground was a blur beneath my feet. I was fuelled by the pain alone.

After an eternity we rounded a corner and in the distance we could see a Land Rover with the staff waiting for us. They were sitting drinking a cup of tea, not expecting to see us for some time yet. Hearing our yells of encouragement to one another they stood up and glanced at their watches. And then they were running towards us shouting encouragement as well.

"Come on lads, only another 300 yards to go, keep pushing, keep pushing."

The body was in complete automatic now. I looked up and the Land Rover was so close I could read the number plate. One last burst and then we were there.

The staff rushed up to take the weight of the stretcher as we came to a halt. As the weight came off my shoulders my legs buckled beneath me and I collapsed to the floor. But I was not alone; around me every member of the team had done the same. Through the pain I closed my eyes and heard the staff announce the new record.

"One hour and forty six minutes. Fucking impressive stuff, gentlemen."

The staff came around with water bottles to ensure that we were fully hydrated. It was only then we realised that the person who had suffered the most was Fraser. He had been bounced around on a wooden stretcher for two hours and his entire body was black and blue. Added to this he had been lying still for the entire period in sub-zero temperatures. While we had all been perspiring with the exertion, Fraser's body temperature had been slowly dropping to such an extent that mild hypothermia had set in. Realising the pain that we were all going through, he did not feel as though he was in a position to complain. He was taken away, wrapped in a warm blanket and given a cup of hot tea to drink. As a reward for our efforts we were all given a mug of tea as well. Sitting in the winter sun, not moving, and drinking a warm cup of tea, I was in heaven and did not want for anything else.

We were given the remainder of the day as rest. Considering the state that I was in, that's all it could have been. I realised that after believing that I had reached the limit on all the other occasions, I now had. I had pushed my body as far as it would go. I was exhausted both mentally and physically and we were now in the state that the staff desired. The following day we moved into the escape and evasion phase. Day seven started with a thorough briefing on the final stage of the exercise. We would now act as singletons. We were behind enemy lines and were to remain tactical at all times. This meant moving at night if possible. If forced to move during daylight we were not to use main roads but had to remain concealed from anyone that passed by. There was a team out looking for us. We discarded our backpacks with the parachutes and spare socks. Finally we had five minutes to copy relevant details from the maps before they were taken away.

However, before the escape and evasion phase started we took part in an exercise with the local police dog handling team. In order to give us an insight into the difficulties of remaining hidden from our canine friends we had to conceal ourselves in a large wood. To ensure that we were well and truly hidden, two hours were allocated to the task. On completion of this time the dogs would come and search us out. I wandered off into the wood and found a large hole that had previously been inhabited by some creature that smelt a lot better than I did at that moment in time. It crossed my mind that if it was true that a dog's sense of smell was a hundred times more sensitive than that of a human then, if I were a dog, I would not want to go anywhere near humans who had spent a week in the woods without washing, until they had all taken a long, hot shower. If the dogs were going to be forced come and smell us out then we definitely got the better deal.

The dogs duly arrived at the allotted time and within thirty minutes we had all been found. I'm not sure who got the biggest fright when the German Shepherd poked his snarling nose down the fox hole and came face to face with pungent smelling *homo sapiens*. Either way it made us both jump. Once discovered we watched the dog handlers use the dogs as offensive weapons. One by one we had to strap a leather protective cover to our forearms and then run off into the woods. The dogs would then be dispatched after us to grab our protected arms (we hoped) and bundle us to the ground. Once on the ground they would stand over us and snarl a lot if we moved. All very impressive stuff.

The end of the exercise was in sight. But our spirits were not lifted by this prospect. Now that we had entered the escape and evasion phase; the much talked about, and feared by all, interrogation was only hours away. Everybody knew that the final day consisted of being captured by the 'enemy' and taken away for interrogation. The whole course was shrouded in a certain amount of secrecy and once it was completed it was an unwritten rule that you did not discuss the dynamics of it with anybody who had yet to attempt it. The secrecy added a certain amount of mystery and glamour to the proceedings. However, most people had an idea about what they could expect in 'the woods' as the course was known – apart from the interrogation. Nobody ever spoke about that phase of the course. We had received extensive training in the classroom concerning what information we would be allowed to give if captured and how, under the Geneva Convention, we might expect to be treated. We had been warned that the interrogation would be conducted by trained professionals and would be very realistic indeed. We watched videos made by the MOD on how they envisaged we could be treated in such situations – it was not a very appealing prospect.

Back in the forest it was all becoming very real. With the dog exercise completed we were each assigned an area in which to build a tactical shelter and this would become home for the night. During the course of the night the area would be searched and anybody discovered would be sent home for an early bath. We guessed that this meant a longer time in the company of the interrogators and I set about building my shelter in earnest. As generations of soldiers had done before me I started digging, for a tactical shelter amounted to not much more than burying yourself in such a way that it did not look like a recently cultivated allotment when complete. As the sun began to set I eased myself into the hole and pulled the pre-prepared branches and leaves over the top of the hole.

For the next three hours I lay motionless as the temperatures began to drop. Initially it was great just to lie there and do nothing but soon the cold began to take effect. First I felt cold. Then, after an hour, I started to shiver. After two hours my whole body was shaking uncontrollably. It was so, so cold that I closed my eyes and wanted, quite literally, to die. Presently I realised the seriousness of the situation – I was not shivering any more as hypothermia was setting in. Bollocks to the exercise. I emerged from the hole looking and feeling like an extra from a Michael Jackson video.

The sound of me emerging from what was fast becoming my own grave was obviously heard by somebody else deep in the woods.

"Who's that?" a rather cold and weak voice enquired from the darkness.

"It's Dickie, listen get out of your hole, it's too fucking cold."

Jerry emerged from the darkness onto the track where I was standing.

"I got out about an hour ago, I was freezing to death."

We sat and chatted for a while and discussed ways to warm ourselves. In the distance we could hear the faint sound of people talking. We decided to investigate and seek help against the increasing cold.

Not surprisingly, it transpired that the voices were those of another group of survivors who had recently emerged from the ground. There were now five from the group of eight and we took the decision to seek out the other three. Already there was concern that, if still in the ground, they could potentially be in serious trouble. We spread out and shouted. After a couple of minutes we found them wandering in the opposite direction looking for the rest of us. No sooner had the whole group reformed when the staff Land Rover arrived on the scene. Realising that the temperature had plummeted to -7°C the staff had arrived to retrieve us from the ground. In the back of the Land Rover they carried a cauldron full of piping hot soup. We huddled around the back of the vehicle and waited excitedly as the soup was distributed. Just warming your hands on the cup was luxury enough; drinking the hot liquid was heaven itself. The staff remained with us for over an hour, checking that we were all fit to continue the exercise. Strangely, even though we remained cold, exhausted and on the very limits of our endurance, nobody wanted to stop. Having come this far we wanted to finish it properly. It was obviously far too cold to continue with the tactical shelters and we were divided into two groups of four to spend another night on a navigation exercise.

Nobody took this seriously; it was too cold. We wandered around the New Forest looking for somewhere warm to shelter. It did not seem like an exercise any more; as far as I was concerned I really was surviving. My group came across a derelict shed situated by the side of a disused railway line. The building did not provide much shelter against the cold but, having a roof over our heads, it made everyone feel better. The group huddled together to try and conserve body heat but nobody really slept as it was just too cold.

As the sun began to rise in the morning we formulated a plan. Now well in excess of a week without eating properly, and with the interrogation section only hours away, we needed some food. One of our number thought he knew the site that had been home for the night, and was fairly convinced that less than a mile away there was a small village. We estimated that we were close to the next rendezvous point and were not due there for another three hours. Two members of the team were duly dispatched to search for the village and locate any food that they could. Meanwhile we waited in the cold. After two hours they had not returned and so we had no choice but to proceed on to the next RV. As was becoming normal for this exercise, once close to the designated meeting place we met the intrepid food hunters. The news was good, they came bearing Mars bars, and lots of them. Resembling Cambodian refugees we sat in the sunlight and dined on chocolate for breakfast as we listened to how the explorers had come across a small paper shop. They had to wait for an hour before the owner arrived but soon persuaded him to part with the chocolate in return for a watch, put down as a deposit to guarantee that the money would be paid on completion of the exercise. Quite what they looked and smelt like to the poor shopkeeper is a mystery, but my guess is that we smelt pretty bad and he parted with the chocolate just to ensure that the food hunters left the shop.

Eating food again lifted us both mentally and physically and I now felt ready to face the final few hours on a full stomach. I also had a psychological advantage for, as far as the staff were concerned, I had not eaten for over a week. But I knew I had just eaten and, rather like a schoolboy who is told a secret, that made me feel very good indeed. I had won the first battle. At the RV point again, we were greeted by the staff. This final part of the exercise was very simple. We had to make it to another trig point ten miles away, only this time there really were people out looking for us. Once at the trig point we had to meet another mystery person and using a code system, just like a James Bond movie, we would make contact. After that, it was anybody's guess. The final part of the brief was that at all times we were to act as singletons. With that the instructor raised his hand and from over an adjacent hill, thirty or so 'aggressors' came in quick pursuit. Instinctively we all fled into the woods.

At least half of the course members were caught in the first few minutes. Some believed that with the 1,000 yards head start they could easily outrun the pursuers. They had not taken into account the fact that being this long in the field had taken its toll physically. Even though it felt as though you were breaking the four minute mile, the fit and rested chasing team easily caught the survivors, like greyhounds chasing a wounded rabbit. For them the escape and evasion exercise was over before it had really began. For me it was to last another ten hours.

As soon as I entered the wood I threw myself into an adjacent fox hole and covered myself as best as I could. The pursuers, all volunteers from a neighbouring naval base and all regular sailors eager to catch a young officer and give him a hard time, stampeded into the woods after us. While there were still runners ahead they chased them and did not spend time searching for people who had taken the less energetic option. As I lay there, trying to gasp for air as quietly as possible, the enemy ran past me and were gone into the woods. I lay there for well in excess of an hour as I wanted to be sure that they had truly disappeared.

Emerging from the hole, I tentatively walked back to the dirt road. I waited by the side for five minutes hidden in some brambles and, when I was sure the coast was clear, walked nervously onto the road. Once in the open I looked left and right, resembling a young child crossing the road for the first time on his own. The caution was not misplaced. Along the road I could see two of the enemy walking in the opposite direction and I quietly retreated back into the woods. Obviously I would not be able to travel using the main tracks. Using all my newly acquired skills, I ascertained which direction I was facing and orientated myself to face the desired way. Sitting in the classroom I had paid little attention to the survival instructor talking about moss growing on the south side of tree branches. Having regarded these facts as something out of a not very interesting episode of *Blue Peter*, now they took on a whole new significance. I formulated a plan. Using the roads was obviously foolhardy, but walking in a straight line, between the two points, ran risks as well as that was bound to be what the enemy were expecting us to do. The cunning plan was to move ninety degrees to the intended direction of travel and hopefully circumnavigate the enemy. For half an hour I walked north when the final RV was west of me. Initially, encounters with the enemy were fairly frequent, however, walking through the undergrowth, I managed to achieve first sighting on every occasion and thus avoid them. Soon the sightings became less frequent until, eventually, I deemed it safe to start heading west.

For the next six hours I navigated using the sun, darting into cover at regular intervals to avoid detection. The chocolate inside my stomach seemed to lift me both mentally and physically and the game of cat and mouse became both interesting and intriguing. While it was still only an exercise, it had gone on for so long that it all seemed real to me and I did not want to be caught. Exercise or not, I was not looking forward to the interrogation and wanted to postpone it for as long as possible. Navigation had always been an inexact science to me and trying to find my way around the New Forest using only a hand drawn map and fungus on trees, I was not entirely sure of my position. However, as the sun started to set on the horizon, I estimated that I was closing on the RV position. The increasing numbers of pursuers that I was having to evade confirmed this fact.

The meeting point had been described as a five-bar gate on a track in the corner of a field. Finding the pre-arranged RV point I approached it with caution and, when I had crept to within thirty yards, I hid myself in a ditch and waited for any sign of activity. Thirty minutes passed with no sign of life. Eventually, becoming bored, I walked boldly up to the gate to investigate. No sooner had I thrown caution to the wind and walked out into the open, than a shout from behind me meant that I had been discovered. Turning around, it was not the mysterious person that I was supposed to be making contact with but a pair of the aggressors. There was no point in running, it was all over. Standing still, I was bundled to the ground, my hands tied together in front of me and a blindfold placed over my eyes. When fully trussed I was marched away, stumbling on the broken ground. The two 'aggressors' said nothing and I was marched silently back down the track. I was later to learn that I was the last person to be captured and was within 200 yards of the RV position but I had mis-identified the correct gate.

After a brisk and uncomfortable twenty minute walk I found myself being bundled into the back of a lorry. I was aware of the presence of people around me as the lorry started up and started to move. For the next two hours I was bounced around in the back, not able to see anything and with the noise of the old five tonner drowning out any possibilities of hearing anything that may have given clues as to where I was being taken. Eventually the journey came to an end and I was bundled out in an undignified manner.

Being led by my hands, the aggressors said nothing. I was aware that I was being led down some kind of passageway. Every few steps I would stumble and fall, each time I would be pulled up again and pushed on at the same remorseless pace. And then we stopped moving. My blindfold was torn from my face. The light was so bright that I could not focus but I was aware of a figure standing before me. "Safeguard, I am a doctor. Before we continue with the next stage of the exercise I have to ascertain that you are fit and willing to do so. Can you confirm that you are Midshipman Boswell and that you consider yourself fit to continue?" The word "safeguard" meant that this was for real, this was not somebody pretending to be a doctor for the sake of the exercise. But for a long time now this had ceased to be an exercise for me. For the last four days I had been genuinely surviving, and, no I did not feel OK and no, I definitely did not want the torment to continue. My eyes began to focus, I blinked repeatedly and remained silent trying to comprehend what was going on. It looked as though I was standing in an old Second World War bunker, I was aware that there was more than one person in the room. The person before me was in uniform, I recognised the red strips in between his gold bars that indicated he was a doctor. "Boswell, did you understand me? We need your consent before the exercise can continue, do you consider yourself medically fit?"

"Yes Sir."

As soon as I had muttered these words a flashlight illuminated the room in a bolt of brightness that returned my vision to its blurred state. Someone had taken a photograph of me. As I blinked, feeling confused in this indistinct world, the blindfold was placed over my eyes again. All of this time I had been standing perfectly still with my hands by my sides, now I was bundled out of the room again and down a corridor. Then I was in another dark and damp bunker. Again my blindfold was removed. Before me was a large desk, behind it a sat a stern faced man.

"Take off your boots and clothes."

The temperature was freezing. I had no idea what the time was but it must have been late at night. I slowly undid my shoes and began to undress. Eventually I stood naked and shivering before him. He looked me up and down by way of examination.

"Put your overalls and boots back on, leave the rest of your things on the floor."

I placed the flying overalls back over my body grateful for the limited warmth that the garment offered. As I placed my boots back onto my feet the blindfold was placed over my head and again I was led out of the room. I had no time to fasten the laces on my boots which made walking even more difficult. Led once again through a maze of passageways I felt confused and disorientated. All of the time I could hear a diesel engine that drowned out any other noise and sounded as if somebody was trying to drill into my head.

Many hours later I lay in a hot bath and contemplated life. How many hours later I had no idea; all that mattered was that I had successfully completed the interrogation phase. The truth is that I actually remember very little about those twelve or so hours bar the fact it felt very real and, in my weakened state, I believed that I had been 'captured' for an eternity. My mind constantly played tricks on me: was this really an exercise or was my thought process just trying to shield me from the true horrors of what had really happened? I recall being dragged from one stress position to another and then from one interrogation to another with no sense of time or place. Perhaps not surprisingly, the most vivid memory I retained is that of being sat on the ground, my legs crossed in front of me and my hands placed onto my head, one on top of the other. I was grateful for the opportunity to sit down, but within minutes the cold from the stone floor started to seep through the thin material of the flying overalls and numb my bottom. I soon discovered that I had another problem. The zip on my overalls had long since broken leaving the front open. Wearing no underwear, as I sat cross-legged on the floor my penis rested on the cold ground. I began to get concerned when I started to lose feeling in it. Exercise or not I was rather fond of it and had no intention of suffering frostbite in my nether regions.

Every time that I moved my arms to try and replace my penis into the comfort of the front of the flying overalls, somebody would snatch my hands back and replace them on the top of my head. I began to worry. Soon this became less of a problem. I could no longer feel my genitals but, trying to keep my hands placed on my head was becoming increasingly painful. Rather like holding your hands in front of you, it was fine for the first few minutes but after a while it became increasingly difficult. Every time the hands slipped somebody would instantly replace them. Throughout this time I could hear nothing but the diesel engine incessantly beating on my eardrums.

Although the exercise never became physical beyond the discomfort of being placed in stress positions for hours on end, the actual interrogations I remember as being extremely real. People yelling at you one minute and then trying to be your best friend the next. Ordinarily I am sure that I would have found the play acting rather comical; in my confused and exhausted state I found it rather sinister.

After an hour in one position, with my arms feeling as though they were going to drop off, I was bustled into another dingy room. Again my blindfold was removed. Before me was another desk, although this time sitting behind it was a charming looking woman. She smiled at once and pointed towards the chair in front of the desk.

"Sit down Richard, make yourself comfortable, would you like a cup of coffee?"

The brief had been very specific: we were only to give our name, rank, number and date of birth. We were not to answer any other questions. I sat down on the chair, grateful to take the weight off my feet.

"Well Richard, would you like a cup of coffee?"

She held up her mug and looked inquisitively. I nodded expectantly. "Does that mean yes or no Richard?" Her tone began to change. I averted my eyes from her glare and looked at the floor.

"I cannot answer that question." This was the only other answer that we were allowed to give.

"Your name is Richard Boswell?"

I sat uncomfortably, not knowing what to do. The irritation in her voice began to unsettle me.

'What *is* your name then?"

"Richard Boswell."

"Well, Richard, do you want a cup or coffee or not?"

The silence obviously irritated her.

"I am trying to be civil with you, what are trying to hide? We found you in the forest. What were you doing there?"

The one-sided conversation continued in this vein with the interrogator becoming more ferocious in her verbal attacks. And then that interrogation ended. Blindfold on, I was led away and back into a stress position with nothing to think about but the cup of coffee I never tasted.

And so the interrogations continued, but never in any particular order. It's called "dislocation of expectation" and is designed to confuse. It worked. Sometimes I would be led away and end up back within earshot of the generator in a stress position. I had no idea of whether I was still in the same room or whether I had been moved to another part of the building. More importantly I never knew what was going to happen next. That is very disturbing. I tried to keep track of time by counting the seconds to myself; as a timekeeping device it was pretty awful but it did keep my mind occupied. After finishing one interrogation I was led away into another room and the blindfold removed. Before me stood one of the members of staff had been supervising us the previous week whilst in the forest.

"Safeguard - exercise over, have a cup of soup."

He handed me a cup a warm tomato soup. I took it without speaking and obviously looked confused.

"The exercise is over. You can talk to me if you like. How do you feel? Would you like to see a doctor?"

Still afraid to speak, I shook my head and took a sip of the soup before it was taken away again.

"Bosers the exercise is over, would you like to speak to some of your comrades, they are next door?"

"Thank fuck for that, I never want to do that again." And I meant it.

It took another twenty minutes for the exercise to finish for the rest of the team. We were then taken around the mysterious building. It was an old open castle. I had assumed that the whole building had been in darkness; in fact the diesel engine was a generator supplying electricity to numerous strip lights illuminating the building. I had assumed that I had been on my own whilst held in the stress positions; in fact we had all been in the same place, just yards from one another. I do not really remember much about the tour or the trip back to Seafield Park where the exercise had begun ten days previously. I remember eating a Mars bar and drinking a pint of beer and feeling sick. It was around five o'clock in the morning so I ran the bath and started to contemplate life. The feeling was out of this world. It was so good to be warm. I fell asleep almost instantly.

I awoke some time later sitting in a freezing cold bath of mud. The water was a thick dark brown and the smell pungent. I could not believe that all of the grime had originated from my body. I drained the water away and the scum stuck to side of the bath. I cleaned it and ran more water to wash myself again. It took four bath-loads of water and a shower before I felt clean enough to go to bed.

The final week of the course was dedicated to sea-survival drills. Reflecting during our passage across the Mediterranean, I realised that, although the course was advertised to us as teaching survival skills, what it actually achieved was far more subtle and subjective than merely instilling the knowledge of what mushrooms to eat or how to catch a rabbit. If you are unlucky enough to be shot down behind enemy lines, then these skills are relatively unimportant. Time and time again it was stressed that the most important aid to survival is the will to survive, but no course can ever teach you this will. What it actually did was push me to my limits: through hunger, discomfort and exhaustion, the personality clothing that hides the real person was stripped away, the 'inner self' exposed. Getting to know this inner person, instilled a new deep-seated self-assurance, the certainty that I could retain my dignity, even in the most adverse circumstances. This is so important. Stripping an individual of all his self confidence is the most effective tool available to interrogators. However, possessing the knowledge that you can retain your self belief, instills a confidence which means the only thing you need fear is the physical pain that you may be subjected to after capture. According to prisoners of war, this is one of the easier factors to cope with. This core confidence, this ability to believe that you can cope with the very worst, although it may not manifest itself in routine day-to-day existence, is what emerges in adversity. This is the will to survive that the instructors referred to. It was a useful tool in my armoury, but even so, I was rather hoping I would not have to use it.

CHAPTER SIX

A Mediterranean Cruise

*Partisans fight for passion – thankfully soldiers and mercenaries
merely fight for a career.*

Friday 18 January 1991 – Mediterranean

This morning I awoke to the news that Iraq had attacked Israel using Scud missiles in what appears to me as an obvious attempt to draw Israel into the war and create World War III. This hit me like someone punching me in the stomach, and I was scared, very scared.

I felt certain that Israel would launch a counter attack in no time at all. However as far as we know this hasn't happened yet. There is a rumour going around that the Americans have put enormous pressure on Israel to exercise restraint and avert mass destruction. I was thankful that we were kept busy all morning flying so that I did not have too much time to contemplate it all.

This afternoon we heard that the first British warship had become involved in the hostilities. It appears that Cardiff's Lynx has been tasked to locate and destroy two Iraqi Fast Patrol Boats, we are still awaiting feedback as to their success. We all realise that soon we are going to get involved in the hostilities and come under fire and I believe that most people have come to terms with this now.

I went to bed this afternoon as I was totally exhausted after a very busy few days. I woke up dreaming about being at home with Jill in our lovely little house, alas I am not but I wish I was.

During this period the ship went from the normal routine into 'defence watches'. This meant that the ship was brought up into an increased state of readiness and so all vital equipment and weapons had to be manned twenty-four hours a day. This obviously required a significant increase in the number of man hours worked onboard the ship each day. To achieve this, with the same number of men onboard, the ship's company was divided into two halves, port and starboard watches. Port watch would man the equipment for six hours while starboard watch slept and ate; they would then change over. In theory this could carry on *ad infinitum*. It is very tiring as during the time off you need to sleep, eat, write and read your letters and complete your ablutions. Times of the day and indeed days become meaningless, the only person you have a regular social contact with is your opposite number who you take over from every six hours. The flight consisted of two aircrew and eight maintainers. As it required both of us to fly and fight the helicopter, the aircrew could not divide into defence watches. We continued to work our own routine, sleeping when we could and flying when required. The maintainers were divided into two groups of four and went into the defence watch routine which meant that there were members of the flight available to work on the helicopter twenty-four hours a day, so that in theory, we would be available to fly at all times.

Along with the defence watches the ship was 'secured for action'. Experiences in the Falklands Campaign had shown that, post enemy attacks, ships were lost unnecessarily. This was due to equipment inside the ship not being secured to the deck. This had two implications: firstly personnel were injured by loose articles flying across compartments during missile and bomb strikes, and secondly the loose articles themselves impeded the damage control efforts. In smoke-filled compartments fire fighters would trip over equipment scattered across the floor, these items would then be sucked up into water pumps as attempts were made to empty water filled compartments. The Navy was determined not to make the same mistakes again and so the ship was 'secured for action': nothing was allowed to be left out unless it was tied down. Pictures had to be removed from walls, chairs were tied to tables unless someone was sitting on them, photographs of loved ones were taken down. All creature comforts were removed, but there were very few complaints since everyone realised the seriousness of the situation.

Coupled with securing for action, we also changed into our action coveralls. This was another legacy from the Falklands Conflict. Naval uniforms contained some and some sailors suffered horrific burns as a result of being caught in a burning ship in their uniform. After the Falklands it was deemed too expensive to change the entire naval uniform so a different solution was sought and found. On sailing into a hostile area all members of the ship's company were issued with two sets of white action coveralls. These were made of double layered cotton and were extremely fire retardant. There was but one small problem with them. When under threat of chemical attack, and everyone had donned their gas masks, we were all dressed in exactly the same clothing and it became impossible to establish the identity of the person you were talking to, causing an element of confusion. Therefore we were required to write our rank and name in big, bold black letters on the right pocket. The Wardroom as a whole lost an extreme amount of street 'cred', when one member spelt his own name incorrectly, although it did give us all a good laugh.

With the introduction of these measures, the atmosphere onboard changed quite markedly. There was no more dressing for dinner and silver service, no more pleasant after dinner conversations; the Wardroom looked bare and impersonal. But people did not get demoralised and they went about their business far more purposefully than before, with everyone taking the situation very seriously, but people retained their sense of humour and the atmosphere, while different, was not unpleasant.

That evening we were tasked to fly between all the ships that made up the Task Group. It was not a particularly pleasant evening for night flying and the atmosphere in the aircraft was tense, if only because the weather was right on the limits and all of the ships were using darkened operations procedures. Night flying in any situation is not enjoyable. "Only bats and twats fly at night" was the common attitude of most aircrew towards night flying, especially from a heaving deck in the middle of nowhere. It does have a strange way of concentrating the mind! For normal operations at night a series of lights are illuminated to aid the pilot while recovering to the deck. Probably the most important of these is the glide path indicator (GPI). It shows green when you are making the correct angle of descent towards the deck, red if too low and amber if too high. When closer to the ship a row of lights, known as the horizon bar, is switched on above the hangar and these give you a good perspective of the ship and indicate how much the ship is moving. When hovering alongside the deck, they make the pilot's job considerably easier as they provide a visual reference to hover alongside. Finally there are some low intensity lights that are shone onto the deck to illuminate the deck markings. In a tactical situation the darkened operations procedure would be used: in order to minimise visual detection the GPI would only be used when the helicopter was within half a mile of the ship, all other lights would be extinguished and the pilot was one hundred percent reliant on the Flight Deck Officer to marshal him over the deck using illuminated batons.

On this evening we flew to HMS *Brave* to drop off some stores which we had collected in Gibraltar for them. *Brave* is a Type 22 Frigate, equipped to carry Sea King helicopters and therefore had a considerably larger deck than the one I was accustomed to operating from. I had never flown to a Type 22 at night before. As the FDO waved me across the deck, I moved the helicopter close to the hangar as I was used to doing. The FDO signalled for me to move back. I moved a few feet but he signalled me to move the helicopter back further. I moved another few feet. Surely by now the back wheels must be close to the edge of the deck; in the darkness I had no idea where the deck ended and the sea started. Still the FDO signalled me to move back further. Had he gone completely mad? Had the ship been hijacked by Iraqis and this was their idea of a sick joke, making me land in the sea? I manoeuvred the helicopter back still further. By now I was totally convinced that no matter how large the deck we must be hovering over the sea. The FDO signalled for me to land. During all of this, Nick hadn't said a word. He knew how hard I was working. I did not want to land, it did not feel right. I quizzed Nick.

"Are we over the deck, mate?"

"I haven't got a clue, it's far too bloody dark, but the FDO seems to think so."

So much for words of wisdom from the experienced aviator. I swallowed and against my better instinct lowered the collective to start the helicopter descending. She settled gently onto the deck for a perfect deck landing in the centre of the spot. Night flying was definitely dangerous enough without some bastard shooting at you. The rest of the flight was just as uneventful but just as scary.

The following morning the daily information signal revealed details about the first Scud attacks on Israel. This was it. Surely the Israelis would retaliate; they are not known as pacifists. I had always respected their attitude in the past if you fuck with us, we will fuck with you, only worse. All of a sudden I felt that this attitude of automatic retaliation would throw the whole of the Middle East into turmoil. If Israel became involved, what would Syria, Egypt and Jordan do? Would they be dragged into the war on the Iraqi side? The consequences of what might happen were unthinkable. It really did scare me.

The other news of the day came later in the afternoon. The first Navy Lynx had been tasked to locate and destroy two Iraqi Fast Patrol Boats; that's what they were out there to do after all. I waited anxiously to hear how our compatriots had faired. Here were two colleagues, drinking buddies of mine, facing enemy fire as they searched the seas to destroy enemy shipping. It all seemed so unreal. I waited up late that night to catch some glimmer of news as to their success or fate, but by two in the morning it became obvious that we were not going to receive news until the following day and I was very tired. I discovered the next day that they had successfully sunk an Iraqi vessel.

Saturday 19 January – Eastern Mediterranean

I usually sit down at the end of the evening, just before I go to bed and write these notes, however today I was so tired that I forgot all about it, so I am writing this the following day. It is amazing how little I remember about the previous day.

I do remember, however, an early start as we were flying between eight and ten o'clock. Most of the flying was involved with a trial about which we know nothing but involves flying around the ship at various distances pointing what looks like a white sandwich box at the ship. I assume that there is some kind of transmitter in it. The remainder of the day was spent trying to sort out the Japfax machine such that it will give me a met picture, sorting out the videos for the closed circuit TV, writing a few letters and sleeping!

We flew in the evening for a couple of hours, the first part of the serial we had our postman hat on and flew around all the ships collecting mail and taking it to Ark Royal.' *The latter part continued with this 'dodgy' trial. After the flying I awarded myself two night flying beers for good behaviour, during which we had a real fire in one of the engines, not that it affected me. I remember the general alarm going off and not even wondering what it was for.*

Sunday 20 January – Eastern Mediterranean

Life seems to continue with some sort of absurd normality at the moment, today was just another ordinary day. The craving for constant news reports has died down quite considerably. In fact I only heard one news bulletin today and that did not contain any news at all, just more speculation.

I didn't get up until reasonably late today, around eight o'clock followed by a morning letter writing and preparing the flying brief. We took off at midday, with our postman's hats on once again, this time collecting all the incoming mail from Ark Royal *and distributing it around all of the ships in the task group. This was followed by practising boarding operations, rapid roping the Royal Marines down, all good fun. In total we flew over four hours today but the time went very quickly.*

The highlight of the day was receiving a letter from Jill, I really hope that she writes as often throughout the deployment. It is quite uncanny how we seem to be on the same wavelength; all the questions I asked in the letter that I wrote this morning, she answered in the letter that I received this afternoon.

The evening was taken up watching a film in the Wardroom. Sitting watching the film it is easy to forget that you are on a warship heading to war.

Tuesday 22 January – Off Cyprus

Today was meant to be a rest day for the ship's company after two long tiring weeks, however it didn't quite work out like that. Overnight we approached Cyprus and the plan was to remain at anchor just off Akrotiri airport to allow a Sea King to Vertrep (vertically replenish) *all of our stores and mail.*

I awoke to a glorious day, flat calm and very sunny, however rumours were already spreading like wildfire. We have been tasked to transit the Suez canal tomorrow and make full speed to the Northern Persian Gulf to assist with the war effort – now it's all for real. I was not totally surprised by the news. I suppose that we all expected it really, but I was still shocked at the prospect, despite all the soul searching I have done about it.

We ended up doing a reasonable amount of flying today, taking stores here there and everywhere and doing a two hour surface search to clear the area ahead for our passage the following day. The other good point of the day was that we received some mail onboard and I received loads, which cheered me up no end.

The day had a bizarre end to it. We were all sitting around watching the Wardroom film when someone politely knocked on the door and informed us that we had gone to air-raid warning red, i.e., air attack imminent. There was no panic, only humour. It turned out to be a false alarm, probably Scud missiles aimed at Israel.

Ordinarily, Royal Navy ships spend most of their time at sea involved with one exercise or another. I had joined *Manchester* six months previously and had spent most of that time involved in an assortment of short exercises. This period of the deployment was quite bizarre in that it was just like any other exercise and we were in the relatively safe waters of the Eastern Mediterranean, with no direct threat to life or limb. Occasionally, however, there were episodes that brought everything back into perspective; on one occasion as we transited past the coast of Libya, I sat and watched the maintainers working on a live torpedo. Gaddafi was known to have an active submarine fleet, and as yet he had not made any indications as to any intent to become involved in the conflict. However he was not known for his sound and rational decision making. It had been assessed that the submarines were a significant threat that merited further surveillance. Anti-submarine helicopters from HMS *Ark Royal* patrolled the oceans for the menacing 'beneath the surface' craft. We prepared our torpedoes such that we could act as a weapons carrier if it was deemed that we needed to sink these vessels.

As I sat in the hangar it occured to me that the long black cylindrical shape seemed to summarise all that was sinister about this particular facet of warfare. It occurred to me that we could be sunk at any moment by an enemy we had never seen and were not even at war with. For some strange reason it just made me laugh.

During this period, all of the ship's company who possessed beards were ordered to shave them off. The reason was very simple; with the chemical threat taken very seriously, a beard prevented a proper seal being achieved between the face and gas mask. The slightest leak in the gas mask would negate its use with potentially disastrous consequences if Saddam chose to use some of the chemical and biological weapons he was known to possess. The whole episode added an element of joviality to the day as old and bold sailors who had grown their beards when they had joined the Navy twenty years previously, had to shave them off. Nick had always been known for his large stature and beard to match. Without it he had a baby face and I began to realised why he had grown it in the first place. I laughed inwardly but not outwardly. He was a Chelsea supporter and significantly bigger than me.

The trial that we were asked to conduct was very odd. Two scientists, looking just as I had imagined scientists to look, had joined the ship in Gibraltar and had installed a black box on the mast. We were then given what looked like a sandwich box and told to fly around the ship, pointing this sandwich box out of the window at the ship. It was the most boring of flying and the scientists in their grey corduroy slacks and home knitted cardigans, kept asking us to repeat the procedure. I was extremely inquisitive as to what the trial was all about but only the mad rocket scientists and the Captain knew, and they were not about to tell me. The sandwich box was quite heavy and contained a very primitive off/on switch, so it obviously contained a battery. The fact that we were required to point it at the ship meant that it contained a transmitter of some description, although more than that it was impossible to say. After many hours flying, the men in corduroys were apparently satisfied that it was working and we dropped them off in Cyprus. On leaving the ship they gave the Weapons Engineering Officer a key. The key opened a door in the black box, behind which was a red light. If the red light went out at any time we were to signal these guys immediately – that's all we knew about the black box.

Carrying out a Vertrep was a far more interesting form of flying. The Lynx is a very powerful helicopter but not that big. Therefore if we were required to move a considerable amount of stores from one place to another, rather than try and load it in the back of the helicopter we would transport it as an under-slung load. Nick would lie down in the back of the helicopter with his head out of the door looking down and talk me into position until the strop was over the top of the load. The stores to be moved would be wrapped up in a net and it was a simple matter of the ground crew connecting the net to the hook on the strop.

Once connected, I would lift the load off the deck and gently transi-

En-route to the Gulf. Driving the ship during a RAS (Replenishment at Sea).

tion away. Flying with a heavy load hanging thirty feet below the helicopter was an art form in itself. The load would act like a pendulum on a grandfather clock. If it was allowed to swing too much it would start to move the helicopter, which is when the fun and games would really start. The pilot would feel the helicopter move and adjust the controls to try and stop the movement. By this time the load would have reached its limit of swing and be moving in the opposite direction. Therefore, because of the lag, the pilot's control input would be in the same direction as the swing exacerbating the problem. If not careful, the pilot could induce such a severe swing that the load would have to be released before it caused the helicopter to crash. Nick being such an experienced observer was an old hand at this type of serial and gave an expert con.

"Height, line and speed are good, fifty yards to run."

At about this time I would lose sight of the drop off area underneath the nose of the aircraft.

"OK Nick, lost contact."

"Roger, height, line and speed still good, ten yards to run."

I would now slowly bring the helicopter to a hover, fifty feet above the deck, with the load hanging beneath us. Nick would continue the con.

"Come forward eight yards and right two yards."

Judging how far three yards is when you are so high over the deck and all you can see is the sea can be quite difficult. However the con would continue.

"Forward three yards, two yards and steady, nicely over the spot, down ten feet."

By coming down I could gently place the load on the deck and allow the ground crew to unhook it. Nick would continue with his head out the window.

"OK load's been earthed, now on the deck, ground crew under the disk and unclipping...Load's clear, you're free to transition."

We would go round again and repeat the whole process. We moved a surprising quality of stores that afternoon, but with three hundred men onboard and no idea when we would have the opportunity to re-supply again, we needed to take as much gear as possible.

On receipt of the news that we were to make full speed to the Persian Gulf, after the initial shock, I was actually quite relieved. Rather like waiting for some bad news, it's almost good news when it arrives as it means that you can stop worrying about it. I suppose deep down part of me actually wanted to see some front-line action. The helicopters from HMS *Cardiff* and *Gloucester* had now accounted for five enemy vessels and appeared to be on top. I wanted a bite of the cherry, but it didn't stop me being scared at the prospect. I believe the same could be said about the rest of the ship's company; certainly the atmosphere was jovial as we watched the Wardroom film.

The knock on the door was not heard first time and hence ignored. The second time the young Radio Operator knocked slightly more purposefully. One of the 'off watch' Warfare Officers answered the door and read the signal, AIR RAID WARNING RED. In an exercise this would have caused people to drop everything and run to their Action Station. Nobody moved. The signal was telling us that an attack from the air was imminent, either missiles or aircraft. The reason for people's lack of enthusiasm was not a state of developed apathy, it's just that sitting here off Cyprus people did not really believe that there was a serious threat of an air attack. Even if there was, we were already in defence watches, all the weapons were manned and the ship was secured for action. Nick and I left the Wardroom, amongst serious banter and went to change from our action coveralls into our flying suits, just in case we had to go flying. That was the ship's total response to be told that an air attack was just about to take place. It crossed my mind that the system obviously worked if nobody needed to run around panicking. It turned out to be a false alarm and we all enjoyed the rest of the film.

Wednesday 23 January – Off Cyprus

A busy day where all the final preps for detaching to our new theatre of operation were completed and we commenced passage to the Suez Canal. We had not been programmed to fly today although, in the end we spent nearly four hours airborne, most of it load lifting – all of it fairly demanding flying. By the end of the day I was shattered.

All of the other ships in the group sent us their best wishes every time we landed on their decks, they all seemed genuine messages of well-being which was very heartening to hear. During the evening I allowed myself a couple of beers as the aircraft is down for maintenance for three days and we also had a little party to see off the old navigator. I found it very difficult to get into the spirit of it all and for some reason ended up feeling very depressed and went to bed a worried man.

I thought about the consequences of dying, of those who I would leave behind and how their lives would be affected. I wondered how I would cope with the prospect of being crippled, spending the rest of my life in a wheelchair perhaps. What frightens me most is that these are real prospects, not just the fruit of my overactive imagination.

This was the last day we would work with the rest of the task group. They had been assigned to remain off the coast of Cyprus and maintain the protective air umbrella in the Eastern Mediterranean. As we flew around the rest of the group there was very much a feeling of leaving old friends, their messages of best wishes all seeming heartfelt and very genuine. It was impossible to ascertain whether they wished they were going to the front-line as well or were glad to be staying in the Mediterranean.

The atmosphere onboard the ship remained strange. The Navigating Officer was leaving after a two year appointment on the ship. His relief had joined in Gibraltar and they had completed the hand-over as the ship crossed the Mediterranean. The party to say goodbye to him, was a small and quiet affair as we were still at sea. Drinking my first beer for a week I just could not get into the mood for having a good time and relaxing. I knew that the Navigator was going home and this made me wish that I was in a similar position. I had not really thought about home and Jill during the previous week as I had thrown myself into the work. Now that I had time to relax and unwind, I just wanted to go home.

CHAPTER SEVEN

Transition to War

Conflicts of the mind are more difficult to win than physical battles.

The ship commenced its transit through the Suez Canal around mid-night. It transpired, much later in the deployment, that intelligence had been received to suggest that the Iraqis might try to close the Canal, hence the reason for our sudden detachment from the rest of the Task Group. They remained completely inactive and bored in the Eastern Mediterranean for the rest of the war. *Manchester* waited until the cover of darkness to slip through the Canal, and so minimise the chance of a terrorist attack. I slept through all of this totally oblivious.

There were a number of modifications that needed to be carried out on the aircraft to bring us up to the full Gulf specification. It was two full days work for the maintainers to fit all of the additional equipment, so we decided to use the Suez transit, where we couldn't fly, as an opportunity to ground the aircraft for two days so that all of the work could be completed. The extra equipment that was fitted included an additional IFF, an infrared jammer and the hard wiring for a passive identification device.

The Identification Friend or Foe system (IFF) was designed to reduce the chance of a 'blue on blue engagement': being shot down by friendly forces. The standard aircraft carried a normal IFF set as do most aircraft both military and civilian, and it is used for air traffic identification. The system is very simple: the ground station sends out a signal to which the aircraft responds. The pilot sets a code given to him/her by Air Traffic; that code then appears on the radar screen so that the controller knows exactly where each aircraft is. The addition-al system known as Mode 4 IFF, that was fitted during this period worked on the same principle but was slightly more complex. When challenged, the aircraft sent an encrypted signal to the ship or ground station challenging it; the encrypted signal would be deciphered by the ground station and would reveal whether the aircraft was friend or foe. It was encrypted such that the Iraqis could not pretend to be a friend-ly unit. With the Iraqis possessing a very effective Air Force, more than capable of sinking many of the allied ships in the area, we assumed that the ships would be a little trigger-happy. Therefore we made a decision very early on that once we got to the Gulf, we would not go flying unless the Mode 4 IFF was working.

The other additional piece of equipment that was fitted was an infrared jammer. However we removed it within a week. Every time we tried to test it, it caused one of the circuit breakers to trip and we could smell burning. A decision was reached that, pound for pound, the extra fuel would be a better bet. I have no idea how much money was spent procuring this equipment which then sat in the back of the hangar gathering dust, but I was impressed at how quickly the new equipment had made it to the frontline. I felt we were not being sent into a war zone to act as cannon-fodder. I guess that if I had thought that infrared missiles had presented more of a threat, I would have insisted that more time was spent trying to make it work.

The Passive Identification Device (PID) was known as Sandpiper. It consisted of an infrared camera that bolted onto the side of the helicopter and produced a black-and-white TV-like picture on the radar screen. Initially I thought that this was going to prove very useful in identifying contacts to ascertain whether they were enemy. The picture it produced, based on the heat differential between objects was very clear. However it was still early in its stages of development and unfortunately the magnification just wasn't enough to make it a useful tool. After extensive trials, it too was consigned to the back of the hangar with the infrared jammer.

Thursday 24 January – Suez Canal

As the aircraft was down for maintenance, in many ways it was a restful day, as we knew that we would not be called upon to fly. Both the morning and afternoon were spent attending lectures on how to fire-fight and repair a ship after it has been hit, and how to survive a chemical attack.

Not surprisingly I found this very thought provoking and the anguish came running back. It sounds very naive and perhaps even childish but I really do not want to die: there is so much that I still want to do with my life.

The late afternoon was spent exercising on the flight deck as the ship passed through the Suez Canal. It has to be said that getting out into the open and stretching the muscles cheered me up no end.

The evening was uneventful. I had planned for an early night but received an invitation down to one of the mess decks and spent the night making light hearted conversation over a few tinnies. I was grateful for the change of company but I really do want to go home back to the ones that I love. July seems just so far away at the moment.

Friday 25 January – Suez Canal/Red Sea

Today was the first really hot day of the deployment. It was another no fly day and one in which I didn't really achieve much but enjoyed myself nonetheless. Most of the morning was spent watching the ship replenish at sea with a large American auxiliary ship. I stood on the bridge wing in the glorious sunshine and generally took the piss out of everyone involved in this seamanship evolution, as I am prone to do. Eventually the fish-heads got fed up with me and made me take the con for half an hour so that I could appreciate how hard they were working. Now I know why I decided to go flying.

On completion I wandered down to the flight deck and watched three Sea Knights recover to the back of the auxiliary's deck, all very impressive. The rest of the morning was spent recognition training. After a quick half an hour sunbathing on the fo'c's'le during lunch time (aeroplane spotting – saw a Sea Sprite and a Viking), I spent the first half of the afternoon sorting out a flight plan for tomorrow's trip into Jeddah. The rest of the afternoon I was back on the flight deck for some circuit training in the sunshine.

The evening was very quiet. There were few people about so I dashed off a few letters to Jill and Mum and Dad. Once again I found it very difficult to sound cheerful with the realisation that some people will not make it back home, although it is sinking in now and I truly believe that I am beginning to cope with it.

Watching the guys on the flight spend a full two days fitting all of this additional equipment, followed by lengthy discussions as to how we were going to use it proved very thought provoking. Yes, it was great talking about how we would use all of these toys to destroy the Iraqi Navy, but this was serious stuff now. In any conflict, no matter how superior your forces are, you must expect some attrition. Ultimately we were being sent round at maximum speed to act as a replacement for when the first RN ship was sunk, or Lynx helicopter shot down. I tried never to display my anguish. The unwritten rule seemed to be to never let your fears show to anyone, but the thought of people shooting at me, either in the helicopter or in the ship made me scared, very scared. The fact that we had been provided with so much extra equipment, aids against being shot down, meant that nobody thought this was going to be a walk in the park; at some point this was going to get dangerous.

With all of this additional equipment the helicopter was in theory a far more capable craft than that which I had trained on. Those days of flying training seemed so far away, and yet the reality was that I had been out of the training pipeline for less than a year. After gaining my wings I had a month's 'holdover' period waiting for the next Lynx helicopter training course to start. I took advantage of the opportunity to attend two adventurous training programmes; those courses that the military seem to specialise in and yet nobody seems to have the time to attend. During the month, I qualified as a top roping and abseiling supervisor and went straight on to learn how to become an expedition leader. Both courses had been run by the Army at their adventurous training centres in North Wales and had provided a welcome break from the mental demands of flying training.

In the February of 1989 I had commenced Advanced Flying Training. The first part of the course consisted of a month in the classroom at the Royal Navy's Warfare School in Portsmouth. Here we learned the tactics involved in fighting a modern naval battle and the role that aviation plays in it. Perhaps rather poignantly, I did not fare very well in this course, having little interest in fighting tactics. On reflection, at that stage in my career, I did not fully appreciate that the Lynx is considered as one of the ship's principal weapon systems. I had just heard that it was great fun to fly and couldn't wait to get my hands on it. The only real memory I have of the course is landing myself in serious trouble when I was caught cheating in the final exam. I could not be bothered to learn the theory behind advanced radar propagation.

From one immensely boring course not really related to aviation we moved onto another: a month spent in the Royal Navy School of Management. Here we were taught how to become Divisional Officers, responsible for the welfare and career progression of the men under our command. This course did have its moments, but in my humble opinion too much time was devoted to learning the fine art of filling in the reporting form correctly, such that the Head of Department would sign it first time without making you re-type it fourteen times. Upon reflection I did learn a little on the subject of man-management. This ultimately stood me in fairly good stead over the next few years, whilst I built upon my management and leadership experience.

I completed the two courses with the other two pilots from my Gazelle course, together with three additional officers who had recently completed their basic Observer training and were to join us for the Lynx conversion course. Rob was an ex- 'lower decker' (naval rating) who had been selected for officer training and, despite desperately wanting to be pilot, had been selected to become an Observer. Joe was also an ex-rating but he had spent many years flying in Wasp and Wessex helicopters as an aircrewman. Hence he was a very experienced aviator in his own right. He was also another master of spinning hilariously funny naval dits. Finally Paul made up the trilogy. Paul had been in the Navy as a Seaman Officer for five years and had recently specialised as an aviator. The course quickly gelled into a team: as always the group consisted of young men with flying as their first and foremost interest.

With the secondary courses complete, the flying proper started. The first part of the Lynx training process lasted three months and was intended to teach you how to fly the helicopter. Again it started in the classroom. This time however, it was deemed that as pilots with wings we did not need to be taught the basic principles behind piloting. The time spent in the classroom was dedicated to teaching us the intricacies of all the different systems and components that made up this modern military helicopter. This ground school was intensive and often tedious, hours spent learning the pressure at which hydraulic valves opened, or the fuel pressure in the low pressure fuel pump. The problem of learning all of the system limitations was further exacerbated by the fact that at the time the Royal Navy operated both Mark 2 and Mark 3 Lynx. The different marks had different engines and transmission systems which therefore necessitated two sets of different limitations to be committed to memory.

The course was joined by a further three aviators, two experienced pilots who joined us from a Sea King squadron for the Lynx conversion and Simon Isbister, who had just re-entered the Navy following a two year sabbatical in the city. Chatting to him, it transpired Simon had joined the Navy at the same time as me, but as an Observer, and after initial training had been selected to fly Lynx. Three months into the course he had became disillusioned with service life and after a lucrative job offer, had left to work in the financial sector. Having carved a successful City career he hankered after the perceived excitement that a military flying career offered. He rejoined the Navy and became a member of 41 Lynx Advanced Flying Training. Simon and I were from totally different backgrounds and yet had a similar outlook on life. I found Simon's company refreshing. He approached service life with a healthy degree of scepticism and maintained an active social life outside the sometimes narrow minded confines of the Wardroom. Not surprisingly, although we all became closely acquainted, Simon and I became friends.

My first flight in the Lynx met with all my expectations: it was fast, manoeuvrable and powerful. Lifting it into the hover, its twin turbines pushing out four times more power than anything else I had previously flown, a wry grin appeared on my face. Regarded as one of the world's most capable helicopters, I was quickly to discover why, as the instructor put in through it paces. With wheels rather than skids to facilitate easy movement in and out of hangars on the back of ships, it was designed to be landed firmly to ensure positive contact with a moving deck. But it was in the air that it came into its own. An abundance of power to enable it to lift off a deck in almost any weather conditions, it was built with a rigid rotor head to give it the control response necessary to operate in the turbulent wind conditions found as air spills around hangars and weapon systems onto the flight deck. The rigid rotor head enabled the Lynx to perform aerobatic manoeuvres that few other helicopters could emulate.

The head of the helicopter is that which attaches the rotor blades to the rotor head of the helicopter. The blades are subject to enormous torsion stresses as they rotate. Traditionally these stresses are relieved by letting the blade move by the use of hinges in all three planes. The Lynx was designed with a rotor head made of one piece of metal, titanium. This enormously expensive and amazing material enabled all the loads generated by the blades to be absorbed and negated the need for hinges. Without these hinges the helicopter responded quickly to control inputs and to fly at attitudes that would cause other helicopters to crash. It was a helicopter pilot's dream machine. The smile on my face took a long time to subside on completion of the first flight.

As usual the hard work started soon after, as I gradually learned to fly this capable aircraft. The course was very similar in structure to that which I had experienced during basic flying training on the Gazelle. This time, however, there were fewer hours allocated to getting it right. This was also my first introduction to two crew operations, although for the majority of the initial phase of the Lynx course we were flying with instructor pilots.

Sitting side by side, the responsibilities of the Pilot and Observer were clearly defined. On the right of the cockpit the flying controls are shrouded by the flight instruments which allow a pilot to fly in all weather conditions. Dominating the left hand side of the cockpit the radar screen and controls allow the trained Observer to locate periscopes in the vastness of the ocean, literally finding a needle in the largest of all haystacks. Between the two seats sits a bank of radio and navigation equipment. On an overhead structure, the system panels allow either crew member to manage the complicated fuel, hydraulic and electric systems. In pride of place between the flight instruments and radar screen sit weapon control panels that allow either crew member to fight the war machine. Below this a bank of dials, which monitor the engines and gearboxes, provide the complicated finale to the impressive bank of instrumentation. The Pilot has prime responsibility for all controls on the right hand side of the cockpit, the Observer the left. Those in the centre are divided equally amongst the two crew depending on the role. At first sight the inside of the Lynx seemed a complicated array of dials, knobs and switches that must surely be impossible ever to master. Over the course of the following months I gradually became more familiar with the cockpit. The impossible list of checks that had to be committed to memory began to make sense; once the logic became apparent the memory managed to retain the checks in the right order. The engine instruments, that initially appeared to whirl around in a nonsensical blur, gradually began to slow down as my eyes became accustomed to looking at the right dial at the right time. By the end of the advanced flying phase I felt that I was within the loop of the aeroplane, knowing when the systems were functioning correctly and able to identify a problem after it had occurred. I envied the skill of the instructors, those who had been flying the machine for many years and were able to sense a problem with the aircraft just by listening to the sounds and feeling the vibrations that emanated from the transmission system and rotor blades. As pilots we were responsible for flying the aircraft, the Observer for fighting it. During the early part of the course we seldom flew with Observers. On the rare occasion that we did they were there merely as safety numbers to assist if problems occurred. We had yet to start the operational phase of the course and therefore yet to realise the skills of the Observer, or the potential as a fighting machine that the Lynx possessed.

By the end of the three months the cockpit had become as familiar to us as the interior of our cars, our hands able to run around it and prepare the aircraft for flight within minutes. Once airborne we had established a feel for the aircraft that allowed us to fly it with confidence, if lacking in panache. Now it was time to learn the skills that gave reason to why vast amounts of money had been spent on us for the preceding three years. Now it was time to justify our existence in the modern fighting force that is the Royal Navy. It was time to hone the skills that would turn the Lynx from a exhilarating flying machine into a deadly fighting craft.

This was the final part of the formal flying training. On completion we would graduate as fully qualified naval aviators, instantly becoming combat ready – deemed ready to fight. Lasting five months it was as demanding as any of the other flying courses that I had attended, although the emphasis was very different. We remained on the same squadron with the same instructors, but now we were treated as fellow aviators rather than students. We cohabited in the same crew-room as the instructors, rather than being condemned to the 'student filth' quarters. As pilots we now very rarely flew with pilot instructors; instead we were crewed up with a student Observer for the duration of the course and flew with an Observer instructor who sat in the back of the helicopter and instructed us in tactical matters. As pilots, if things started to go wrong, it was down to us to land in safety back onboard either air station or ship.

I never appreciated the full extent of this responsibility until the first occasion when things did not go according to plan. For the final two weeks of the course we embarked on a Royal Fleet Auxiliary ship. The objective of this part of the course was to gain a thorough insight into shipborne operations. Although, by this stage, I was relatively comfortable with flying the helicopter, I was by no means entirely comfortable with operating from a heaving deck in the thick of night. Simon and I had been programmed to fly with an instructor on a night anti-surface unit sortie. Simulating war conditions, we were to make a tactical launch from the ship, remaining 100 feet above the water and silent on all radars and radios until a safe distance from the ship, so as not to compromise its position. Once established in our sector we began the surface search, using the radar to locate contacts, and then running in to identify them visually using the powerful searchlight, whilst remaining low and fast over the sea. The theory was that running in fast and low from the stern of the ship would minimise any chances of being engaged by enemy fire. This was a routine that we had rehearsed on a regular basis over the previous five months. Being so low over the water, flying with sole reference to instruments, demanded an extraordinary amount of concentration, both from the pilot who was required to control the helicopter and avoid flying into the water, and the Observer who had to con the pilot onto the required direction to ensure approaching the ship from the stern. On this particular evening, as we descended to 100 feet and began to close the ship at 130mph, the stabilisation system failed. As helicopters possess no inherent stability within their design, gyro controlled stabilisation systems are fitted to more advanced helicopters to ease pilot workload. Although the helicopter would fly without the 'stab' system engaged, it became extremely difficult to control.

As the system failed my immediate reaction was to climb away from the water. At a height of 100 feet, the slightest mistake could result in the helicopter impacting the water below. Once a safe altitude had been reached we tried to rectify the problem but with no success. Thousands of miles out to sea we had no choice but to return to the ship and attempt a landing. Flying with forward airspeed the helicopter was relatively docile even without the stabilisation system, however as soon as it was brought into the hover it began to dance around the sky. Gyrating over the flight deck I knew I was overcontrolling but there was little I could do to relax myself. Both Observers, student and instructor tried to calm me with words of reassurance. It was then that I realised their lives were firmly in my hands. The oscillations were becoming increasingly severe, a real danger now existed that the rotor blades would impact with the ship sending the helicopter spiralling into the sea. I began to doubt whether I would be able to land the helicopter on the rolling deck. The words of my instructor came back to me as the deck heaved and pitched and the helicopter cavorted of its own accord.

"Dickie these oleos will take an inordinate amount of abuse. Provided you land with no lateral movement, you will get away with it."

I retained the memory of him forcing the collective down and the aircraft slamming into the ground from the ten foot hover, jolting my back and leaving me convinced that the machine must surely be left irreparably damaged.

"There you go, that won't even have worried it, don't be afraid about landing this lady firmly."

Now I must surely put that to the test. Unable to maintain anything that even remotely resembled a hover, there was no way I could ascertain whether we were going to land moving sideways. Lateral movement on impact would cause the helicopter to roll on its side, the rotor blades smashing themselves into the deck and the fuselage tumbling into the cold dark sea.

"I'm going to land."

This was the only warning that I gave the two Observers. I closed my eyes and pushed the collective lever down. The wheels impacted the deck as it pitched up, throwing me out of the seat such that the harness dug painfully into my shoulders. But the helicopter was on the deck. By some stroke of unbelievable luck the flying machine had remained upright. I had never been so grateful to be back on the ground. I turned and looked at Simon. His expression of ultimate relief said it all.

"Thanks mate, well done!"

"Don't thank me, I nearly fucking killed us."

"Yeah but you didn't."

The instructor spoke from the back.

"Listen guys, I'm going to have to climb over the seats and climb out of your doors."

I looked over my shoulder at him as the lights on the flight deck were illuminated.

"Why?"

He didn't need to reply. The helicopter had landed so close to the edge of the flight deck that had he deplaned without checking, he would have surely fallen into the sea thirty feet below. The wheel of the helicopter sat on the very edge of the deck. We had been unbelievably lucky.

Somebody was indeed looking after me on that trip. For the following night Simon and I were due to take another helicopter over, on a 'rotors running crew change', a procedure whereby the previous crew would land the helicopter on the deck and we would take over from them whilst the engines and rotors remained turning. As we briefed for the sortie I noticed that Simon was looking pale and reserved, he was not his usual chirpy self. I wondered at this stage what effect the previous night's experience had had on him. By the time we were waiting in the hangar for the aircraft to return to the deck, Simon had deteriorated considerably; there was no way he was in any fit state to go flying. We cancelled the sortie as he began to vomit over the side of the ship. His was the first case of the food poisoning that was to plague over half the ship's company over the following week.

With the sortie cancelled the helicopter was shut down and towed into the hangar for the night. During a routine inspection of another helicopter, one of the engineers noticed oil dripping onto the hangar floor from the tail of the helicopter that we had been due to fly. On closer inspection he discovered a crack in the tail rotor gearbox, the gearbox that drove the tail rotor and prevented the helicopter from spinning uncontrollably around its own axis. Almost all of the oil had escaped. The aircraft would have remained airborne for five to ten minutes before the gearbox seized and the aircraft became uncontrollable. There are no indications in the cockpit of the oil quantity and pressure in the tail rotor gearbox. The reality of the situation was simple – had Simon not been taken ill with food poisoning, the helicopter would have crashed into the sea, period. We counted ourselves extremely lucky but neither incident put either of us off flying.

As it worked out, Simon and I operated as a crew for the duration of operational flying training and we became not only close friends but an effective and close knit team. Simon was a bit of a maverick, he was never insubordinate but he questioned things if he believed they could be conducted more efficiently. He was also extremely sharp. Although the Mark 3 Lynx was fitted with a capable radar, it possessed no computerised tactical system to track and identify targets. This necessitated the Observer locating contacts on the radar and transferring their position onto a plotting board. Six minutes later the process would be repeated again and from the two sets of positions the Observer was able to calculate the course and speed of the targets. This was identical to the tactics used by the old bi-planes in the Second World War, however it was never quite as simple as it seemed. In busy areas the radar screen would be infested with green dots, out of which the Observer had to make a sensible picture. This information then had to be transferred accurately and quickly to the plotting board. The second 'snap shot', for tactical reasons, often could not be taken from the same location. Therefore the Observer was looking at the same jumble of green dots but from a different perspective, not to mention that the dots had moved in relation to one another anyway. From this minefield of information one of the Observer's jobs was to make sense out of it and ascertain accurate course and speeds such that the future position of each contact could be predicted. In addition, the cockpit of the Lynx was not particularly conducive to fast, accurate work. Noisy and constantly moving, the vibration made it very difficult to annotate the plotting board with the degree of precision that was required. There was no comfortable chair with a desk on which the plotting board could be laid. With the board resting upon his knees and hunched over the radar screen the sitting position was an osteopath's nightmare.

Simon had the ability to see the big picture. He possessed a tactical awareness that many experienced Observers never achieved. I had complete confidence in his tactical skills and the night of the stabilisation proved that he had faith in my flying ability. Flying with Simon turned a course that had the reputation for being a long, hard slog, which many failed, into a fun and rewarding five months. It came as no surprise when he was awarded the prize for both the best student on the course and the best student of the year.

The early part of the course was devoted to basic anti-surface unit procedures, learning how to locate and identify enemy units, and then how to destroy them using the helicopter's Sea Skua weapon system. We never had the opportunity to fire the real missiles; at half a million a time they were deemed too expensive to be used unless it was for real. Anti-surface unit warfare was the Lynx' primary role although it was capable of fulfilling others. Later we learned anti-submarine procedures, carrying a variety of torpedoes and depth charges, before moving onto those involved in flying the helicopter over land in a tactical environment. Here we learnt nap of the earth flying skills, contour flying, fighter evasion, and how to land the machine in forest clearings with only inches between the rotors and the trees. I was gradually becoming the complete helicopter pilot and Simon and I were becoming a competent crew. Towards the end of the course we learned the skills required to land the helicopter on the back of a ship, with a postage stamp for a deck, in all weathers, by day and by night. For the final two weeks of the course we embarked on the Royal Fleet Auxiliary to simulate a war environment and combine all the skills we had accumulated throughout flying training.

The course, as always was hard work. Some students failed to make the grade: Paul failed and returned to the main stream Navy to drive ships again; Rob made it to the end of the course but it was deemed he had not reached an acceptable standard to graduate. Usually this would have meant an end to his flying career and possibly an end to his naval career. Rob was lucky. After excessive amounts of haggling by the squadron Commanding Officer, he was given the opportunity to start the course again. It meant going back to the beginning of operational flying training and starting all of the blood sweat and tears again. He took the bit between his teeth, swallowed his pride and, as the rest of us graduated into the fleet as qualified naval aviators, he restarted the course as a student. To his credit he worked even harder second time around and five months later graduated as the top student.

Throughout the course and over the next few years, Rob and I became good friends. Whereas Simon was the independent thinker, Rob was very much the company man who thrived on fast cars and fast women. We remained in close contact throughout the following years. All of our careers proved to contain certain amounts of excitement. Rob was sitting in a helicopter that was tossed off the back of a ship as it manoeuvred through rough seas. Fortunately both he and the pilot managed to escape from the inverted helicopter before it sank to the bottom of the Bay of Biscay, never to be recovered. It was rumoured that Simon had found himself involved in covert operations in and around the Barents Sea. These operations were classified as Top Secret but I could tell by the glint in his eye that the flying had been pretty exhilarating. I found myself onboard HMS *Manchester* sailing towards what I firmly believed was going to be a long and bloody war wondering whether I was really mentally prepared for it.

It was when I was on my own that I started to think about it, so I tried to spend as little time on my own as possible. I would go to circuit training and concentrate fully on the exercises, throwing myself into them wholeheartedly. If I received an invitation to one of the mess decks I would always accept it, if nothing else, just for the change of company. The officers generally lived in their own cabin; the senior ratings shared, three or four to a cabin; the lower ranks lived in mess decks, often in excess of thirty men living and sleeping in a room no bigger than twenty by twenty feet. The space was cramped to say the least. The situation was made even more difficult by the fact that we were in defence watches which meant that at any time of the day there would be people who were trying to sleep after a busy watch, and others who were trying to entertain themselves in their off-duty time. The mess decks would be divided up amongst all the different specialisations; all of the Stewards and Caterers in one mess deck, all the Mechanical Engineers in another. Hence each mess deck had a very different character. They were people's homes, therefore you could not just stroll into them without an invitation. If I received an invitation into a mess deck it usually involved the drinking of beer, however in this situation when I was never sure when we would be called on to go flying, I never drank more than a pint unless I knew that the helicopter was unserviceable. The men were allowed two tins of beer per man each day. Officially it was not allowed to be stockpiled, although every mess deck did. This generally meant that if the helicopter was down and I was invited to a mess deck, I would come out pissed. The conversations down in the mess decks were very different to those in the Wardroom: some of the very young and junior guys would be intimidated by you just because of your officer status; some of the more experienced guys would go out of their way to take the piss out of you because you were an officer. I did not mind that and generally reckoned that on the banter front I could give as good as I got. I made some firm friends with the guys in the lower ranks.

Saturday 26 January – Red Sea

Another glorious sunny day, the temperature is really starting to rise now. Today saw an early start for an eight o'clock launch to take two of the warfare officers into Jeddah, a Saudi city on the Red Sea. The flight lasted about two hours in total. We did not shut down on arrival, just dropped the passengers and left.

The city itself appeared a complete hole surrounded by desert. The airport was partly taken over by the Americans and there must have been at least twenty B-52s lined up on the taxi-ways. Very impressive. On our return we went straight into Action Stations for two hours. I spent most of it trying to find a cool place in the hangar to go to sleep in! The afternoon consisted of a two hour surface search, it still seems like a big exercise. The surface search revealed nothing more than an abundance of merchant shipping.

During the evening we had a Wardroom film evening and watched Desperately Seeking Susan *starring Madonna. I really enjoy these film sessions as you can distance yourself from the real world whilst watching them. The only problem is returning to normality, or rather reality, as soon as the film ends, then the anxieties return.*

Sunday 27 January – Off Yemen

Each day now seems to follow the same pattern. I wake up and feel depressed that I am still in my cabin and still at sea with another five and a half months before we are due back home. As the day progresses I cheer up and by lunchtime I am generally confident that I will make it through the war, and in some way, very proud to be part of it. As the day wears on I generally get scared about what the immediate future holds, realising that it is only a matter of time before ships start to be sunk and sailors get killed and injured. I normally lie in bed worrying about it.

Today was no exception. The morning started with fire-fighting drills on the flight deck using charged hoses, great fun and a very worthwhile exercise. Let's hope that we do not have to use the skills learnt. The remainder of the morning was divided between writing divisional reports, recognition training and chatting with some of the ship's company. The afternoon continued in the same vein with a good hour's fitness training on the fo'c's'le. The evening was very dull and I went to bed feeling very miserable and generally fed up.

Monday 28 January – Indian Ocean

I achieved very little today. After waking up I wandered down the hangar to have a chat with the boys and ended up playing computer games for most of the morning. Nick eventually retrieved me for half an hour's recognition training and the morning was finished off by reading reports to two members of my Division.

It is the first time that I have actually been responsible for writing reports on anyone so I spent a lot of time preparing them, not wanting the lads to feel, as I have done on occasions, that the composer of the report had no idea about the subject.

For the remainder of the day I locked myself away in my cabin and calculated some new range and endurance figures for the aircraft, now that it has all of this new equipment fitted. This was not before a quick half an hour on the fo'c's'le soaking up the sun. During the evening I watched Tall Guy *on video which I really enjoyed and think is an exceptionally funny film. However yet again I couldn't help thinking about Jill and the occasion that we had watched the film together. I miss her and went to bed wanting to be with her again.*

Whenever we were not programmed to fly, I felt like a fish out of water, and although there were lots of things that I had to do, I would tend to squander my time a little. I would find that until I was desperately behind with the paperwork, it was very difficult to sit down and get on with it, probably because I believed a lot of it to be unnecessary, especially in this type of environment. The two things that I did take very seriously were the recognition training and the divisional report writing.

We held a complete bank of recognition slides on board and concentrated on learning those ships and aircraft we might encounter during the forthcoming few weeks. I was the expert on the aircraft and Nick on the ships, although we both tried to learn them all. If the programme permitted we would try and sit down for at least an hour a day. I figured that the recognition training kept my mind active and the circuit training, my body. As it transpired, the many hours spent looking at slides of ships did pay dividends later on.

The Divisional system is the bane of every naval officer. Each officer is responsible for a Division of men. The responsibility includes ensuring that the man carries out his duties correctly but more importantly, looking after his career progression through the Navy. As such we were called upon to write an annual report on each man, or whenever a man left the Division. The reports were very detailed and covered both a professional report and a general report, together with a points scoring and recommendation system. The number of men, per division, averaged around fifteen which meant a lot of additional work for the officer over and above his primary responsibilities. I was lucky that I only had five men in mine all maintainers on the flight, so guys that I knew and trusted. As such I would try and spend as much time on the reports as I could to make them as accurate as possible. I genuinely felt that it was my responsibility to spend as many hours on the Divisional system as I could; I regarded the guys on the flight as friends rather than subordinates.

Tuesday 29 January – Indian Ocean

Today was a good day. Firstly because we heard the news that for the first week at least we have not been programmed to go too far north in the Gulf, secondly because the coalition forces have declared air superiority and thirdly because it was a R&R day and I let my hair down for the first time in a long while.

The morning started with a fire at around 0200 and, although I was not directly involved, the main broadcast kept me awake for a few hours. When I eventually got up I spent the morning ground running the aircraft and attending some more lectures on chemical warfare. The afternoon was devoted to time off and enjoyment. It started with flight deck sports followed by a BBQ. I thoroughly enjoyed myself and got chatting to one of the Royal Marines on board. It transpired that we went to the same school at the same time in Rhodesia. It really is a small world. Over a couple of beers we had a really good chat about mutual friends that I haven't seen for years and all the worries disappeared into the starlit sky. I could have been anywhere.

Wednesday 30 January – Indian Ocean

A long and busy day in which we flew for almost seven hours. In the morning we flew a gunfire support sortie, spotting for the ships 4.5 inch gun, practising for a situation I hope we do not find ourselves in for real. After landing I just had time to file a flight plan for the afternoon trip, followed by a quick bite to eat, before launching again for some more spotting. That lasted for a further two hours before we were tasked to fly to RFA Resource to pick up two pas-

*sengers. On completion we had a rotors running refuel and were off again to
fly into Seeb to pick up another passenger.*

*The Air Force guys at Seeb were very friendly indeed and came rushing out
with cans of Coke as soon as we landed – most welcome. By the time that we had
returned to the ship I was absolutely exhausted but the good news was that I had
ten letters waiting for me including four from Jill, so naturally that lifted my
spirits. I dashed off a quick couple of letters in reply followed by an early night.*

The ship left the Red Sea and progressed towards the Straits of
Hormuz to enter the Persian Gulf. I had not worked particularly hard
for the previous week, but the rest of the ship's company certainly
had. Defence watch is in itself fairly tiring simply by virtue of the fact
that you are working twelve hours a day every day; the whole of this
week the ship's company had been working long hours to ensure that,
materially, the ship was totally prepared to enter the war zone. Before
we entered the Gulf, the Captain ordered a rest and recuperation day
(R&R) to give people the chance to relax a little and unwind.
Everybody needed it; it was a great decision.

The day itself was an immense amount of fun. We played sports on the
flight deck during the afternoon – volleyball and deck hockey. For the
volleyball, a net was set up across the deck and a string tied to the ball so
that it would not be lost over the side. The deck hockey was a lot more
physical. It's a great naval game and one in which there are very few
rules. The hockey sticks are fairly primitive bent walking sticks and dis-
posable pucks are used, made out of paper and masking tape. You need
a good supply as they get lost over the side on a fairly regular basis. It's
a great way of letting off steam and you always end up with a few bumps
and bruises by the end of the game. The weather was brilliant and everyone had a fantastic time in the sun. This type of afternoon is fairly common on long deployments. The whole ship's company forgot that we
were just about to enter a hostile area; we all just lounged around on the
flight deck, playing sport and drinking the odd tin of beer. I had noticed
that one of the Royal Marine detachment had a Southern African accent
so I quizzed him about it during the evening.

When I got chatting to Sean I was amazed to discover that we had
attended the same school in the middle of Africa. It seemed so ironic,
sitting on a British warship in the middle of the Indian Ocean and
meeting someone you had gone to school with in the middle of
nowhere. It was a great way of escaping for me, as we talked about old
teachers, and mutual friends, and sang old school songs and war cries.
I did not think about the Gulf, or going to war, or dying, or anything
related to it. It was just what I needed.

The next morning I awoke with the faintest hint of a hangover, having
drunk more than I had intended the previous night, but felt relaxed and
refreshed. We briefed early for the forthcoming Naval Gunfire Support
(NGS) serial. The Principal Warfare Officer (PWO) outlined the plans.

"This may be our last opportunity to practise this before we are
shelling Kuwait for real."

My first sight of an oil rig.

Already the rumours were that we were going to be part of a large amphibious assault group, forming to retake Kuwait from the sea.

"Three-six-zero[1] will launch and carry out a surface search to ensure the area is free from other surface contacts before we start the serial." This was standard procedure. The last thing we wanted to do was inadvertently sink a passing merchantman – very bad for PR.

"Once the area is deemed safe, Three-Six-Zero will drop one marker marine approximately ten miles from the ship, pass its position and call for the start of the serial." The marker marines were flares that fitted underneath the aircraft. When dropped in the water they began to smoke, giving us a marker in the water for the ships 4.5 inch gun to fire at. The idea was that once the position had been passed, the ship would fire a single round at it and the wind, on the day, would dictate how close to the target the shell would land. It was then our job to pass corrections back to the ship until the shells were directed onto the target. The PWO continued.

"We intend to fire the fifty remaining practice rounds such that on entry into the Gulf we can replenish at sea and refill the magazine with High Explosive shells."

He ended with the standard, "Any questions?" There weren't any.

We took off and cleared the range. There was no other shipping in the area so we moved into the serial. I dropped the flare and established the helicopter in the hover about half a mile away, where we could still see

[1]*The call-sign for HMS* Manchester's *Lynx.*

the flare and were not in the flight path of the shells that were about to rain down on us. A standard radio procedure was used so that we could call for gunfire support from either a ship or an Army artillery position and everyone would be talking the same language. We called for the first round and waited for the ship to reply. "Fire" meant the round had been fired from the ship, "Shot," it was just about to land and "Splash" the shell had hit the water and we should be able to see the splash. We would then pass the corrections in yards.

"Right 400, drop 600." There was no completely accurate method of measuring the distance, it was just a matter of guessing and trying to bracket the target. As we waited for the next round to be fired, Nick and I contemplated doing this for real. Nick aired his fears.

"If we have to do this in a war zone, we're going to get shot out of the sky before we have a chance to target the rounds anywhere near where they are supposed to be."

"No shit Sherlock, got any ideas about what we're going to do about it?" He was the ideas man after all. He looked across and smiled.

"Claim the helicopter's gone 'tits up' and let some other bastard claim the posthumous VC."

I laughed and shrugged my shoulders, I wasn't sure if he was being serious. The next round landed about twenty yards from the smoke. I spoke on the radio.

"On target, ten rounds fire for effect."

The water erupted into a bubbling turmoil around the smoke target as ten high explosive 4.5 inch rounds were fired into the same piece of water in quick succession.

From our side the sortie went well, a simple matter of talking the rounds onto the target. For the crew onboard the ship it was a far more complex serial. There were numerous calculations that had to be made, both manually and by the system computer to ensure that the rounds hit the target. Considering that the ship was moving in the water all of the time, and hence was firing each shell from a different position and the fact that the barrel of the gun was moving with the ship each time it rolled over a wave, the system was remarkably accurate. However, to ensure that everyone was entirely happy with the procedure we repeated the serial in the afternoon and finished off the remaining practice rounds. For the rest of the afternoon we supplied a taxi service bringing people to and from the ship. We collected the two chaps who we had delivered in Saudi four days before from RFA *Resource*. They had been attending lectures on operating procedures within the large multi-national force that made up the Allied Task Force, and now returned to brief the rest of the ship's company. We then flew into Seeb, in Saudi Arabia, to collect a chap who was going to give the Warfare Officers a brief on the airways that had been established to ensure the smooth running of the bombing campaign, which had been underway for two weeks.

Flying into Seeb, it was great to see dry land again. We parked in the corner of the airfield and I remained in the helicopter, keeping the engines running, while Nick jumped out and tried to locate our passenger. As I sat in the helicopter, one of the Air Force ground crew came running up to the helicopter and handed me a can of Coke. It was a small and yet significant gesture. There has always been a healthy rivalry amongst the three services, especially in the air world, as each service has its own flyers, and they are all convinced that they are the best. The cheery smile and the can of Coke, made me realise that petty differences had been forgotten and that everyone was pulling in the same direction to ensure the speedy resolution of the conflict. That one small gesture filled me with confidence for the rest of the trip.

CHAPTER EIGHT

In the Box

It is difficult to know what is worse; dying or the thought of death.

Thursday 31 January – South Persian Gulf

Today saw us "on station" for the first time. We have commenced a new routine of an early flying brief at 0615 followed by Alert 15 all day.

During the morning the guy we had picked up the day before gave us a fairly detailed brief, concerning how the airspace is divided over the Gulf area to help avoid a blue on blue engagement. All very tactical.

The rest of the morning was spent chasing my tail, trying to get people to make a decision on when the ship wanted us to launch, such that I could file a flight plan. It eventually happened in the afternoon and we flew to Dubai to return the tactical chap from whence he came, then straight into a surface search. This was preceded by a very welcome nap on the flight deck over the lunchtime period.

All in all a fairly average day but somehow I felt ill at ease all day and must admit I was very short tempered. It's the first day in the war zone and I am bored, pissed off and want to go home.

Alert 15 (AL 15) is an indication of the state of readiness of the helicopter; there are three alert states that are used. AL 15 was the most commonly used during this period and its implications were that the helicopter could be airborne within fifteen minutes of being 'actioned' – told to take off – which was initiated by a broadcast over the tannoy system of "ACTION LYNX – ACTION LYNX". We would brief early in the morning to cover the rest of the period that the helicopter would remain at AL 15. The brief would begin with a weather forecast for the rest of the day, given by myself, and the helicopter controller would then cover all of the tactical information, such as other units operating in the area with call signs. Nick would then cover any additional information pertinent to that day's flying. Then, for the duration of the Alert 15 period, the helicopter would remain 'ranged on deck', which meant that it was fully fuelled, armed and sitting on the deck ready to go. We were required to be dressed in our flying clothing, with the only additional equipment needed, prior to flying, our life jackets and helmets. We were free to roam around the ship as long as we remained fully kitted out. On hearing 'Action Lynx' we would make our way to the hangar as quickly as possible. I would give the aircraft a pre-flight inspection while Nick

strapped in and spoke with the operations room, via telebrief, to ascertain the reason for the launch and obtain a tactical update. As soon as I had finished the pre-flight inspection, I would strap into the aircraft and commence the start up procedure. Once both the engines were running and the generators were on line, we could update all of the navigational and internally test all of the important systems before engaging the rotors. Once fully 'burning and turning' we would request permission to take-off. The ship would then stop any manoeuvres and indicate that it was happy for us to launch by illuminating a green light on the flight deck. I would release the harpoon that clamped us to the deck and pull in power until we left the deck. Fifteen minutes was the maximum time the whole process should take. As Nick and I had now been flying together for eight months, we knew exactly how each other worked so there was no need for unnecessary chat and we would generally be airborne in less than ten minutes.

Launching for an operational sortie.

At the end of the Alert 15 period the helicopter would be returned to the hangar. This process took up to thirty minutes as the rotor blades had to be folded back on themselves and the tail unhinged and folded so that the helicopter would physically fit inside. It would then be secured with chain lashings to stop it moving around inside the hangar and colliding with the bulkheads. With the helicopter in this state we were deemed to be at Alert 45, i.e. it should take no longer than forty-five minutes for the ground crew to prepare the helicopter and for the flight crew to change into flying kit, receive a flying brief and start the helicopter. All the time the helicopter was serviceable and we were not at any other alert state, we were deemed to be at Alert 45. We did not need to be in flying clothing all of the time, but as we should be ready to fly at forty-five minutes notice, drinking was not allowed. I did, on the odd occasion after a particular taxing night flying sortie, allow myself one beer before going to bed, if for no other reason than to help me relax and sleep after the trauma of night flying from a deck.

The only other alert state was Alert 5 where we were required to be airborne within five minutes. We would be sitting in the helicopter, without the engines running but with all the pre-flight inspections completed, and all we needed to do was start the engines and go. Two hours was the maximum time that we were allowed to remain at Alert 5. This was because it was mentally very draining strapped in the helicopter with nothing to do but try to remain alert – you could be actioned at any time. In the heat of the Gulf, it could also become quite physically draining. The Lynx had an endurance of two and a half hours, therefore if we were actioned at the end of the alert period we would be strapped into the aircraft for a minimum of four and a half hours. In the intense heat, fully dressed in protective clothing, it would become extremely hot and uncomfortable.

Being at Alert 15, Nick and I were free to attend the brief on airspace division, given by a Navy Air Traffic Controller. With an overhead projector he produced, on the wall of the Wardroom where fine paintings had previously hung, an amazing work of art that depicted all of the air routes in and out of Iraq and Kuwait. I sat listening to the brief becoming increasingly confused. The whole system was designed to ensure that all of the ships operating in the northern Persian Gulf would be able to differentiate between friendly units, returning from bombing missions, and Iraqi jets launching a raid on the Allied Fleet. It was an amazingly complicated and yet effective system. However there were occasions during the course of the next month when Allied pilots exited Iraq on the wrong route. This left Warfare Officers with an agonising decision to make; assume it a friendly unit – and risk the ship being sunk if it was an Iraqi aircraft launching an attack under the cover of an allied air raid – or take the safer option of assuming it was an enemy aircraft and engage it – this ran the real risk of a blue on blue engagement. Nobody wanted to have to live with the thought of knowing that you had shot down a friendly aircraft returning from a mission over enemy territory.

For the immediate future all these decisions were being made by other ships hundreds of miles to the north. *Manchester* had been assigned to an area of the sea that was to become known as the Brit URG Box. Situated in the southern part of the Gulf, it contained all the British support ships that had accompanied the initial Task Group. The system was that the ships on the front-line would periodically drop back into the box to restore and refuel while still at sea. Hence the name: the British Underway Replenishment Group Box. Our job, as an air defence ship, was to protect the Group from hostile air attack as the support ships had only limited independent defensive capabilities. As such this was our first day with an active role to play so, applying the lessons learned from the Falklands, every member of the ship's company was required to make up 'battle bags'. These bags were carried at all times and consisted of a gas mask in its haversack. Contained in the haversack was a spare filter for the gas mask, a self administered injection to be used in the event of breathing in nerve gas, a set of anti-flash hoods and gloves similar to those worn by Formula One racing car drivers and finally a plastic mug strapped to the outside to drink one's tea from! Not surprisingly people were particularly diligent about preparing and maintaining their battle bags.

Friday 1 February – Southern Persian Gulf

Another busy day and another day in which I am becoming increasingly annoyed at being treated like shit and given no responsibility, combined with being bollocked for no reason at all.

I am fed up with life, not with being out here. I realise that there is a job to be done and we are here to do it. Every decision that I make is perceived as wrong and someone changes it. The flying is boring and routine, you could get a monkey to do my job, AND I still have another five months of this to go. I believe that it's only my own morale that is low and not the whole ship's company – which is encouraging.

As to what I actually did today, four hours of flying consisting of two hours surface search and two hours playing at being a taxi driver. The highlight of the day was receiving more mail, including two parcels from Jill, and letters of support from people I do not know or hardly remember, either way they lifted my spirits no end. I really expected today to be a good day, it is the first of a new month which means another month behind us and only five and a half months to go before we get home. Today I am looking forward to that so much.

Saturday 2 February – Brit URG Box

A fairly short day in terms of flying, only two and a half hours but a very interesting day. The morning followed the usual routine of early start followed by a surface search to "sanitise" the area. This was followed by a flight to HMS Brazen *to drop off the Captain and Operations Officer. Whilst we were there we managed to have a quick chat with their aircrew Jon Reed and Mike Perry.*

They agreed to pop over and visit our ship in the afternoon to give us an insight into what they have been doing out here since September. For one reason or another they ended up staying for the whole of the afternoon during which we continually picked their brains to get all the information we could about operating "up north". It was an extremely worthwhile afternoon and in many ways it put my mind at rest although in others it scared me even more.

They were very relaxed in their approach to operating in a real war environment which is reassuring. However actually speaking to people who had been shot at for real meant a resurgence of all the fears about being a coward when it's my turn to face the fire.

Sunday 3 February – Brit URG Box and Jill's Birthday

A good day with a reasonable amount of flying and a lot of laughs. The day was supposed to start with the usual early morning push however the aircraft decided it did not want to get up early and refused to start which resulted in a 0900 launch.

So followed an interesting surface search. We found a turtle which looked just like a mine, picked up a HMP[1] from Brazen, *carried out a little winching practice and at the end were actioned to investigate a suspicious object in the water that turned out to be a fridge.*

During the afternoon the ship conducted another Chemex[2], during which we were actioned again to assist a Sea King that had gone downbird on the coast of Qatar. However by the time we arrived there were another two Sea Kings on station assisting from the same squadron so we returned to mother[3].

During the evening I wrote a letter and watched Alienation *in the Wardroom. Overall not a bad day and considerably better than the preceding few. The fact that today is Jill's birthday made me sad, I would have much rather spent it with Jill having a romantic day/night. Such is life, only another five and a half months to go.*

Everyone has a bad day once in a while and I had very few during the course of the deployment. However, the first full day in the Brit URG Box, was one of them. It was a combination of finally arriving on station and finding that we were consigned to be REMFs (Rear Echelon Motherfuckers.) We had always known that this was going to be the case. I just had not anticipated how boring and infuriating it would be, having mentally prepared myself for combat. Secondly, as an inexperienced pilot I was making bad decisions, not airborne, but in the administration of the flight. I felt infuriated that my decisions were continually being overturned. Fortunately the bad temper only lasted one day and then I was back to normal.

The opportunity to chat with another flight who had experienced flying in the Northern Gulf was very well received. They had been dogged with bad luck. The processor unit that controlled the interface between radar and missile on their helicopter had not been fitted or maintained properly. This had resulted in three unsuccessful attacks on enemy shipping. On the first occasion the missile had simply flown into the sea shortly after launch, on the second it had disappeared into the horizon in completely the wrong direction and, on the final attempt, the missile had climbed away from the sea and headed towards Baghdad becoming the first inter-ballistic Sea Skua missile. They were obviously a little infuriated but were very good natured about the situation. As they recounted the stories I laughed so much that I eventually induced a stitch. It was really good to see the chaps and provided a welcome break from the fairly boring routine we had been operating.

[1] *HMP – Helicopter Machinegun Pod. Pod containing 0·5in machinegun and ammunition, attached to the side of the helicopter.*
[2] *Chemex – Chemical Training Exercise.*
[3] *Mother – Code for a helicopter's home ship.*

Monday 4 February – Brit URG Box

The day began with the usual early morning brief followed by an early morn-
ing sortie. We had been due to carry out a surface search but somehow we never
achieved it and once again ended up being a taxi for most of the morning. The
afternoon followed in a very similar manner, in fact we ended up flying for
about six hours today, the majority of which was HDS-'ing.[1]

Throughout the day I had a headache that was steadily getting worse and by
the early evening I was feeling quite poorly. During the evening I had my sec-
ond Anthrax jab. The evening was spent watching a film in the Wardroom
slowly feeling worse and worse.

We received mail onboard today but I didn't get time to read it until I was
in bed, by which time I was feeling absolutely lousy. The mail consisted of a let-
ter from Chris's father and not one but two Valentine cards from Jill which real-
ly cheered me up.

Tuesday 5 February – Brit URG Box

I really thought that I was going to die today, and not as a result of an Iraqi
bullet but poisoned by our own doctors.

After going to bed feeling terrible I woke up just past midnight feeling
absolutely awful: I had a migraine, I felt nauseous, I swung from sweating
profusely one minute to freezing cold the next, basically I was a total wreck. I
attempted to get out of bed at about ten in the morning but collapsed on the
floor and it took a monumental effort to climb back into my bunk.

I tried again at lunch time and failed once again. Eventually managing to
surface at 1700, I felt extremely weak. It's now 2100 and I still feel very ill but
at least I feel half human.

Wednesday 6 February – Brit URG Box

A pleasant day really. Because of my illness over the last twenty-four hours,
there was no flying scheduled until late morning to give me maximum recovery
time and, as it transpired, we did not actually take off until 1230. The morn-
ing was devoted to tying up a few loose ends on the niffnaff and trivia front
and generally wasting time chatting in a pleasant kind of way.

The majority of the flying was devoted to NGS spotting, interspersed with the
usual surface search and HDS. We also flew one of the ship's company to film
the ship from the air for a video that is being put together to send to families
back home. It proved to be really good fun.

We learnt today that on Friday we are due to sail north and relieve the
Gloucester. I don't think the implications of that have sunk in yet. Fairly soon
we will actually be involved in fighting a war instead of watching from afar.
I'm still scared.

After we landed on this evening, the aircraft was found to have a crack in
one of the plates that holds the tail rotor drive shaft in position, so it was imme-
diately grounded, and therefore tomorrow should be a quiet day. The evening
was spent sorting out some niffnaff and trivia and writing letters.

---

[1] *HDS – Helicopter Delivery Service.*

Thursday 7 February – Brit URG Box

As predicted, a reasonably quiet day for the aircrew whilst the rest of the flight team carried out the repairs on the aircraft. The majority of the day was spent sorting out film and video returns – a very boring and tedious task.

The good news about today; was that we received mail onboard and I received another couple of letters from Jill plus one from Mum and Dad and one from Chris.

There was no real highlight of the day, it just plodded along quite nicely. We came alongside HMS Herald *to transfer some stores, so it was good to have a look at her again from close quarters.*

I also found the time to go to fitness training which was painful but enjoyable. One thought provoking incident occurred today. HMS Gloucester *just narrowly missed a mine, so the dangers of our present situation were reiterated. We also heard news about the bombings in Downing Street. It sounds pretty dangerous and made me realise that we are not the only ones facing potential danger.*

The evening was spent watching the video Highlander, *generally sorting out paperwork and writing a letter.*

Friday 8 February (In transit to the North Persian Gulf)

The day started earlier than expected with a call saying that we were required to fly and had a brief in half an hour. After a mad rush we sorted the briefing out, however didn't actually get airborne until mid-morning to carry out a Vertrep *with RFA* Orange Leaf. *After lunch we had a quick recognition session followed by another two and a half hours flying, a half hours HMP shoot, which was very successful and a surface search.*

The HMP shoot was going to be cancelled. However, with a gentle bit of persuasion (i.e. losing my temper), it was reinstated. I could not believe that they wanted me to go to war with a gun that had not been tested or sighted.

It was quite a psychological day in many ways as today saw the ship begin its transit up north where the action is. By lunch-time tomorrow we could be shooting missiles and firing guns at a real enemy. As we transit north the level of activity from friendly units increased dramatically. The ship encountered a number of friendly aircraft, both fixed and rotary wing, flying by throughout the day. With the increased activity the level of anxiety amongst all of the ship's company noticeably increased.

The whole week proved to be odd on a variety of different levels. Physically I reacted badly to the injections, which left me feeling extremely ill for the first few days and then lethargic for the rest of the week. The end of the period saw us moving closer to the action, where I had thought I wanted to be, away from the mundane flying around the support ships. However, the atmosphere onboard the ship was similar to that experienced when we first sailed from the UK. Maybe it was the mail drop with Valentine's cards from loved ones, perhaps it was the final realisation that Manchester *did have a role to play and which might mean being in the firing line: either way, once again there was little euphoria, just quiet contemplation.*

CHAPTER NINE

Taking the Hot Spot

There is no feeling of power that compares with having your finger on the trigger, and no greater feeling of vulnerability that compares with the knowledge that the guns are pointing at you.

Saturday 9 February – On Station – North Persian Gulf

We did not fly today but it was an interesting day nonetheless. Having arrived on station in the NPG, Nick and I reached the decision that it was not a good idea to fly until we had received a full brief on operating procedures from HMS Cardiff, *our buddy ship. Her aircraft transported key personnel from* Manchester *to* Cardiff *during the afternoon, for what proved to be a very enlightening series of briefs. We managed to have a long chat with their aircrew who already have four confirmed kills to their name – they are obviously very proud.*

Overall a stimulating day and I now feel that there is a actually a job for us to do and, perhaps more importantly, a reason for us being out here.

Sunday 10 February – NPG

A busy day. During the morning Nick flew north in Cardiff's *aircraft to ascertain how things operate in the hot area, whilst I flew the aircraft on my own, providing a HDS service between the 'Mighty Manch',* Cardiff *and* London. *We actually completed the handover today and so are now 'on the job'. The afternoon was spent with the inevitable paperwork and domestics and I even managed to fit in a circuit training session which made me feel a lot better. I am now looking forward to getting airborne and flying north to do the job in hand.*

As the very north of the Persian Gulf was thought to be heavily mined it was deemed too dangerous to have more than two ships sitting in a minefield at any one time. Therefore only two suitably equipped ships were stationed just off Iraq to provide a radar picture, while the other ships were stationed 80–100 miles to the south of them. The ships were rotated around every three or four days so our time was to come, but initially we were still 120 miles south of Kuwait. It still felt more interesting than being in the Brit URG Box. Everyone was glad to be out of it. We were excited, if a little apprehensive.

It had been deemed necessary that a two day handover would be required in order for *Cardiff*'s crew to give everyone who needed it a thorough brief on the routines and procedures at the sharp end. *Cardiff* had been stationed in the Gulf for ten of the last twelve months, and they had been operating in the north since hostilities commenced. All the ship's company looked exhausted but they remained an extremely worked-up and efficient fighting unit from whom we all had a lot to learn.

After the main brief, during which the members of *Manchester*'s warfare team were given a general overview of the tactical situation, Nick and I sat down in a quiet corner and quizzed their aircrew.

"Where are the areas to avoid?"

"How much radar activity is there?"

"What's it like being fired at?"

We both had so many questions and we wanted to glean every last bit of information from them. They were the 'old hands' up here and we were the new boys. We didn't want to mess up on our first sortie in the hot area.

"Why don't I fly north with you tomorrow and you can show me the sights?" Nick suggested to *Cardiff*'s flight crew. They were due to fly one last patrol on the following day before the ship set sail back home. We had been tasked to continue flying personnel between the two ships to complete the handover.

"I'm happy to fly the transfer trips on my own, if you want to go," I chipped in. I loved flying on my own and took advantage of every opportunity to do it, besides, I had absolutely no desire to be stuck in the back of an aircraft with no controls while someone took pot shots at us. It felt good that we were actually getting involved at long last as this was what I had been mentally preparing myself for. I was still scared but, deep down, I was actually glad that we were going to get the chance to fly in the war zone proper. I wanted the chance to fire a missile in anger.

The following day *Cardiff*'s aircraft flew over and collected Nick. I stood on the deck and waved them off but I felt very nervous for him, wondering what would happen if they were shot down and, how long would it take to get another Observer out here for me to fly with? How would I cope with having to rebuild the bond of mutual trust that had built up between us? I hoped that they were going to be OK.

The ground crew pushed the cab out of the hangar and prepared it for flight. Suddenly I felt nervous. Although this was going to be a simple trip of shuttling people between the two ships, twenty miles apart, what if I got lost? What if I stumbled across an Iraqi vessel making a dare-devil raid? The Lynx can be flown with only one person but requires two to fight it. I wished the ships had been closer, as that would have enabled me to physically see *Cardiff*. Perhaps I wasn't the experienced aviator that I thought I had become after all.

As I strapped into the cockpit the operations room called me on telebrief.

"PWO to Pilot"

"Go ahead PWO, what's the problem?"

"Slight change of plan, can you go to *London* first and pick up SNOME[1]. He wants to sit in on the handover briefs today."

---

[1] *SNOME - Senior Naval Officer Middle East.*

It was an order not a question. Shit, *London* was miles away, halfway back down to the Brit URG Box. Without the Observer the radar cannot be used – there is only one set of controls and they are out of reach from the pilot's seat. Without radar, the navigation over the sea is all done on the Tactical Air Navigation System (TANS) and dead reckoning. TANS is a doppler driven navigation system, which is inherently inaccurate, while dead reckoning involves holding a constant speed and heading, hoping you arrive in the right place. Getting lost around here and wandering around the skies struck me as very dangerous. If you didn't wander into enemy airspace you would probably get shot down by your own side. The IFF was supposed to indicate to other ships that you were a friendly unit but, having been locked up[1] by friendly units on more than one occasion, I didn't trust it. Most ships had the point defence systems set on automatic: wander into the airspace surrounding the ship without telling them and they would shoot you down – period.

I thought for a minute.

"Pilot to PWO, sure I can do that, no problem."

What had I just said? This bravado thing was getting out of control. I spoke to the helicopter controller and programmed TANS, making double sure that the co-ordinates were entered correctly, not that it made much difference as the ships were never where they said they would be anyway.

As I departed the ship and set off in the direction of HMS *London* I felt very lonely sitting in the aircraft on my own; normally I would have loved it. Those Jaguar pilots, flying daylight missions over Iraq, must have felt very alone indeed. After forty-five minutes flying I switched frequencies and called *London*. I was extremely grateful when she replied and even more grateful when she came into view on the horizon a few minutes later.

I landed on *London* and could see Commodore Craig waiting in the hangar. As he strapped himself into the aircraft he seemed genuinely pleased that Nick was not in the aircraft. Nick and the Commodore had a mutual dislike for one another that stemmed back several years. I never got to the root of it but, apparently, the Commodore had been instrumental in having Nick court-martialled some years before after an 'incident' at a Chelsea match in which Nick and a police constable had experienced a slight disagreement.

On our arrival in the Brit URG Box we had been tasked to spend the afternoon acting as an airborne taxi for the Commodore. Neither Nick nor I were particularly happy with this as I figured that I would rather be involved in the tactical side of the conflict rather than playing at being an airline pilot. Nick simply did not like him and therefore had no desire to spend any time in his company. We carried an inflatable seat in the back of the aircraft that was used for transporting passengers. However, this was difficult to get in with all the additional equipment that had been fitted within the rear of the aircraft. We came to a command decision that we would not fit the seat and instead would throw a cushion into the

[1] *Locked up* – *Locked onto by a weapon targetting radar.*

back of the aircraft for the Commodore to sit on. I did not know the man so held no grudges against him, but I must confess that the look of disbelief on his face when he opened the back of the aircraft to see a cushion waiting for him was hilarious. Initially he thought we were just taking the piss and that we had a seat hidden somewhere. When he realised that he was actually going to have to spend the afternoon sitting cross-legged on the cushion, like a five year old schoolboy, he was less than impressed. He sat in the back and said nothing, but our taxi service role was relinquished at the end of the flight.

As I said, I'm not sure whether the dislike was mutual or whether it was simply because, after the cushion incident, he was just grateful to have a seat. Either way he looked happier with the fact that Nick was absent. The journey back was uneventful and I tried to make polite conversation but he obviously had other things on his mind. This suited me as it meant I could concentrate on accurate flying and looking out for other ships. Having the Senior Naval Officer Middle East shot down by an RN ship because of the pilot's cock-up would have been acutely embarrassing.

After dropping Commodore Craig off, I received an updated position for *Cardiff* and set off to the north. This time the transit was only twenty miles and I was very keen not to stray any further north than that. As soon as she appeared out of the haze I flew straight towards her and relaxed a little. As I approached closer I noticed that her flight deck nets were still up and the hangar door was closed. Normally the nets, which surround the deck and prevent people falling off, are lowered for flying operations. The hangar door, similar to that of a rollover garage door, should have been half open for two reasons; first it enables the pilot to see the white line painted on it, indicating the centre of the deck, and secondly it allows the ground crew in the hangar to have an unobstructed route to bring weapons, fuel and stores to the helicopter.

"Echo-Two-Juliet this is Three-Six-Zero. The flight deck doesn't appear to be ready to receive me," I quizzed the Helicopter Controller. I watched a solitary member of the ship's company standing on the deck, nonchalantly watching me.

The HC sounded confused.

"Negative Sir, we've been closed up at Flying Stations for the last half hour."

As he said this I started to look around and, about a mile away, I could see HMS *Cardiff* – I had made my approach to HMS *Gloucester*! Fortunately *Gloucester* had been briefed that *Cardiff* was taking part in flying operations and had realised my error. I felt hugely embarrassed and it wasn't something I mentioned to Nick on his return. I also realised how lucky I had been. If I had made an unannounced approach to an American ship, the reaction might have been somewhat different.

By the time I had finished the transfer, Nick was back on the *'Mighty Manch'*. As I shut the aircraft down, I could see him waiting to speak to me in the hangar.

"So how was it Nick, what's the score up north?"

"I think we've missed the boat. The Iraqi Navy doesn't want to play anymore, they have had their arses kicked once too often. Bar the odd oil rig and wreckage it's all pretty dull."

I was disappointed: to come this far, endure all of the preparation and not a get a bite at the cherry was irritating. As the afternoon progressed, I had time to think it through. During the circuit training on the flight deck, pushing out press-ups, a sense of relief came over me. It would be preferable to return in one piece, having seen no action, than to be shot down and killed or captured.

I entered the Wardroom after a particularly physical fitness training session. The First Lieutenant didn't like us in the Wardroom all smelly and sweaty, so I did it deliberately to rile him. Not that I didn't like him, I just thought that it was my home as much as his. Unfortunately he wasn't in; outside of watch change over times there were very few people around. Nick sat in the corner on his own reading a piece of paper. It was an intelligence signal from the Americans. He passed it over.

"You might find that interesting reading."

I skimmed through it. It outlined the latest intelligence concerning the naval battle. Amongst other things it indicated that the Iraqis were very anxious to shoot down an Allied helicopter; because of the carnage that the Lynx had already caused amongst their fleet, a Navy Lynx was their prime target. Our role was to protect the naval forces amassing to the south of our position for the inevitable amphibious assault. It crossed my mind that the Iraqis might be very keen to interview a Lynx crew and discover more about our capabilities.

"About this signal. What do you think is the best method of personal defence if we get shot down?" I enquired. As he had seen action in the Falklands as well, I figured he would have a good idea.

"*Cardiff*'s crew are flying with personal 9mm pistols, but I'm not convinced its really worth it."

"Why the fuck not?!"

"If they do want to shoot down a helicopter and interview the crew, we're hardly going to fight off the Iraqi Navy with a peashooter and twenty rounds. The best we could hope for is to shoot one of their mates, which isn't exactly going to improve our reception committee."

I thought it through; sitting in a life-raft in the middle of nowhere, a pistol would not exactly be a lot of use when trying to discourage the advances of an Iraqi ship looming down upon us. I could not envisage a scenario where all the escape and envasion techniques that we had learnt would come into good use.

"I think we should carry something, just to make me feel better." It was about the only reason I could think of for carrying a personal weapon.

"Why don't we sling a couple of SLR's[1] in the back of the aircraft. If we end up on land somewhere they might provide a little more fire power than a pistol, and we won't have the hassle of flying with a pistol and holster strapped to our sides."

---

[1] *SLR – Self Loading Rifle, predecessor to the SA80, the combat weapon used by the British Army.*

I liked Nick's suggestion.

"Sounds logical mate. I'll go and sort it."

As I stood up to leave the Wardroom, Nick called across.

"Ask them to stick alternate tracer in."

I couldn't think of any reason why, so quizzed him.

"What the hell for?"

Nick smiled, "If we stumble on an Iraqi helicopter, I'll have a go with the SLR, the tracer will be helpful when trying to hit a moving target."

I smiled and left, but I liked the idea.

Monday 11 February – NPG

Well, what a day. It started at 0300 with a telephone call saying that an Iraqi fast patrol boat had been found and that we were to come to Alert 15. As our chaff and flare dispenser is not working, Cardiff's aircraft was tasked to go north and subsequently hit the target, bringing their total to five.

We were stood down at 0630 and I immediately went back to bed. I arose again at 1000 and we briefed to go flying at 1100 but we did not actually take off until 1145. It was supposed to be just to clear the deck whilst they received another aircraft but we ended up remaining airborne for an hour whilst we completed a Photex[1] with Cardiff. After a quick fifteen minutes for lunch we were up again, this time with two live missiles, on our way north for a surface search. We landed on the American ship USS Paul F. Foster, to refuel before commencing the patrol, and were informed that there was a possible target to the north. After communicating with an American Seahawk, they vectored us in and we fired a missile which was assessed to have hit the target.

We were then vectored in to another target which we fired at. However, it was assessed as a miss. We have now fired our first shots in anger and undoubtedly killed our first victims of the war. How do I feel? – surprisingly unaffected. During the attack I was scared, afterwards jubilant, now I am back to normal.

We were greeted on our return with half of the ship's company cheering us in the hangar and the Captain with some champagne. It made me appreciate how much the rest of the ship's company are identifying with us and relying upon us to perform for the ship. It was a special moment but there is still lots of work to be done so we must not become complacent, but I suppose it still feels good to have pressed home a successful attack.

My diary entry here conveys a degree of self-assurance and calmness about this day and I guess, whilst writing the diaries, that's how I felt. The only reason I was writing them was to let Jill know how I was feeling in my last days. If I died next, I didn't want her to know how scared I had been. I did not want her to think that I had died a coward. Therefore the diaries left out a lot of details. However, even now, I remember them fairly vividly.

We were woken early, the Principle Warfare Officer had been informed by a maritime patrol aircraft that they held a contact on radar, making its way at high speed towards the Allied shipping. The details were sketchy and we were brought to Alert 15. Getting dressed into my

[1] *Photex – A flight to take aerial photographs.*

flying overalls at three o'clock in the morning, I felt nervous but not scared, but I always felt a little nervous before night flying from a deck. I caught up with Nick in the operations room talking to the PWO.

"The contact's believed to be some eighty miles to the north, that's about all we know." The PWO looked excited. I'm not surprised, I thought, he doesn't have to fly off in the pitch-black darkness and get his balls shot off.

Nick looked concerned,

"We don't know what type it is or what it's armed with, and our chaff and flare dispenser's not working."

The chaff and flare dispenser was an additional piece of equipment that all Gulf aircraft had been fitted with. The unit itself was strapped on under the tail boom of the aircraft and controlled by a black box in the cockpit on top of the instrument panel. The unit contained flares that burnt at a high temperature and bundles of thin strips of tin foil called chaff. If a radar controlled missile locked onto the helicopter we would fire the chaff. The bundles of tin foil would be fired into the slipstream and bloom into a highly reflective radar cloud. The theory was that this cloud would convince the missile that it was a much bigger and better target and it would be seduced towards it, leaving the aircraft to escape. If a heat seeking missile locked onto us we would fire the flares and hope that the missile could be convinced to track towards the flares and not our jet pipes. I could understand Nick's reluctance to investigate the contact without the protection that the chaff and flare dispenser afforded. He was senior to me, he called the shots.

"*Cardiff*'s aircraft is at Alert 15 as well, what do you reckon, ask Camera Bug to launch *Cardiff*'s aircraft?" the PWO suggested, looking at the two of us.

Nick nodded his approval. I wasn't sure whether I was happy or disappointed. This might be our one and only chance to fire a missile in anger and we were turning it down. It doesn't come much more yellow-bellied than that. Tactically it was the right decision; *Cardiff*'s crew knew the score as they had been operating up-threat since before Christmas and, in addition, had four kills already to their name. Most importantly, all of their equipment was working.

We were now under American control as they were running the show up here, and any tactical decisions had to be cleared by them over the radio. They used the call sign 'Camera Bug'. God knows why.

All communication on the tactical net with Camera Bug was made using secure speech, a system whereby the outgoing transmission was scrambled and, without a decoder, all you could receive was a loud hiss. With secure speech you could pass tactical information in plain language, safe in the knowledge that the enemy would not be able to listen to you. In the Lynx it had one major disadvantage; the way the radio was wired into the aircraft meant that only one person could listen to it. As Nick was in charge of the tactical situation, he got the encrypted radio. At times I found it dreadfully infuriating not being able to monitor the tactical situation while airborne. Here in the operations room we did not have that problem.

We sat down and listened to the radio as their sortie progressed.

"Camera Bug this is Navy Four-Zero-Five, Contact 001, position Hotel 325 896, possible Zuik-class patrol boat." The whole of the Gulf was divided up into one big grid to make the passing of positions easier.

"Navy Four-Zero-Five this is Camera Bug, weapons free contact 001", replied the Texas drawl.

"Roger, weapons free, contact 001."

There were a couple of minutes silence before the next call.

"Fox-trot Five Mike this is Four-Zero-Five, bruiser[1] loose contact 001."

That was the helicopter telling her mother that the missile had been fired; it was now skimming across the sea towards the target.

"This is Navy Four-Zero-Five. Contact 001 confirmed hit, large explosion seen on the horizon, returning Mother."

That was it; as simple as that. We could have done it. I was envious as I went back to bed.

I arose again at mid-morning and we briefed for the day's flying. The plan was that we would launch just before midday to clear the deck and enable a Sea King helicopter to deliver some stores to the ship. As *Manchester* had such a small flight deck, it meant there was barely enough room for one helicopter to operate from it, never mind two. As we were at Alert 15 the helicopter was required to be sitting on the deck ready for action. To receive another helicopter the ship had two options: either stand the helicopter down from Alert 15 and fold and stow it back in the hangar, which required a lot of work; or, alternatively, launch the helicopter. We opted to launch and clear the deck.

While airborne we were called on the radio by *Cardiff*. Their helicopter was airborne carrying two Sea Skua missiles. As we had now taken over and they were just about to set off home, would we care to take some photographs of their helicopter with the ship in the background for PR purposes? It seemed like the least we could do for the boys. The whole serial ended up taking longer than an hour. Eventually our ship called on the radio with a message to return, politely reminding us that there was actually a war to be fought. Our presence was required up north to carry out a surface search.

As mentioned earlier, although we were now officially 'on station' in the North Gulf, we were still 120 miles south of Iraq. There were just two ships stationed at the very north, their role being very much that of first line of defence, co-ordinating the air and sea picture over and around Kuwait, hence a very precarious position, a prime target for Iraqi fire and well within range of Silkworm anti-ship missiles.

On top of all of this, the area was heavily mined. As this was deemed such a dangerous area to be working in, the ships would rotate round with an average length of time spent in the "hot area" lasting three or four days. The remainder of the ships acted as support and platforms for the helicopters. This meant that in these initial days of our patrol, each sortie would start with a 120 mile transit to the north. This would take about an

[1] *Bruiser – Codeword for a missile. Loose – Fired.*

hour, so to give us maximum time on patrol, we would land on one of the northernmost ships to refuel before commencing each patrol.

Despite the excitement of the night before, we were still 120 miles down-threat and having just completed a routine photographic sortie, it was still difficult for me to imagine that a real enemy actually existed. Onboard the ship we did not receive the constant CNN news reports that covered all the minute details of the conflict and so we had little idea of how the war was progressing outside of our own horizons. Our sorties were very strange in that, unlike the Tornado pilots who had been allocated a target to attack before they launched, we never knew how the trip would progress and what, if any, enemy activity we might encounter. On this day I learned the first lesson of war – things can change very quickly.

The hour transit was event free. However as we approached the American ship USS *Paul F. Foster* I could see Nick talking on secure speech and smiling. Shit, it was infuriating not being able to listen. Once he had finished talking he switched back over and spoke to me.

"A Sea Hawk has been engaged by a small Iraqi fast patrol boat and they want to know if we can assist."

When it came to locating and tracking the enemy, Sea Hawks were very capable helicopters, but bar small calibre machine guns, they were unarmed.

Nick was grinning.

"I've told them that when we land on to refuel, I'll pop down to the control centre to get a tactical update."

I was getting excited. I looked out of the window at the missiles. They looked very menacing.

As soon as we landed on the ship, Nick unstrapped and jumped out. I sat in the cockpit keeping the helicopter running and waving at the guys on the deck like a schoolchild. As they were completing the refuel I saw Nick come running into the hangar. It was the first time I had ever seen him run. As he was strapping back into his seat the American sailor who had been conducting the refuel, came up to my window and waved a jamjar full of fuel at me. I obviously looked confused because he waved it in my face again. Not knowing what was going on, I simply gave him the thumbs up and he wandered off quite content.

"What the fuck was that all about?" I enquired of Nick as he plugged his helmet back into the intercom.

"He's showing you a sample of fuel so you can check that there is no water in it before taking off again."

It was so obvious, I should have known. For the second time in two days I felt very embarrassed.

Nick, however, was very excited.

"The Sea Hawk is tracking the FPB twenty miles to the north. It's already engaged them once so they are keeping well out of its way. I've got a rendezvous position for them. They are going to lead us into the target."

Now I was excited. We might get a chance to fire a missile and there was no fear at this stage. We decided to communicate with the Sea Hawk by the ordinary radio rather than the secure speech. The Iraqi vessel knew that someone was out there as they had already attempted to shoot down the American helicopter. By not using secure speech, at least I would be able to take a much more active part in the proceedings.

Nick called the Sea Hawk, call sign Oceanlord Two-Seven. The reply was instantaneous,

"Roger Three-Six-Zero you're loud and clear. Suggest you RV our position, we'll take you right in."

It was evident that they were old hands at this operation and were completely in control of the situation. They had suggested that we rendezvous in such a way that we would not have to use our radar. It made sense as by now the Iraqis would associate our Sea Spray radar with the Sea Skua missile. To the Iraqis that would mean trouble and we didn't want to show our hand too early. By not transmitting on the radar until the last minute we could, hopefully, lead them into a false sense of security and then attack before they had a chance to jam or decoy our fire control radar.

Nick replied, trying to sound as laid back and as smoothly British as possible. He had never been a *Top Gun* fan.

"Roger Oceanlord Two-Seven. We are presently five miles to the south, with you in two minutes."

I accelerated the helicopter to the maximum permissible speed. I didn't want to give the FPB a chance to get away and so miss another opportunity to launch an attack. I was beginning to feel excited, overlaid with an element of fear. The sight of the Sea Hawk orbiting on the horizon

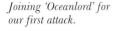
Joining 'Oceanlord' for our first attack.

reassured me that things were going to plan. I joined the other helicopter in close formation. One of the crew was leaning out of the back door waving and taking photographs.

"Oceanlord Two-Seven, Navy Three-Six-Zero is now aboard," I transmitted, indicating to the Sea Hawk pilot that we were now in close formation and ready to move off towards the target.

"Roger Three-Six-Zero, contact bears 005 at 15 miles."

The Sea Hawk rolled out and headed to the north. Nick entered the position of the enemy ship in TANS and then we were left with nothing to do so I handed Nick my camera from a pocket in my flight suit.

"Take a quick snap of Oceanlord for me, I'll stick it in my album." It seemed bizarre taking photographs again as we ran in towards the enemy. In close formation I wanted to keep my hands and feet on the controls.

"Contact bears 002 at 12 miles – from Camera Bug, you have weapons free on the target," the Sea Hawk updated the enemy's position. Nick updated it in TANS.

"I'm going to have a quick sweep on radar to confirm," Nick informed me. He set up the radar so that with one sweep he would be able to locate the target. I glanced across at the radar screen as he pressed the transmit button. Exactly where the Sea Hawk had said it would be, a green blob appeared on the illuminated screen. Nick transmitted again.

"Roger Oceanlord Two-Seven we have the contact on radar, many thanks for the service."

"Best of luck Navy Three-Six-Zero." The Sea Hawk broke away and we assumed it was going back to its mother. It felt very lonely again. Nick and I had a quick discussion to decide at what range to fire the missile.

"We will fire closer than usual to maximise the chance of success," Nick commented.

"OK mate, but let's not go inside five miles." We still had no idea of what we were up against except that it was an Iraqi Fast Patrol Boat. Therefore we had no idea as to what type of anti-aircraft guns and missiles she might be armed with. What we did know was that the Iraqis were equipped with SAM 5, a hand-held heat seeking anti-aircraft missile with a range of five miles, and we had to assume that all vessels would be equipped with them. We eventually agreed on a range of six miles.

Nick turned the radar on for another sweep. As he turned it off we both heard it through our headsets. A short bleep, followed by a pause and then another bleep.

"Fire control radar, band three," Nick said almost nonchalantly. My pulse noticeably quickened, I did not need telling. I had heard it as well and had glanced at the screen on our electronic support measure equipment, known as Orange Crop. A series of lights on the third row up indicated that the enemy was looking for us with the radar that controlled the missile system: they must have realised that an attack was imminent. I started a gentle descent. Because radar relies on radio waves, flying lower over the sea minimises your chances of being detected as your radar return becomes confused with the ground 'clutter'. I levelled at fifty feet.

"OK Dickie, two miles to run." Nick had his radar on all the time now.

I was feeling nervous, I could feel my hands becoming very sweaty. I looked down at them: I had a vice-like grip on both the cyclic and collective. I took a deep breath and tried to relax. I remembered my old instructor's words, from when I was learning to hover and tensed up on the controls; "Take a deep breath and try to relax from the arse upwards. If you can unsqueeze your cheeks, you will start to relax". I tried it. It worked, a little.

Bleeeeeeeeeeeeeeeeeeeeeeeeeeeeee. The noise was so familiar. I had heard it a hundred times before on the simulator. It sounded like the whine of the television when left on as the transmission ceases. It was the Orange Crop again: we had been locked up. The sound made us both jump. Shit, I must break lock before weapons can be fired at us. I descended even further. I was now flying lower than I had ever dared before. It felt like the wheels should be in the water – this was seriously low. The whining stopped, we had broken lock. Nick offered some encouragement.

"OK mate another mile to run." He didn't comment on the lock up but I could sense the slight apprehension in his voice. We were both scared but controlled. In order to fire the missile we would have to climb again. To attempt to fire at this height would result in the missile simply dropping into the sea.

"Half a mile to run." Nick was now running through the pre-fire checks and activating the missile. I was concentrating very hard on unsqueezing my cheeks and trying to relax.

"Point two of a mile." That was my cue.

"Roger, starting climb," I informed Nick. It all sounded very professional and rehearsed. I was thankful that my body had gone into automatic, overriding the fear and excitement.

I slowed the helicopter down to less that forty knots, I didn't want to continue closing the enemy at almost 150 mph while at this height. As we levelled, I knew that we were sufficiently high to ensure that the missile would have enough room to fall from the weapon station and ignite when fired. The system works thus: the missile fire button is pressed and, within a second, it receives all of the information from the aircraft and internally tests its own systems; it then drops away from the weapon carrier and falls clear, before the burners ignite and it tracks towards the target. This ensures that the helicopter is not engulfed in flames of burning liquid fuel.

I looked across at the radar screen. The little dot indicated that our radar had successfully locked onto the ship. I could hear the bleep, bleep of their radar as they tried to lock us up. It was in rhythm with the heart beat I could feel pounding in my chest. We were now just waiting for the two lights to illuminate on the missile control panel that would indicate the missile was locked onto the target and ready. The two seconds seemed like an eternity. Time was moving at a tenth of its normal speed. Who would win this aerial chess game depended on who would shoot first. We had the advantage as they had yet to lock onto our helicopter again, but the continued regular bleep through the headset indicated that they were frantically trying. Then the 'locked' and 'ready' lights illuminated.

Our missiles had now received all the information from the system computer, knew where to look for the target and wanted to go. Nick pressed the fire button. Nothing happened.

I looked across at Nick as he pressed the fire button again. Still nothing happened. The bleep continued through the headset – they must surely lock up soon. I reached forward to press the fire button on my side. As I moved my arm towards the switch I felt the aircraft twitch laterally as the missile fell from the weapons pylon. Shit. Of course. The missile takes a few seconds to complete an internal self-check before it releases!

Time was moving very slowly indeed. The missile must surely have fallen uselessly into the sea by now. Then it ignited. I had never fired a live Sea Skua before so wasn't ready for the burst of energy, heat and noise as the fuel ignited. It caught me by surprise. I tried to watch but instantly it disappeared into the haze. Almost immediately I turned and descended the helicopter. The helicopter radar must be kept pointing at the target so that the radar waves returning from the contact can guide the missile now thundering towards it. The radar is situated in the front of the helicopter and rotates through ninety degrees either side of the nose, enabling me to turn away from the Iraqi vessel – I did not want to get any closer – while keeping the radar pointing at it. I descended to try and avoid detection by their radar, but we couldn't descend too far and risk losing our own missile.

I glanced in at the missile control panel. The bank of 'time-to-run' lights slowly extinguished as the missile flew towards the ship. Nick *The missile impacts.*

counted them out loud.

"Five lights to go...four...three...two...one...all lights out."

We both looked anxiously in the direction of the ship. With the visibility at less than five kilometres we had never been in visual contact with it, however, exactly when the 'time-to-run' lights in the cockpit indicated impact, an explosion was visible on the horizon, followed shortly afterwards by a thick plume of black smoke.

"Yes!" I punched my clenched fist into the air.

We had achieved our first kill. I felt elated that we had actually achieved the job that we had been dispatched to do. The nerves had gone completely. I relaxed a little and started to shake.

I took a deep breath to calm myself and quickly checked around the cockpit to ensure that all the systems were still working routinely. Good airmanship dictates that this should be done every five minutes or so and I hadn't done it since we left the refuelling ship. While I completed this, Nick reported the engagement back to the controlling authority using secure speech. I was hoping that we would be tasked to close the ship for damage assessment. It's helpful to know how much damage has been done such that you can ascertain whether the target is out of action or not.

Nick finished on the radio and came back on to the intercom.

"There's another contact that they want us to go and attack 25 miles to the north-west. I've been given the position. It's been reported by the SUCAP and believed to be a Boghammer type vessel."

The Boghammer vessels were large military speedboats with four 20mm anti-aircraft guns fitted to the front. They were a real hazard because of their size; small enough to be very difficult to locate, both with the radar and the naked eye, and yet with enough fire-power to really ruin your day. The standard Sea Skua missile skimmed across the sea at about twelve feet, which meant that the missile would pass right over the top of one without impacting. Fortunately we were carrying a variant of the missile that had been developed especially to counter this type of threat. Its performance parameters had been changed to ensure that it was capable of engaging smaller targets. SUCAP was military jargon for Surface Unit Combat Air Patrol, the American jets assisting in the search for enemy vessels. They were armed with normal free-fall iron bombs. Apparently, hitting a small ship with an unguided bomb proved very difficult and they achieved only very limited success.

This time there was no friendly contact to lead us in. We had no way of knowing how long ago the vessel had been sighted and therefore no indication as to how valid the positional information was. Nick had his radar on pretty much all of the time as we ran in towards the last reported position. He was getting noticeably agitated at his inability to locate any sign of enemy activity amongst the clutter on the radar screen. I kept my eyes firmly glued out of the window, peering into the haze to try and find something visually. We were both concerned that if the intelligence received the previous night, was correct there could well be a number of these vessels around, armed with SAM 5 missiles and with the single objective of shooting down a Lynx helicopter.

Nick spoke again.

"I've think I've got a weak return about seven miles away. It's in the location of the position previously passed."

I glanced across at the radar screen but from where I was sitting I couldn't make out anything.

"OK Nick, I'll hover here and keep pointing towards it." Now it was my turn to sound nonchalant.

Nick was still hunched up over the radar screen, but I could see his lips moving and as he wasn't talking to me, I assumed he was talking on secure speech to Camera Bug. I was right.

"We've got weapons free. Start flying towards it."

Things were a lot calmer and slower with this attack. There was no indication on Orange Crop of any enemy radar activity in the area. We agreed that we would fire at five miles.

Nick counted me down again.

"Seven miles to the target, still a weak return," he informed me. I was flying at fifty feet – no point in flying at five feet when you don't need to.

"Six miles, still a weak return on radar." I glanced at Orange Crop; still no sign of any radar activity from anybody else.

"Five and a half miles." That was my cue. Again, I started to climb and when levelled at optimum height, brought the aircraft into the hover and called 'on condition'. I could tell that Nick was concerned that he might not be able to lock the radar onto the target as it was still such a weak return. In the end he locked on without any problems. With no fire control radar trying to locate us, the 'locked' and 'ready' lights took no time at all to illuminate. The fire button was pressed and this time I was ready for the delay. It seemed very short this time and I was ready for the missile igniting. There was no point in turning away and I held the helicopter in the hover. Once again we watched the 'time-to-run' lights count down. As the last one extinguished I looked into the haze with anticipation: there was no explosion, no plume of black smoke, nothing happened. I felt disappointed. Nick played around with the radar, the contact had been so weak he could not accurately assess whether it had disappeared or not. I looked at the fuel, we were beginning to run low. Nick passed me a heading for the USS *Paul F. Foster* and I turned towards it. After all the excitement of the first attack this had been a complete anticlimax. We discussed the possibility of what might have happened enroute back to the ship.

"It could have been a very small craft and the missile passed straight over their heads," I suggested, "so at least we would have given the rag-heads a shock."

Nick remained less convinced.

"I think we fired at a navigation buoy. There are a lot of them marked on the chart around there."

We were both deflated, but Nick lifted the mood.

"We smoked that first bastard though."

It brought a smile to my face and made me feel good. The American ship began to appear out of the haze.

I landed on the ship and the ground crew commenced the refuel. Noticing the empty weapon pylons they signalled thumbs up inquisitively. We returned the thumbs up and they started jumping and dancing around the deck. They obviously approved of the action. The return flight back to *Manchester* seemed to take forever – in fact it took about forty minutes. The rest of the sortie had taken about three hours but it had felt like ten minutes. It was not until afterwards, when I sat down with Nick, that I had any idea about where we had actually been. It is the Observer's responsibility to look after the navigation, but I used to pride myself in having a good seat-of-the-pants feel as to where we were (extremely difficult when flying over the sea in haze with no landmarks to identify your position). However, on this occasion I really did not have a clue as to where we had been, I had been concentrating so hard on just flying the aircraft safely.

I rejoined Mother in my usual punchy manner, although this time with real reason. The ship was heading towards us, so I flew along the starboard side at maximum speed, just feet away. As I passed the stern of the ship I pulled up into a steep climb. Reaching the top of the climb at 400 feet I rolled the helicopter on its back and pulled it through to head in the opposite direction back towards the ship. As I moved over the deck I looked into the hangar and saw that it was full of the ship's company: it made me feel very proud. As soon as the helicopter was shut

We return home.

down the Captain came out onto the flight deck clutching a bottle of champagne and a handful of glasses. It was a wonderful moment. We shared the champagne amongst the flight and toasted Three-Six-Zero; she had behaved impeccably. The helicopter controller arrived in the hangar from the operations room with a big smile on his face. It really made me realise that all of the ship's company had been sharing my feelings of boredom and wanting to get involved. Now that the ship's helicopter had seen some action we all had a reason to be out here and we all had a reason to smile. Apparently when the report had been received back on the ship that the first attack had been a success the whole operations room had started to cheer spontaneously.

A handshake from the Captain on our return from our first 'kill'.

Tuesday 12 February – NPG

After yesterday's excitement, today proved to be a busy yet boring day. We flew for five hours, but all of it was oil slick reporting, not exactly the most riveting of tasks.

After another early start we were airborne at 0630 until 0930 looking at oil terminals that were pumping oil into the sea. The rest of the morning was spent between squandering time and a quick nap before lunch. Most of the afternoon was wasted in the same fashion as the morning, followed by another two hours' oil search. An early night followed due to a headache. Overall a normal day after yesterday's very abnormal day.

The flight enjoy a glass of champagne before going back to work.

Wednesday 13 February – NPG

Today proved to be more exciting than yesterday but not nearly as exciting as the day before. It started with the inevitable early morning surface search, a little bit more stimulating this time as we were working a long way north which got the adrenaline going again.

On our return we landed on USS Princeton, an American Aegis class cruiser for a Lynx/SH60 brief which proved to be both very useful and interesting. On completion of the discussion I was shown around the ship and was impressed beyond all belief. It was only a shame that we could not stay longer and the hospitality offered by the Americans was tremendous.

The rest of the morning/early afternoon was spent with recognition training/record book articles and a pre-lunch nap. We then remained at AL15 from 1600 until midnight which included being actioned at 1700 to investigate two suspicious targets. Unfortunately by the time that we arrived it was getting dark, so we were only able to positively ID one target as an oil rig and then were forced to return. On the way back we were locked up by a friendly unit and that was pretty scary as well.

The remainder of the evening was taken up with watching videos and letter writing, complaining as I received nothing in the mail drop today.

The oil slick reporting was a task we were called upon to do on a fairly regular basis. The oil came from a number of sources including a damaged oil rig and a stricken oil tanker. We plotted the position of the slick

The helicopter waits for another attack...

simply by flying around the edge. However, the slicks were generally so large, extending over hundreds of miles, that we could not circumnavigate them in one sortie. It proved a very tedious but necessary part of the operating requirements in the North Persian Gulf.

The next day we flew back up to the very north again. After the excitement of our previous visit the adrenalin was pumping even before we took off. However this time we conducted our two hour search but saw nothing more interesting than oil rigs and the wreckage of vessels that had been hit previously. We had arranged to land on the *Princeton* and discuss how the two types of helicopters would operate, so that we could maximise the merits of both. They too were relative newcomers to the Gulf and were as anxious as we were to get things right. We sat in the Wardroom and, over coffee and doughnuts, talked tactics.

"Our radar's very good at locating reasonable size targets, but it's these smaller Boghammer types that we have problems with in rough seas," Nick informed the attentive audience of the eight flight crew of the *Princeton*.

"What we need is an accurate up-to-date position if we are to succeed in attacking these guys. Once we know exactly where they are, we have both missiles and guns that can blow them out of the water. Ideally, if you find a contact let us know both where it is and where you are. We will rendezvous with you and follow you in until about twelve miles. That way we do not have to use our radar until the last moment and hopefully

... and so do I.

we can maintain the element of surprise. We tried it a couple of days ago and it worked a treat."

"What kind of information do you need to know in order to target the missile?" enquired one of their Airborne Tactical Officers.

"Just a range and bearing from our position," Nick continued, "plus the type of vessel if you know it. It helps us select the final skim height of the missile to cause the maximum amount of damage."

"How many missiles do you carry?" asked one of the pilots.

"Up to four," Nick replied, "but generally, unless it's a specific task, we will only take two and use the extra weight to carry fuel or guns."

"Tell us more about the guns."

I interjected. "The guns are the pilot's responsibility. We can carry up to two, one on each weapon station. The guns themselves are half inch calibre with explosives shells to maximise their effect. They are manually aimed, using an old head-up display stolen from out-of-service jets and mounted on the pilot's side. They were introduced a few years ago to counter the threat of the Boghammer. To the best of my knowledge they haven't been tested in anger yet, but I wouldn't mind a go."

The audience looked impressed.

"Want to swap helicopters buddy?" offered one of the American crew.

"No thanks mate, I'll stick with the Lynx: you find them, we'll waste 'em."

That summed up the meeting quite nicely. We left for a tour of the ship.

During the flight back to Mother, Nick and I discussed the tour around the ship. We had both been tremendously impressed. She carried a variety of weapons that made our own ship look about as useful as the proverbial chocolate fire guard. The Control Centre was something else. Surrounded on three walls by enormous blue screens, the Captain had an amazing range of information at his fingertips: press a button and all of the air assets currently airborne would appear on a large map of the Gulf; press another and all the surface units appeared with an arrow indicating course and speed. This was impressive stuff.

On our way back Nick and I were talking about the amazing fire power that just one ship could carry when the Orange Crop suddenly went berserk.

"Lock up, band four!" Nick yelled.

Instinctively I lowered the collective, turned the helicopter and descended. The best way to break lock with this type of radar was to descend below its coverage. The whine in our ears continued, we hadn't broken lock yet.

"Who the fuck is that?" I yelled.

"I haven't got a clue but it's a friendly unit." Bollocks, what a way to go, wasted by your own side; I continued to weave and descend; Nick fired off the chaff. The whine started to become intermittent; it couldn't hold lock continuously, but could it hold it long enough to get a missile off?

"I thought the IFF was supposed to stop this shit!" I was getting angry more than scared.

"So did I." Nick replied. Suddenly the whining stopped. We exited the area as soon as possible. It turned out to be a Dutch ship.

CHAPTER TEN

The Light on the Dark Side of Me

Given the choice between death or glory, I'd rather have neither.

Thursday 14 February – North Persian Gulf

Not really the way I would ordinarily choose to spend St Valentine's Day, but an interesting day none-the-less. Today I experienced another all time first – someone shooting at me!

The day began with the first lie-in for a very long time, and most enjoyable it was too. I eventually arose at 1000 and generally sorted myself out before a flying brief at 1130. A Sea King HDS was followed by lunch which in turn was followed by a launch at 1500 for another surface search.

We were airborne for ninety minutes and were tasked to do some battle damage assessment on a contact half way between Faylakah Island and Kuwait. However, on investigation, there was nothing there. We returned to Mother to refuel and were sent out again with an updated position, further up the Kuwait/Faylakah gap. We eventually sighted the vessel but, due to the poor visibility, could not positively identify it by type and were not given weapons free.

While running in for a second visual inspection we were engaged by hostile fire. We terminated the run and as we were still unable to obtain weapons free we returned to Mother. On our return we were held off as she thought that she had found a mine which eventually turned out to be an empty life-raft.

I went to bed at around 2200 in preparation for an early start the next day.

Faylakah Island is situated some ten miles off the coast of Kuwait. It is part of Kuwait and as it had been occupied by the Iraqis it was heavily fortified. It was believed that an amphibious assault to retake Faylakah Island would herald the commencement of the ground offensive, hence *Manchester* had moved to a position twenty miles east of the Island. Each time we conducted a surface search in the area we always encountered a significant amount of radar activity. After an uneventful sortie, Nick and I were on our way back to Mother when we bumped into an American Sea Hawk. Like us they had finished their patrol and so were fair game for a mock dogfight. We spoke to them on the radio and switched to a secondary frequency so that our idle chit-chat would not disrupt the war effort. The Lynx being considerably more manoeuvrable than the Sea Hawk, we very soon had the better of them.

"Shit buddy, I gotta learn to fly one of those." The American pilot spoke in a deep Southern drawl as we looped the aircraft above him, bringing our unloaded guns to bear.

I loved this sort of behaviour and indulged in it whenever the opportunity arose. Nick just closed his eyes and hung on, he wasn't that keen on flying upside-down. There was a serious element to it as *Gloucester's* aircraft had encountered an Iraqi helicopter flying towards Faylakah a few days earlier, but both helicopters had turned and fled. I was slightly more ambitious, so consequently we flew with the HMP (helicopter machine gun pod) on the side of the helicopter whenever weight permitted. If we stumbled across an enemy helicopter I wanted to shoot it down. To my knowledge there had never been a reported incident of two helicopters engaging in air-to-air combat with one being shot down. I wanted to put that right and this was the ideal environment, so I took every opportunity that arose to practice my air-to-air combat skills on another helicopter. The dawning had finally begun. Military pilots are there to kill people and the skills necessary to achieve this objective are great fun to learn. But one has to accept that the enemy are within their rights to do the same to you. I wanted to fly with the HMP and shoot down another helicopter before someone did the same to me.

In this particular instance, as the Sea Hawk was no match for the Lynx, it had degenerated into an impromptu flying display. I was in the process of demonstrating the Lynx' aerobatic abilities when we were called on the main radio.

"Three-Six-Zero you are to return to refuel immediately, we have further tasking for you."

I immediately rolled the wings level and Nick called a heading for

Sights during a typical sortie. A stricken tanker.

Mother. I said goodbye to our American audience and they appeared to have been suitably impressed with the flying display.

As soon as I landed the aircraft, the telebrief cable was attached.

"Hello chaps, this is Ops. We have information on a vessel which has been sighted five miles south of Faylakah by the SUCAP. It's believed to have been hit at some stage. Can you close for battle damage assessment?" His accent wonderfully British.

This sounded like the opportunity to fire another missile and Nick eagerly copied down the position while I gave the hand signals to commence the refuel. We were airborne within five minutes and once again there was an air of excitement in the cockpit, but this time it was short-lived. It took us less than fifteen minutes to transit to the position given, only to find a large area of empty sea. Nick was on the secure speech talking to Camera Bug and I liaised with Mother.

"This is Three-Six-Zero. Nothing seen in position given, awaiting further instructions."

"Roger Three-Six-Zero, keep us informed."

Nick came back on the intercom.

"I've been given another position, It's halfway between Kuwait and Faylakah."

I turned the helicopter to the north and, as we were less than twenty miles away from the updated position, Nick used the radar to look for any sign of the ship. The visibility was its usual five kilometre in haze and this meant there was no chance of seeing anything at this range.

"There's a radar contact in the new position. Sat that close to Kuwait, it's got to be enemy."

Nick sounded quite excited as he informed the Americans and I spoke to Mother.

"This is Three-Six-Zero, new position passed by Camera Bug. Have identified contact on radar to the west of Faylakah Island. Presently closing for visual assessment."

The voice that replied was not the voice of the helicopter controller (HC) who was our usual point of contact with the ship. The HC formed part of the flight team. His role was that of a tactical air traffic controller for helicopters and his calm and reassuring voice always portrayed a sense of cool karma – not having his reliable voice on the other end of the radio was quite disturbing. Instead I was talking to one of the Fighter Controllers (FC), who usually looked after the jets. He had obviously been dragged in to cover for the HC.

"Er Roger, what's the position?"

"This is Three-Six-Zero. Contact presently lies between Faylakah and the mainland."

"All right mate, be careful."

I smiled. I didn't need to be told that and I had no intention of being a hero. We were now closing on the Kuwait/Faylakah gap and I could just make out the coastline on either side of the helicopter. It was the first time I had sighted Kuwait. Nick was hunched up over his radar again, talking to me. I had reduced the speed to forty knots as I did not want

to find myself within anti-aircraft missile range until we were ready.

An abandoned Zuik class.

"OK Dickie, we are six miles from the contact."

I looked out into the horizon and squinted. Far in the distance I could make out the shape of a ship on the horizon.

"Nick, I believe I'm visual with it."

He looked up from the radar screen and squinted at the horizon as I scanned the Orange Crop. As we were getting close to the enemy I thought somebody must be getting interested in our presence, but although there was a lot of radar activity, from both the island and the mainland, nobody seemed to be targeting us. I quizzed Nick.

"What do think it is? It looks like some kind of tug to me."

"I reckon it's some kind of resupply vessel running across the gap. Keep closing, we'll go into five miles."

I eased the helicopter forward and at five miles I brought it into the hover pointing towards the ship – we still couldn't positively identify it but in this position we were just outside the five miles from the island, ship and mainland. Nick spoke again.

"It's definitely military and, in its present position, it's got to be enemy. I'll try and get weapons free."

He went off the intercom as he spoke on the radio and I turned the aircraft around and opened up from the target. I felt we had been in one position for long enough and it struck me as a good idea to clear the area, obtain weapons free and then run it at low level for the attack. Thirty seconds later Nick was back on the intercom.

"We are still weapons tight. They want a positive ID by type."

I turned the helicopter back towards the target. At five miles I re-established the hover but still neither of us recognised the ship, and we would have to get inside the five mile limit to have a closer look. My eyes were beginning to hurt from continually focusing at infinity so I turned to look out of the side window and give them a break. As I looked at the sea there was a large explosion in the water about 300 yards away. I thought I was seeing things but then it happened again only closer and my first thought was that we were flying over a minefield and the downwash from the helicopter was detonating them. Another splash only closer still.

"Nick, what do you reckon this is."

Another explosion, this time almost under the helicopter. Fuck! Some bastard's shooting at us. I turned the helicopter away from the ship and accelerated in the opposite direction. Nick was smiling.

"I suppose you've worked out that it was enemy fire."

I started to laugh. The pair of us were giggling uncontrollably and I had to take a deep breath and compose myself. Nick spoke with the Americans again while I radioed Mother.

"This is Three-Six-Zero. On closing for damage assessment engaged by enemy fire from Faylakah Island."

There was a stunned silence for half a second, then the FC replied.

"Three-Six-Zero, GET THE FUCK OUT OF THERE!"

I guessed that was fighter speak for 'clear the area'. Helicopter drivers may not be as cool or punchy as their fighter colleagues, but at least we had a sense of humour. I didn't like to inform him that we had already made that decision on our own so I replied rather casually, trying not to giggle again.

"Roger, Three-Six-Zero is getting the fuck out of there."

We still could not get weapons free, so returned to Mother.

Friday 15 February – NPG

Today we achieved our second successful attack.

After a flying brief at 1130 we took off at 1300 for a surface search. There was very little activity so we returned around 1500, only to be told that a contact had been found in the area of interest, in a similar position to the ship that we had located yesterday.

Gloucester's Lynx was already on the scene. She had to ascertain the identity of the vessel due to the improved visibility. It was a Russian built Spasilac tug-type vessel, which intelligence had indicated had been converted to a mine layer. After much haggling she finally managed to obtain weapons free and engaged. The attack was unsuccessful and the missile assessed as a miss. She broke off the attack and returned home. We had already re-launched as a stand-by aircraft and shortly afterwards we pressed home a successful attack.

On completion of the attack we closed for battle damage assessment. Although she had definitely been hit (we saw the missile impact followed by thick black smoke) she did not sink. Therefore it was impossible to ascertain whether her anti-aircraft guns and missile were still operational. We tried to use binoculars hovering just outside of the assumed range for the weapons that she had, but still being unable to ascertain her fighting effectiveness from that range we were called back to Mother.

We completed three hours flying today and I'm pretty tired. I once again feel unmoved by this attack. Whilst flying, waiting to see whether the first attack had been successful, both Nick and myself were hoping that it would fail such that we would get another chance to press home an attack. I guess it's a combination of getting used to being at war combined with feeling that the target was ours (we had found it yesterday) yet we could not get permission to fire, despite being fired upon.

The surface search sorties were now getting fairly routine and even slightly boring and the majority of the early afternoon sortie was spent arguing with Nick about a small aerial I had seen on one of the oil rigs.

"Listen, I'm telling you mate, that aerial was not there yesterday. I'm totally convinced." I tried to explain to him but he remained unconvinced.

"Those rigs have been deserted since the outbreak of hostilities. Who do you propose is using them?"

"Well it's not going to be Japanese tourists is it, you git."

He turned his head and stared at me across the cockpit. From his expression I could tell he was unimpressed. I suppose he thought that I was behaving like an over-enthusiastic character from a *Boys' Own* comic. I obviously looked hurt by his stern stare and he tried to placate me.

"I'm sure that, if the Iraqis are using the rigs as observation platforms, we would have been informed about it."

I remained insistent.

And a tanker with a hole.

"Who's going to tell us about them. We're the only fuckers flying around these parts?"

He gave me one of those 'shut up kid and eat your candy' looks and I decided that I would not fly unnecessarily close to the oil rig unless I absolutely had to. It was one of those situations where I was glad that I had the controls in front of me. Many weeks later, after the cessation of hostilities, it transpired that Iraqi special forces had been using the rigs as forward observation platforms to monitor Allied shipping and aircraft. It's entirely possible that we could have been engaged by a concealed sniper as we circled the rig arguing about it. I guess we will never know. If they did shoot at us then they certainly missed.

The atmosphere in the aircraft had improved dramatically by the time we returned to the ship, which is just as well as an ambience of tension was not conducive to a good working environment within the confines of the cockpit. Once the aircraft was secured on the deck and the telebrief connected we were called by the Operations Officer. I had got into the habit of not shutting the helicopter down until I had ascertained that we were definitely not required to re-launch again.

"Keep the helicopter running chaps. We believe that the guy you found yesterday is out and about again. *Gloucester*'s flight has been tasked to investigate."

Rather than shut down I signalled for a refuel. We waited patiently and, after ten minutes, we were told to relaunch and hold ten miles south of Faylakah Island, pending further instructions. The atmosphere in the cockpit was significantly better now with the last argument well and truly forgotten. We listened intently on the radio and heard that *Gloucester*'s helicopter had found a contact in exactly the same position as the one we had discovered the day before. The visibility was far better today and they had positively identified it. Very shortly afterwards they were given weapons free.

"Miss you bastards, miss," I murmured under my breath. They had five ships to their name, we only had one. This should have been ours. And then our prayers were answered: they had missed. We both shouted excitedly as I turned the aircraft north towards the target. We were passed weapons free almost instantly. At six miles I brought the helicopter into the hover again and we could see the target quite clearly on the horizon, but I was more inclined to keep checking out of the side window this time. The 'locked' and 'ready' lights illuminated and Nick pressed the fire button. The missile dropped away and ignited as I kept the helicopter pointing towards the ship and transmitted on the radio.

"This is Three-Six-Zero, bruiser loose."

Once again, exactly on time, there was a large explosion on the ship followed by a thick plume of black smoke. There was no mistaking that our missile had hit and I transmitted again.

"Bruiser hit. Closing for damage assessment."

Rather than fly straight towards the burning ship I turned away and opened up from it, before turning round to run in at low level. The logic was quite simple. There was no doubting, on anyone's part, that we were here now. Due to the attack our position had been compromised and, if any of the weapon systems on the ship were still working, the ship would undoubtedly try to attack us – they certainly would not be too pleased to see us. I wanted to clear the area from which the attack had been launched and run in at low level, below their radar horizon. Nick was using the binoculars and could see that she was on fire but more than that he could not say. Orange Crop indicated that her radar was still working if nothing else. There was complete calm in the cockpit and so we stopped at five miles and considered the possibilities. Nick pondered for a while.

"Even if all the ship's weapons have been taken out, they could still nail us with a SAM 5 if we go much closer."

I was continually looking out the side window.

"They may well nail us from the mainland if we get much closer."

"The options are simple: we either close at low level for a quick pass or fuck off back to Mother now. Either way sitting here is achieving nothing more than giving the rag-heads some target practice."

The radio answered our dilemma.

"Three-Six-Zero, you are not to close for damage assessment but return immediately."

Deep down I guess I wanted to make one quick pass to see how much damage a missile makes.

"Next time it's my turn to press the fire button," was the only thing I could think of saying.

The drama was not quite finished for the day as, on our return, we were refused permission to land. Operating this far north the ship was well and truly in minefield territory, the defences against which are minimal, bar having a sailor on the fo'c's'le with a pair on binoculars looking at the water, the aim being to spot the mine before the ship ran into it. On this occasion the lookout had seen something in the water and the ship had applied full astern power and stopped before reaching the object. We were held off. If it was a mine and the ship struck it we would be required to airlift any casualties to the hospital ship 100 miles to the south. It was an odd feeling being glad that I wasn't onboard and yet concerned about friends and colleagues who were.

After much tentative investigation the mine in the water turned out to be a harmless life raft. It did however, make us all think; returning to the ship had always been regarded as returning to a relative safe haven from the dangers of flying in the northern territories. It made me realise that it was not always going to be the case. For the past three days HMS *Manchester* had been operating further north than any other ship and we were still under American tactical control, being used as the front edge of the anti-aircraft barrier. Each day the ship had been ordered a little further north and our migration, from the relatively safe areas one hundred miles to the south, had almost gone by unnoticed, but here we were, the prime targets for the enemy. Perhaps more dangerously the ship was operating in and around the minefields.

Saturday 16 February – NPG

A truly rude awakening today. The day started early, very early when at 0200 I was woken to be told that we were being actioned to attack a target that was trying to recover the tug that we had hit earlier.

It transpired that, once again, Gloucester's Lynx had been airborne on a routine sortie and had been first on the scene. Their attack however was unsuccessful due to hostile fire. We launched, successfully put two missiles into the target and returned, but I can quite honestly say that it was the most frightening experience of my entire life. I eventually got to bed again at 0600.

I had a second rude awakening at 0830 when I awoke to the racket of the three inch chaff rockets going off and assumed that we were under attack. It turned out that it was only the system being tested.

Two mine searches followed and a very welcome afternoon nap. Whilst remaining at AL 15 for the rest of the day I wrote a few mailies and watched Gorillas in the Mist. *In bed by 2300, once again feeling knackered.*

"Sir, wake up, you're required to brief immediately."

It must be a bad dream. I awoke from the deepest of sleeps and tried to focus on the HC as he attempted to wake me.

"Spike, what the fuck is the time?"

I was never at my best just after being woken up but the HC was wide awake and had obviously been awake for some time, following the developing situation. He replied with some authority.

"It's two-thirty, we've got another target for you. The Captain wants you to get a met picture and brief as soon as possible."

I jumped out of bed and into my flying suit.

"Tell the Skipper I'll be down in ten minutes with the brief."

By the time I had woken fully, collected my thoughts, dressed and looked at the weather, less than ten minutes had passed. I rushed down to the operations room where the Captain, PWO and Nick were huddled around the radar screen listening to the radio. I donned a headset and joined the group. Nick was talking to *Gloucester's* aircraft on the radio and I caught the tail-end of the conversation.

"There's a lot of activity. We climbed to fire the missile and were engaged by both the ship and the mainland, but couldn't break lock and came bloody close to flying into the sea while trying to evade. It's dangerous out there. They obviously do not want that ship sunk and we lost both of our missiles while trying to evade their attack."

David, *Gloucester's* pilot, was trying to sound cool and collected but there was no disguising the fear in his voice. He had seen more action than any other Lynx pilot and, by the inflection in his voice, it was obvious that they had been extremely lucky to survive. No matter what they did they could not break lock from the enemy fire control radar. It was a pitch-black night and they had watched the missile coming towards them but, at the last moment, he had banked the helicopter around and the missile had passed within feet before exploding behind them. The manoeuvre to evade the attack had been so severe that they had come within seconds of flying the helicopter into the sea. They were extremely

shaken but David received the Distinguished Service Cross for his action
that night. Despite their lucky escape, they had been tasked to return to
mother ship and re-arm; it was blatantly obvious to all of us listening to
David's voice that they had no desire to return to the battleground on
that night. Both aircrew subsequently needed counselling as a result of
their experiences during the campaign.

*A captured Silkworm
missile.*

After the radio call the Captain spoke.

"Dickie you missed the brief earlier but you have been tasked to attack
the minelayer while they re-arm. We think that the minelayer is a converted Polnochny assault vessel and it appears that someone wants it
sunk, but don't do anything stupid. I want you both back here at the end
of the sortie. What's the weather like?"

I quickly ran through the met brief. This one was going to be scary as
the Iraqis knew that helicopters would be returning to reattack and they
would be waiting for us. If I had been given the option not to fly this one
I would have taken it, and I ambled down to the hangar hoping the mission would be cancelled by the time I arrived. I walked onto the darkened flight deck where the helicopter was ranged on deck, armed with
two missiles, but I could not see it very clearly, the night was too dark.

I always felt a little nervous strapping into the helicopter prior to going
night-flying and, on this occasion, it was immeasurably worse. I tried to
concentrate on just going through the checks and procedures to get the
helicopter started and flying, but it wasn't easy. The position of the contact was passed, only twenty minutes flying time away, and we launched
into the darkness. In the soft green light of the cockpit I glanced across

at Nick who looked solemn. He opened the conversation by discussing the options in a composed manner, but he sounded nervous.

"Flying in at a hundred feet is going to put us right in the anti-aircraft missile envelope."

A hundred feet was the lowest altitude you flew over the sea at night during peacetime operations. With only a small radar altimeter and precision flying preventing you from flying into the sea at 130 mph, that was quite low enough.

"We'll have to go lower." It was stating the bleeding obvious but I guess Nick needed to know whether his comparatively rookie pilot was prepared to give it a go.

"Will you be happy at fifty feet?"

"Either happy or dead." It was the most accurate answer I could think of. Much later Nick admitted that there were very few pilots he would have trusted enough to fly that low at night: it was the greatest compliment of my flying ability that I had ever received. We were now fifteen miles from the enemy ship and already we could hear their radar looking for us. I lowered the collective and descended to fifty feet and, as we descended below their radar coverage, the Orange Crop went quiet. The plan was quite simple. We would sneak in under radar cover until we reached the maximum range of the Sea Skua. I would then climb the aircraft and hover while Nick fired the missiles. I would maintain the hover while descending back to a height where, hopefully, our radar could continue to control the missile but the enemy would not be able to lock onto us with its fire control radar.

At twelve miles from the ship we heard the bleep of the fire control radar again, obviously we were not low enough. Decision time: continue at fifty feet – that would be madness since *Gloucester*'s aircraft had shown that the Iraqis were more than capable of shooting you down if they held you on radar; turn and run – that would mean some other bastard would have to come and do it – or descend still further. Without discussing it and with both eyes glued to the altimeter I lowered the collective again and descended another twenty feet. At this height just sneezing on the controls could cause us to fly into the sea. I was working extremely hard but the Orange Crop fell quiet again.

I saw them first out of the corner of my right eye. Two white flashes followed by two white lights on a constant bearing. Two missiles launched from Faylakah Island screaming towards us. I didn't dare take my eyes off the instruments to have a good look.

"Can you see those Nick?"

He looked up from his plotting board and paused for a second.

"Yep."

"What do you think they are?"

"Spotlights!"

"You lying bastard."

I was not as afraid as I thought I would be and just concentrated on flying the helicopter. Then the lights went out and the missiles splashed into the water short of their target. We were obviously outside range.

Staying five miles from all points of land had paid off and the next two, seen once again out of the corner of my eye, didn't scare nearly as much.

I was concentrating so hard on flying the aircraft that time became irrelevant. Again Nick spoke.

"Start the climb now."

I pulled back on the control column, relieved to be climbing away from the water, concerned about flying into enemy radar cover. As we passed through a prearranged height I called to Nick that he was clear to fire the missile. Maintaining the hover at night with no visual references proved to be very difficult and the helicopter danced around the sky. I had to keep the nose of the aircraft pointing towards the target so that we could fire. Deep breaths and relax, I kept trying to remind myself.

"Firing now." Nick called.

I felt the clunk as the missile released, a pause for a second then the burners on the Sea Skua ignited. The light was so intense compared to the deep blackness before that I was totally blinded. I blinked furiously as I tried to get my eyes to work and fly the helicopter at the same time.

"Firing the second."

I kept my eyes closed this time and just held the controls where they were. After I heard the whoosh of the missile igniting I tried to re-establish the hover.

"Turn the fucking cockpit lights up!" I yelled at Nick. My night vision was destroyed and I needed some lights on the instruments to try and see them. I did not dare take my hands off the controls and start fumbling around for the rheostat that controlled the cockpit lighting. The bleep of the Orange Crop was becoming more frequent and it was only a matter of time before they obtained lock. I wanted to descend as soon as possible but needed to be able to see the altimeter before I could do that. Nick realised what had happened and reached for the rheostat to turn the lights up to full brightness. I settled the helicopter back down into a fifty foot hover.

Once again Nick counted down the time to run lights. As the last light extinguished, curiosity overcame me and I looked up at the horizon where a large bright explosion illuminated it. There was no doubt that the missile had hit the target and, about four seconds after the first explosion, the second missile struck. The magnitude of this explosion shocked me and, quite literally, the whole area was lit up for several seconds. It was what I imagined a nuclear explosion to look like. I can only assume that the missile hit a magazine containing mines, or a fuel tank. Either way, there could not have been any survivors. There was never any trace of the vessel again. I turned the helicopter and descended, heading back for Mother at maximum speed. Once clear of the of the immediate danger area and when the lights of Mother were visible, Nick spoke.

"I'm sorry Dickie, it was your turn to press the fire button but I was working a bit hard and I didn't have time to think about it."

"Trust me mate, that was the furthest thing from my mind. Besides, I didn't have a spare hand to press it with."

Seeing the lights of our own ship was the most welcome sight in the world and I began to relax, the first time I had ever felt relaxed while

Ship-mounted anti-aircraft guns.

night-flying to a deck. I set the helicopter up for the final approach, a simple procedure of positioning a mile behind the ship at 400ft above the sea, descending the helicopter towards the ship and gradually reducing the speed. I was looking forward to getting back on deck and having a cigarette – I hadn't smoked for a year. During the last part of the approach I noticed that the ship was approaching quicker than usual. Something wasn't quite right. I glanced in at the instruments. I scanned each instrument in turn as I tried to determine what was happening. As I looked at the airspeed indicator it became obvious that I had forgotten to slow the helicopter down. I was 200 yards behind the ship and should have been flying at around 10 knots but I was still doing around 100 knots. I couldn't believe that I had made such a fundamental error but there was no time to ponder on it. I banked away from the ship and passed about ten yards down the side of it at thirty feet, praying that I would not hit, and pulling in power to try and climb away. We missed the ship but I was extremely shaken. How could I have relaxed so much and been so foolish. Nick was on the radio requesting that we reverted to the normal lighting as opposed to the darkened operations procedure; I must have scared him as well. I did not actually kiss the deck when we landed on but I wanted to. The guys on the flight thought I was a hero and they had assumed that I had given the ship a fly-by as was the norm when returning from a successful attack. I did not have the heart to inform them that not even I would be foolish enough to attempt such a stunt at night. When I got back to bed it took me a long time to get back to sleep as there was too much adrenalin pumping around my stomach.

When I did manage to dose off I entered the world's deepest sleep. The second rude awakening really did startle me. *BOOM* right above my head and then the same again. It was the chaff dispensers being fired. Much the same as the helicopter, the ship carried chaff dispensers to distract incoming missiles. I assumed that we were under attack and were trying to evade. I wanted to hide my head under the duvet and pretend that things would be OK but the survival instinct would not let me so I jumped out of bed and ran down to the flight deck. It wasn't until I arrived there that somebody informed me that it was just a routine test. In my half asleep state I felt foolish but relieved.

Sunday 17 February – NPG

A relatively quiet day today in which I could have been busy, but when I realised it was a Sunday I slept a lot instead.

The flying was not very interesting and only two hours of it which made a pleasant change. All of the excitement came in the evening when, after watching Naked Gun, *it came through that the Iraqis had two Silkworms on the launchers pointed in our direction. Fairly frightening stuff. I went to bed in my overalls and socks just in case I had to get up in a rush. As it transpired, nothing happened.*

Monday 18 February – NPG

Today started badly but got a lot better. It began with a flying brief at 0600 which was interrupted by Hands to Action Stations, the first time for real.

A radar associated with a Mirage F1 (associated with Exocet attacks) was detected. At first we thought (and hoped) that the ship would launch the heli. They didn't so we waited nervously but remarkably calmly, I thought, strapped into the helicopter on deck. Anyway, nothing happened.

The next drama of the day came when we received a report that USS Tripoli, *operating just to the west of us had hit a mine. A few hours later USS* Princeton, *who was now operating in exactly the same position as we were yesterday, struck another. The initial reports are that there are few casualties but the ships have suffered severe structural damage.*

The rest of the day followed the usual, now well established course, very much lightened by the fact that I received two goodie parcels, one from Jill and one from Mum and Dad which, as always, made me feel very happy. The evening was spent writing thank you letters.

Tuesday 19 February – NPG

A very busy day, up at 0400 and airborne at 0500. In total we flew almost five hours today, all of it surface search, so generally it was pretty dull, although we did have one moment of excitement when a SUCAP found six small speedboat type craft and we were tasked in the HMP role to go and have a go at them. Unfortunately the speedboats were only one mile from the Iraqi coast. After a discussion over telebrief where both Nick and I pointed out that neither of us minded going on a suicide mission, but we would have preferred it to involve a little more glory than trying to sink a speedboat, and that in our opinion this mission was not absolutely necessary, we did not go in the end and both the

speedboats and the helicopter lived to fight another day.
A quiet evening with another hour's night-flying and then straight to bed.

This was very much a transitional period for both me as an individual and physically for the ship. The threat of mines had been taken more and more seriously until eventually the two ships that we were operating in close proximity with, struck them. Psychologically this both shocked and lifted me. Yes, the threat of mines was a very real one, there was no doubt about that anymore, and clearing a passage through the minefields became a priority. We were placed back under UK tactical control and assigned to escort the Royal Navy mine clearance vessels that had been waiting in the wings. The ship's role changed quite markedly. We now took on a defensive posture, playing big brother to the smaller mine sweepers and the auxiliary vessels that were supporting them. We were assigned to operate in an area about twelve miles off the coast of Faylakah Island where the sweepers started clearing a route through the minefields. The position was defined using the grid system that had been devised to divide the area up for tactical purposes. The box that we were to operate in was known as Hotel 32. For the next week we sat as prime targets in the box, sailing around in circles, in the middle of an assumed minefield, waiting for the amphibious assault to begin. People started becoming quite superstitious about the box, and then quite protective as later on other ships moved into the area – this was our piece of water. The whole concept of Hotel 32 became a private joke which lasted for the rest of the deployment, a joke that – without fail – was never understood by anyone else. A classic case of really having to be there to appreciate it.

The journey I unknowingly travelled was far more psychological. Other ships and aircraft had been hit by a very real enemy – of that there was no doubt, but we were not going to come to any harm. Deep down, if I really thought that I was going to get shot down during the night attack, I would have returned instead of flying lower. The Captain had given us the 'get out of jail free card' but I continued because I knew I was going to be OK. Despite all my previous worries, when the crunch came, I did not contemplate any harm coming my way. Being shot down or flying into the sea was something that happened to other people not me. Much the same logic was applied to the ship hitting a mine. *Manchester* must have been just a few yards away from the mine that *Princeton* hit but we sailed harmlessly past it.

I was not going mad, I just wasn't a hero. Had I not subconsciously assumed this air of invincibility, if I had thought there was even the remotest chance of being hit by enemy fire, I would have been too frightened to operate efficiently. The invincibility allowed me to see the enemy missiles rushing towards me and yet ignore them and carry on concentrating on the flying. And yet this attitude was not totally illogical. In all our flying Nick and I had decided to minimise the risk of getting shot down. We always stayed outside five miles from any enemy unit or point of land, therefore out of range of hand-held heat seeking missiles. For that I had Nick to thank. He had calmed my gung-ho attitude; we had become the thinking-man's crew. It was for this reason that we did not want to attack the Iraqi speedboats. Had they been in the middle of nowhere it would have been different, their guns against ours – a gentleman's battle. It would have been a challenge that I would have accepted, hoping our speed and agility would give us the upper hand. But that close to the coast, the odds were stacked in the speedboats' favour. Up to that point we had only attacked when the odds were on our side neither of us saw any reason to change that. We were not brave men and we certainly were not stupid. Had we ultimately been ordered to go we would have gone, but now we were back under UK tactical control, our own ship was in charge of us, and it gave us the option to question what we believed to be foolhardy tasking. 'Death or Glory' was not for me. I'd rather go without either.

It was this invincibility that allowed me to sit in the helicopter on the back of the ship, waiting for an Exocet missile to rip through it, laughing and joking with Nick. After a few minutes it was obvious that we were not going to be launched to jam the missile as we had practised so many times. We felt the ship turning. The standard procedure was to turn the rear quarter of the ship towards the direction of the enemy attack, thereby minimising the radar cross-section. It also meant that if there was an attack taking place, sitting in the helicopter on the back of the ship, the missile would impact us first. Nick and I were thinking exactly the same thing. Without speaking we casually unstrapped from the helicopter, jumped onto the deck and signalled for the rest of the flight to follow us. In silence we casually walked around the upper deck to the front end of the ship. If the missile was going to hit the back of the ship, it made perfect sense to me to be at the front, as far away as possible. A Lynx had been lost in the Falklands when an Exocet missile ripped through the helicopter, which was sitting on the back of the ship.

The guys on the bridge saw the whole flight huddled on the fo'c's'le and started to laugh and jeer at us. In their position I would have done the same. We took a lot of stick about it over the next couple of days, but I liked a bit of banter.

Wednesday 20 February – NPG

Almost a day off today. I was just about to get up at 0500 when Spike the HC knocked on my door and informed me that we were not required to fly until 0900, so I went straight back to sleep.

The morning continued with the usual drudgery of war, writing letters and a bit of revision. The afternoon was split between afternoon tea on the flight deck and recognition training followed by a 1600 launch. We then flew for one and a half hours on the usual surface search. It appears that the Iraqi Navy have now decided that it is too risky to put their ships to sea with the losses that they have suffered recently. Once again today there was no enemy activity.

Early to bed with another early start due tomorrow. The weather was very English today; wet and windy, which made a very pleasant change.

Thursday 21 February – NPG

Today should have been a really busy day but as it transpired it was quite relaxing. An early start, 0400 for a flying brief and AL15 until 0630. We launched at 0630 for a surface search but found nothing. On return I managed an hour's sleep. We were due to launch again at midday but whilst preparing for take-off we discovered a fault with the aircraft; the engines tried to start on their own every time ground power was connected. The cause of the fault was quickly discovered but with no spare part in theatre it could not be repaired. That put paid to flying for the rest of the day. A relatively lazy afternoon ensued followed by a film in the Wardroom, in bed by 2300.

Friday 22 February – NPG

Today was definitely one of the quietest days of the entire deployment so far due to the helicopter remaining u/s for the entire day. I completed a little revision for my commercial licence exams, read my FLYER magazine and watched a couple of HDS trips (we were re-supplied with more Sea Skua from Brilliant *and* Exeter*) wishing I could go flying, followed by recognition training and letter writing.*

A couple of hours were devoted to a futile attempt at trying to clear the backlog of crap constantly covering my desk, without much success. I did get a little annoyed this evening after being told off by the Jimmy (First Lieutenant) for watching a Chubby Brown video as apparently it is "unsuitable for the Wardroom" – how pathetic.

After flying up to six hours a day for the past fortnight, having an unserviceable helicopter was unbearable. I wandered around the ship looking for something to do that would give me an excuse not to do the work that I really should have been doing. It had become more or less evident to us that the much promised amphibious assault was not going to happen. I assumed that the minefields had caused the change of strategy. I had no idea that it was all part of the master plan devised by men far more intelligent than me, and that there had never been any intention of an assault from the sea.

As we waited for the spare part to arrive, with nothing to do I became very irritable. The saving grace was that Iraqi naval activity had ceased. With a big head I rather assumed that the last attack had been the straw that had broken the camel's back. They had suffered heavy losses throughout the war and it must have been demoralising to have their heavily defended minelayer, operating under the protective umbrella of their extensive coastal defences, literally blown out of the water in the middle of the night. Perhaps, more logically, Saddam had seen the writing on the wall, and rather than have his Navy totally destroyed, he decided to keep them in harbour, maybe to be used in another war at some other time against another opponent.

CHAPTER ELEVEN

They Think It's All Over

*The most difficult part of climbing any mental mountain is the
descent on the other side.*

Saturday 23 February – North Persian Gulf

*I intended to use my time wisely today but ended up squandering it in the same
manner as yesterday. The helo is still u/s and we are still awaiting the spare
part. The morning was spent on the bridge driving the ship during a RAS and
helping out on the flight deck during a Vertrep. It made for a bit of a change.*

*The afternoon consisted of recognition training, a little revision, writing a
few letters and then fitness training. The evening – more letter writing and
then I watched a brilliant documentary about leopards and cheetahs. I have a
real desire to return to Africa at the moment and spend some time in the bush
as I did as a child. Time is beginning to drag now. It has become blatantly
apparent that the First Lieutenant is expecting me to volunteer for more secondary duties during this relatively quiet period for me. I have no desire to do
so. I am enjoying the rest.*

Sunday 24 February – NPG

*The big news of the day is that the land offensive has finally started. We are
led to believe that the push has begun from the south through Saudi. Does this
mean the amphibious assault is not going to happen? Rumour control is once
again running wild.*

*During the afternoon we completed another spell of recognition training fol-
lowed by a session circuit training. The good news is that the spare part has
finally arrived for the helicopter and we successfully fitted it and ground ran the
helicopter during the early evening. During the course of the ground run we
were forced to stop because of a suspected raid inbound. It was strange how we
are no longer scared by these matters, they are regarded as a mere encumbrance.*

*During the last couple of quiet days I have adjusted to being at sea again
and no longer possess a yearning for a run ashore somewhere.*

Monday 25 February – NPG

*We had been expecting a busy day today now that the helicopter is serviceable
and the ground offensive is well under way. In the end it turned into another
relatively quiet one. The morning began with the flying brief where we were
informed, somewhat to our surprise, that no tasking had been received from the
powers that be. I wandered down to the hangar to inform the rest of the team*

and ended up indulging in a game of cricket. This was eventually interrupted when we sighted HMS Herald *on the horizon and I hastily arranged a flight to pop over and exchange some films and videos. This was interrupted in turn when we received an order to go and investigate aeroplane wreckage that had been sighted some way to the north – we found nothing.*

A quiet afternoon spent writing a couple of letters. Continued reports have been received about Gloucester *being fired upon. No-one gets excited about it anymore.*

Tuesday 26 February – NPG

Finally a busy day, one dominated by the news of the ground offensive and the Iraqi withdrawal from Kuwait. We have all been surprised by the speed of events over the last couple of days. We were kept busy all day and completed in excess of six hours flying, all fairly boring and mundane, transporting torpedoes between Manchester *and* Gloucester *– hardly the most demanding of flying operations.*

Everyone's morale has been lifted by the encouraging news being received from the front-line on the ground offensive; I just hope that it is all true. I remember the first reports from the initial air raids. That seems like an awfully long time ago now.

Wednesday 27 February – NPG

Again the entire day was dominated with news being received from the ground offensive, there is very much a feeling that it will all be over very, very shortly.

On a more personal note we were kept busy again today, transporting the remaining torpedoes to Gloucester *– this afforded the opportunity of another dogfight with David flying* Gloucester's *helo. I definitely had the better of him this time and considering that my aircraft was much heavier because of the torpedoes, and he has considerably more experience, I felt relatively happy with my achievements. Anyway it was all good fun.*

There was one particularly harrowing experience of the day. Whilst airborne we heard an American pilot eject and make a call on the emergency frequency as he was descending. He kept repeating that he was parachuting towards the burning factory, the one he had just attacked. The fear and horror in his voice was blood-curdling. We did all we could relaying the messages to the search and rescue organisation and trying to comfort him with calm words. It was very extremely distressing.

Thursday 28 February – NPG

Yet again the day was dominated with news from the ground, this time of the victory. It really does appear that it is all over now.

In between listening to the radio and reading the signal log we did go flying, initially a two hour surface search over lunchtime. We were in the process of launching for another two hour sortie when another problem appeared with the helicopter. We landed back onboard the ship and spent the rest of the day trying to sort it out. This resulted in numerous check test flights but we still had an unserviceable helicopter at the end of the day.

The following day we managed to repair the aircraft and were tasked with collecting SNOME from *Brave* and bringing him to *Manchester*. The purpose of his visit was to inform the ship's company exactly what was going on. We all assembled on the fo'c's'le and he started by thanking us all for our efforts over the previous month. He then proceeded onto the news that we wanted to hear from the horse's mouth. The Iraqis had withdrawn from Kuwait, the United Nations had achieved their objectives and hostilities would now cease. With that in mind the ship was officially released from its station and we were to proceed to Jebel Ali for a few days rest and recuperation before returning to Kuwait to assist with the clean up operations. The ship set sail as *London*'s helicopter departed with SNOME.

In a strange way life just continued as normal. There was no great party. Over the last few days the whole ship's company had felt that with the lack of naval activity we were no longer involved in the war effort. The formal announcement of the cessation of hostilities had been expected and came as no great surprise. There was still a threat of mines as we made our way back down the Persian Gulf. We could not relax completely.

The following day the ship had moved sufficiently far south and the threat of mines was deemed small enough for the ship to fall out of Defence Watches. It was a strange feeling indeed dressing in a shirt and trousers for dinner. It was the first time that I had been out of a pair of overalls since we had arrived in the Gulf. In the morning we flew into Bahrain to pick up some mail – it was a great thrill to fly over land again. During the course of the flight we spotted a herd of camels, their coats blackened by the oil fires that had recently been lit by the departing Iraqis. It was the first sign of the horrors that we were to witness on our return to Kuwait the following week.

Rather ironically, as I dressed for dinner for the first time in a month, I opened a parcel that had been sent by the British Legion. It contained a tin of soup and potatoes. Although it made me laugh. It also made me reflect on how valuable the constant mail drops had been. Obviously receiving mail from friends and loved ones was extremely important, but it was the letters of support and encouragement from complete strangers that were often the most moving. On one occasion I received a parcel from a distant second aunt whom I had never met. She had heard through the grapevine that I was on active service in the Gulf. She contacted Mum and discovered that I was partial to a slice of fruitcake. An elderly lady, she was not particularly mobile and of very modest means. However, she had saved her money and made a special effort to make her way to the shops. I later learned that it was the first time that she had left her house in many months. Buying the ingredients she made me the most wonderful fruit cake which she then carefully packed and sent to the Gulf. Remarkably it arrived in one piece and was thoroughly enjoyed. It did bring a tear to my eye when I received it and reflected upon the effort that a complete stranger must have gone to.

After dinner Nick and I met in the hangar office with the rest of the flight team. We opened a few beers and spent some time talking and reflecting upon the deployment so far. Already the fact that we had been involved in the conflict was becoming irrelevant and we spoke about what lay ahead in terms of the rest of the deployment – the trip was less than a third complete. As the beers started to take effect the mutual appreciation club started. We congratulated each other for hard work undertaken. For the first time I learned that we were the only flight not to switch to wartime maintenance.

During periods of conflict, when the helicopter is called upon to be utilised the demands well beyond that of normal peace time operations, it can become extremely difficult to find the time to service and maintain the aircraft. The stringent inspection criteria are relaxed and 'wartime' maintenance is introduced – a policy of fix it if it breaks, otherwise leave it alone. The Senior Maintenance Rating, the guy in charge of maintaining the helicopter in cooperation with the rest of the team, had undertaken to continue with the normal servicing, despite the fact that this necessitated a punishing work schedule for the maintainers. During the month of February I flew in excess of one hundred hours, normally I would have expected to fly less than twenty.

To continue with normal maintenance with this kind of usage, whilst in defence watches and with such a small team, meant that the engineers had been working unbelievably long hours. It suddenly crossed my mind that every time I landed the guys were ready to receive the helicopter, refuel, reload and service it. I would then retire to the Wardroom or my bed. The following morning the helicopter would be ready for service again, with the same guys still working on it. I had not really been fully aware of all the behind-the-scenes work that had been continuing throughout the previous two months. I looked at their faces. It struck me that they looked very, very tired. I enquired why they did not switch to wartime maintenance like the rest of the Lynx flights operating in the area. The answer was simple. They thought that flying in this environment was dangerous enough and they wanted to ensure that they did everything possible to ensure our safe return. I was genuinely touched and pondered on the reasons why a period of conflict brings out the very best in people.

I remember wandering down to the hangar late one night when I couldn't sleep. I was surprised when I found the hangar light on and Bob, one of the 'grubbers' (an engines and airframe specialist) wandering around the aircraft with a torch. We chatted for a while. I quizzed him on what he was doing tinkering with the helicopter when he should have been enjoying some well earned rest. He took time to explain that the aircraft had been operating at, and sometimes above, its cleared maximum take-off weight, by the time we had loaded it with guns, missiles, fuel and secondary equipment. Bob reasoned that although the engines were powerful enough to lift the helicopter into the air, he was unsure as to what demands it was placing on the rest of the transmission system. He spent hours inspecting the gearbox and drive shafts and it was Bob who eventually discovered a supporting bracket that had cracked. It was Bob who manufactured a new stronger one to keep us flying.

The ship came alongside in the port of Jebel Ali. Despite the fact I was nominated as the liaison officer for the trip, I spent the next three days pretty much out of my face with alcohol. During the second day alongside we were joined by *Gloucester* and spent the afternoon drinking beer with their aircrew. It was the first time that any of us had had the opportunity to discuss our feelings with fellow aviators; people who could relate to what you had been through by virtue of the fact that they had been through it themselves. We talked about what we had experienced – we discussed thoughts and emotions. Inevitably the subject of the night attack came up. They had seen considerably more action than *Manchester's* flight as they had been on station from the moment Saddam's forces invaded Kuwait. These were the friends that I had anxiously waited to hear about as they launched for the first successful attack and we powered around to the Gulf to join them. Even so it was that night attack that we all spoke about with introspective fear and loathing. They repeatedly mentioned how good it was to express themselves with people who were prepared to listen, people they could communicate with and they complained that their Captain had had little time to discuss their operations. He worked them extremely hard without considering the physical drains of flying eight hours a day on top of the mental anxiety of flying in a hostile environment. It was these guys who also subsequently suffered from Post Traumatic Stress Disorder and received psychiatric help on their return to the UK. They seemed perfectly normal when I spoke to them.

For the next three days I relaxed, unwound and drank a lot of beer. There were few lasting memories of the visit and I was generally too drunk to recall anything. I do remember one evening spent talking to an ex-pat teacher who had remained in Dubai throughout Operation Desert Storm. I was drunk and, sitting in a quiet corner of the bar, I somehow found myself talking war stories with her. It felt good to talk to somebody who was not connected to the military, but she left very quickly. I guess that she was bored with pissed service men trying to relive their war experiences with her. On the last day of our visit the USS *Mobile Bay* docked alongside *Manchester*. It was their pilots who were the voices behind Oceanlord Two-Seven the helicopter that had led us in for our first attack. I took time to visit the pilot and swap some aviation stories. It transpired that they had witnessed the missile impact and, after leading us in towards the target, the Sea Hawk peeled off, and, unbeknown to us, slotted in behind our helicopter. Equipped with high definition gyro stabilised binoculars they visually tracked the missile until it exploded when striking the Iraqi Fast Patrol boat. The ship sank fairly shortly after being hit. Witnessing survivors jumping from the sinking wreckage they flew towards the sailors in the water. While the Sea Hawk attempted to winch them to safety, the Iraqi forces on Faylaka Island turned their guns on them. Maybe they had no idea that the helicopter was on a mercy mission rescuing their countrymen, maybe they didn't care. Either way the Sea Hawk cleared the area before they had time to begin their rescue mission.

It was the first time that I allowed myself to contemplate the human element in the horror of warfare. To me the ship was a dot on the radar screen that had been removed. To the guys in the water it was their means of survival that had been savagely ripped apart by an enemy missile, leaving most of them dead and the remainder floating in the water with little hope of staying alive. I was glad that I had not witnessed the drowning sailors. The following day we departed Jebel Ali and made our way back to Kuwait.

Sunday 10 March – En route to Kuwait

A very enjoyable day's flying. It started with a check test flight in the morning and ended up with a massive wingover session and a Photex of the ship escorting a Russian tanker taking fresh water to Kuwait. The afternoon comprised a combined [1]HMP/GPMG[2] shoot which was enormously rewarding. A good day's flying and I enjoyed myself.

When we first sailed from Jebel Ali I was really homesick and July seemed further away than it did in January. However, today I feel much better about it and I am sure that the rest of the deployment will pass really quickly.

Monday 11 March – En route to Kuwait

A quiet day all round. We did not fly. Scheduled to fly in the afternoon, it was cancelled when Nick went across by sea-boat to Brilliant *for a meeting and discovered that all of the aircrew are now flying with personal weapons due to the current state of unrest in Kuwait. This resulted in a quickly arranged small arms shoot to qualify us to legally carry pistols. Seems somehow ironic. I also managed to get to circuit training which was most enjoyable.*

Coastal defences. Stakes in the sea, mines and trenches along the entire Kuwaiti coastline.

[1]*HMP – Helicopter Machinegun Pod.*
[2]*GPMP – General Purpose Machinegun. Hung out of the back door like the helicopters in Vietnam.*

Tuesday 12 March – Kuwait

Iraqi tanks wait for the amphibious assault.

The very first day I wrote this diary I remember commenting on the preparation for war – today I witnessed the aftermath first hand. It was one of the most harrowing and yet interesting experiences of my entire life.

The day started early with the flying brief. We were then sent to pick up a passenger from Brilliant *(their Padre, a nice old guy) and take him ashore to Port Ash Schuaybah, on the way dropping one of our guys off on the* Sir Galahad. *Sounded easy enough. However after landing on the* Sir Galahad *we suffered a radio failure and were forced to return to Mother to have it changed. On our return we were commandeered by the Captain of* Brilliant *– both of his aircraft were u/s – to fly him and an ITN film crew to Port Ash Schuaybah.*

As we approached the coast I was shocked to see how dark and cold it was becoming under the thick black cloud of burning oil. By the time we had finished filming the first Allied ship to enter Kuwait it was almost totally dark, despite the fact it was still early in the afternoon. After the filming we were used as a taxi for the rest of the day but did get the opportunity to fly into Kuwait International Airport (for which we had to make a night approach, it was so dark) and witnessed the well-heads ablaze in the distance. We then flew up and down the coast looking down on the incredible scenes of mass, seemingly pointless, destruction. Almost all of the houses had either been looted or razed to the ground; all of the cars and pleasure craft had been destroyed; along the beach miles of barbed wire, surrounded by anti-personnel mines provided coastal defence, backed up by multitudinous tank and gun emplacements.

We flew for over eight hours today so at the end of it I was completely shattered. It was an incredible day.

Wednesday 13 March – Kuwait

Another varied and fascinating day's flying, with two particularly interesting experiences. Initially we returned to the airport, however this time we landed and had the opportunity to have a good look around some of the 'sights,' including the remains of the British Airways 747; only the engines and tail remained.

As a pilot I found it a sad and distressing sight. Then we spoke at length with the Navy EOD[1] team and saw first hand some of the munitions they had collected including six Silkworm missiles (we spotted two launchers on the beach on the way in).

Overall a busy day with varied and interesting flying; meeting the EOD team and listening to their exploits and what life is now like in Kuwait is fascinating.

Thursday 14 March – Kuwait

Well, the days just get better and better. Another long flying day with the usual HDS but the highlight of the day was definitely visiting 845 squadron in the desert and flying around seeing some of the battlegrounds. A genuinely portentous sight, words really cannot describe it all, so many tanks and artillery pieces scattered around the desert, it was truly remarkable.

Seeing 845 squadron was a real treat. I managed to catch up with a lot of buddies from the Gazelle course plus numerous other faces that I recognised. Overall a completely exhilarating and eye-opening day. Witnessed the road to Basra, a scene of such destruction that was beyond description.

Friday 15 March – Kuwait

Me and the 'tart'.

As we fly around Kuwait, each day reveals a new sphere of the war. It really is quite remarkable. We flew over the desert again today, witnessing similar sights

[1]EOD – Explosive Ordnance Device.

as yesterday in addition to some military airfields with hardened bomb shelters that had been blown apart. Even stopped to collect some 'gizzets'[1] in the desert. Today's highlight was visiting O Battery and driving an OPV plus motorised gun. They gave us a full brief on their part in the war. We were really well looked after and it was a day that I will remember. When I have more time I will write more about today.

The biggest bonfire night in the world.

I retain vivid memories of this particular week. You cannot witness such scenes and be unaffected by them. As we approached the coastline for the first time I could see the oil cloud obscuring the horizon and, as we flew below it towards the harbour the temperature began to plummet to near freezing levels. We had flown into the set of a horror movie. Nobody in the helicopter spoke as the atmosphere was not conducive to polite conversation. The oil smoke not only removed all heat and light from the air but it also acted as a blanket against the wind causing the atmosphere to be calm: deadly calm and quiet. The bodies that once littered the harbour had been removed, but everything else lay destroyed; cars gutted and burnt, buildings looted. Bullet holes and pools of dry blood filled your vision everywhere you looked. The divers who had been clearing the harbour of mines told stories of how they continually discovered bodies at the bottom of the harbour, often mutilated. On the cold, still, polluted air you could smell death, it was all around you. This was Hell. This was the Apocalypse.

Flying into what remained of the airport, the horror continued: the burnt out wreckage of civilian aeroplanes, destroyed on the ground by the retreating forces; the bombed out terminal building and control

---

[1]*Gizzet – Naval slang for souvenir.*

Kuwait international airport.

No way BA. The remains of a Jumbo.

tower, destroyed just because they were there. Flying along the beaches; it was the miles of barbed wire, the trench that had been constructed along the entire length of the Kuwaiti coastline, mirrored in the sea by metal stakes pointing seawards to prevent amphibious craft landing; guns and tanks everywhere that one looked, all pointing seaward.

Flying inland towards the desert, the tarmac roads constructed by Iraqi forces to resupply the desert fortresses led to extensive underground bunkers. Scattered across the desert floor was a blanket of used shell cases and the remains of air-launched anti-personnel weapons. Every few hundred yards a burnt out tank would protrude from the sand. Until this moment my world had consisted of patrolling the sea areas. I had been aware of the land and air battles but the scale of what I now saw shocked me. The remains of the battle along the road to Basra were truly disturbing. The Iraqi forces based in Kuwait City had learned of the advancing Allied forces speeding across the desert towards them, dismissing their border defences with unexpected ease. Realising that their position as occupying forces was now dangerous and precarious they rampaged the city, looting shops, homes and offices alike, loading goods onto military and civilian vehicles. Then they fled home towards the city of Basra on the Iraqi border. The road winds out of the city before straightening out and climbing towards Iraq. The Allied forces, receiving intelligence concerning the retreat, despatched the British 1st Armoured Brigade to intercept them. Moving quickly over the desert the Brigade outflanked the retreating forces, attacking and immobilising

The Kuwaiti desert becomes the biggest scrap metal site in the world.

Trying to look cool in the heat of the desert.

the lead vehicles: the road became blocked. With the remaining forces congesting behind, vehicles packed with troops and looted equipment tried to bypass the carnage by fleeing across the sand. These vehicles quickly became stranded in the desert, leaving the forces completely immobilised and in terminal disarray. By this time American Thunderbolt ground-attack aircraft had arrived and the now infamous 'turkey-shoot' began, the aircraft attacking motionless ground forces who appeared not to have the will to retaliate. Eventually they pulled off, unable to justify attacking troops who refused to fight back and the vast majority of Iraqi forces continued safely on their journey. The scene of the battle remains a vivid and disturbing sight in my mind: vehicles piled up as far as the eye could determine; looted furniture scattered across the desert floor; bodies lying decomposing in burnt out cars; belts of machinegun ammunition wrapped around a stolen child's doll.

The debate as to whether the Allied tanks and aircraft should have continued the attack and destroyed the Iraqi war machine forever will continue for decades as the political situation in the Middle East remains unstable. My views remain the same now as those which I formed at the time after witnessing the scenes of destruction. I fully understand why the American aircraft pulled away from the scene of the attack. I would not have liked to have been involved in it, and ultimately would have probably reached the same decision. Should the remainder of the Iraqi Army have been allowed to escape back to friendly territory? Destroying the Iraqi war machine had never been part of the UN mandate, perhaps that's where the problem lies.

For the month following the ship's return to Kuwait we flew around the country assisting with the operation to return the country to some kind of normality. Each day we would fly inland on a new tasking in support of the clean-up operation. Some days whilst in the course of resupplying the troops on the ground I would meet with old Navy friends and we would swap 'war stories'; it would all be a great laugh. Other days we would witness further scenes of death and destruction that would leave us emotionally drained. In many ways this was possibly the most dangerous time for us all. There was an unbelievable number of weapons left discarded by the retreating Iraqi forces. Some of these fell into the wrong hands and, for a period, gang warfare erupted in and around the city of Kuwait. Initially we would fly at low level down the city streets, revelling in the opportunity to be a hooligan over the skies of a modern city. This foolhardy behaviour was soon curtailed when we learned of other helicopters being engaged by random fire from the ground. The reason why we were instructed to carry personal weapons, despite the fact that hostilities had officially ceased, was becoming apparent.

During the early days we would land in the desert to collect 'war trophies', be it a used brass shell or an Iraqi battle hat. We stopped this practice immediately, when we saw an Army officer's map that illustrated most of the Kuwaiti desert as one large minefield. The officer in question then rather casually informed us that most Iraqi gun and tank emplacements were booby-trapped. With hindsight the dangers were all too apparent. At the time the risks inherent in having a complete

The road to Basra is reopened.

The remains of a beach hotel. We think this was being used by the Iraqis and destroyed by the Allies.

This oil container burned for days before it eventually melted and collapsed.

arsenal of weapons lying around for anyone to pick up never crossed my mind. Landing at a desert outstation – a refuelling depot – I was presented with an AK47 assault rifle, a case of 'buy a tank full of fuel and get a machine gun free'. After spending a week working with the 4th Armoured Brigade I was given another AK47 with 5000 rounds of ammunition. I was not quite sure what I was supposed to do with it, but on return to the ship I suggested to the Weapons Engineering Officer that we arrange a small arms shoot off the back of the ship to give members of the ship's company the chance to fire the Russian-made weapon. He almost fell off his stool and insisted that I throw both weapon and ammunition over the side. Sitting onboard the ship anchored off the coast I guess it was difficult for him to imagine what life was like in post-invasion Kuwait.

The other weapon we had 'made safe' onboard the ship. All of the working parts were removed and the barrel welded up. On return to the UK, Nick and I presented it to the squadron as a war trophy. One of the permanent squadron staff accepted it and locked it into his safe whilst he arranged to have it mounted on a wooden plaque. Unfortunately he forgot to lock the safe and, during a routine security inspection in the middle of the night the weapon was discovered. I arrived at work the following morning to find the office sealed off with 'scene of crime' tape and discovered that the new proprietor of the weapon was being held in the MOD police cells under the Prevention of Terrorism Act. I thought the whole episode was hilariously funny until I too was arrested later in the day and interviewed for three hours. Following the interview my house was searched by the MOD police. Jill took great exception to coming home from work to discover an MOD policeman rooting through her underwear drawer. The whole scene got totally out of hand and to the best of my knowledge the AK47 was never returned to become a squadron trophy.

The cloud of burnt oil was ever present. If the wind was blowing in the right direction the smoke would be blown away and it would become a smear obscuring the horizon. If the wind reversed direction the whole country would be plunged into a cold, black darkness that restricted the breathing and blocked the nasal passages. Flying through the cloud of burning oil would result in the aircraft becoming coated in a film of oil that dulled the paint work and obscured the view out of the cockpit. We flew experts in the field of oil-well fires to the burning heads and gradually the smoke started to abate, but the site of oil-coated flamingos trying to fly off mine-covered beaches left a bitter and vile taste in the mouth which did not lessen as the smoke abated.

The defence and line of communications systems that Saddam had established in and around Kuwait were phenomenal. On one occasion, escorted by a British Army officer I was taken to one of the underground Command and Communication bunkers that had been constructed by the Iraqis during the course of their occupation. From the outside the only sign of human dwelling was a wooden door partly obscured by sand. Walking through the door one entered an Aladdin's cave complete with Persian rugs on the floor and marble bathrooms. It was from luxury

Emerging from the five-star bunker.

palaces like this, built underground in the middle of the desert that it was assumed the Iraqi military high command ran the war. The amount of money and effort that must have been spent preparing these underground luxury hotels was amazing. I thought back to the previous autumn when I had tried to convince Jill that Saddam was serious in his promise to withdraw his troops. Whilst he told the world that he had no intention of remaining in Kuwait he must have been building tarmac roads to transport Persian rugs and marble tiles to the middle of the Kuwaiti desert.

Shortly after arriving back in the North Persian Gulf we had the pleasurable task of spending a day flying Lieutenant-General Sir Peter de la Billière between all of the ships that made up the Royal Navy Task Group. At the end of the day we were scheduled to fly him into the airport. With time on his hands before he was due there, he expressed an interest in flying around Kuwait City to see for himself the extent of the destruction and what remained of the Iraqi defences. A mild-mannered and affable man, I found nonetheless it surprising that he was as shocked at the degree of devastation, on viewing Kuwait from the air, as I had been on my first viewing. I would have liked to have been afforded the opportunity to speak further with this man of great dignity and decorum, but the opportunity never arose.

During their occupation of Kuwait the Iraqis had occupied all of the military sites including a number of airfields situated around the city. Presumably these airports had either contained military aircraft or the Iraqis were operating their own military aircraft from them. This was evident by the fact that the Allied aircraft had made a determined effort to destroy all of the hard shelters. The accuracy of the modern laser-guided bomb is amazing. Each hard shelter, a dome constructed of about twenty feet of sand sandwiched between two layers of fifteen foot thick reinforced concrete, designed to withstand the force of a nuclear explosion, had a hole blown through the centre. The contents of each and every shelter had been totally obliterated. We would fly around these deserted and desolate airfields, bringing the helicopter into the hover over one shelter after another peering through the bomb hole into the carnage below.

I felt that the sights that I was witnessing on a daily basis ought to be seen by as many of the ship's company as possible. As aircrew we had always been fortunate enough to have a better insight into the tactical situation. Now that the conflict was over the ship was escorting the mine clearing fleet off the coast. Every morning we would transit to the desert, returning each evening with stories of battlefields and underground palaces. All the rest of the ship's company had to look at was a blackened horizon and an oil-polluted sea. I believed that it was important for as many individuals as possible to witness first-hand the destruction that had taken place. If the aircraft was not required for any tactical flying I would organise 'jollies', half hour flights for members of the ship's company, taking them on a guided tour of Kuwait City and the surrounding battlefields. I must have flown at least thirty of these trips along similar routes and each time I flew the route I noticed something different, be it a speedboat marooned on the beach with a machinegun mounted on the front, or a car that had been completely squashed by an adjacent tank. Small things, but they illustrated the total devastation of the country.

From our point of view it was a strange existence. Virtually every day was spent working with the Army in the desert. Many of these guys had been out in the field for in excess of three months without a warm shower or cold beer. Their living conditions were often less than comfortable. At the end of the day they would return to their camp-bed in a tent illuminated with a paraffin lamp. We on the other hand would fly back to the ship for a hot shower prior to dressing for a silver service dinner and a cold beer. We then returned to the same tired, smelly soldiers the next day. As the ship was due to come alongside in Kuwait, the completed mine clean-up operation allowing Allied ships into the port, we organised for some exchange visits, members of the ship's affiliated regiment visiting the ship whilst some of our ship's company travelled into the desert to spend a day at the Army base camp. As I had spent considerable time off the ship I offered to remain onboard and assist with the hosting of the Army. The day was a roaring success, turning into a bit of a piss-up as the squaddies had not been able to access alcohol for a very long time. At the end of the day the sailors returned onboard, we threw the drunken soldiers off onto the waiting transport, and the ship sailed back out to sea.

Inevitably a few hours later a drunken squaddie was found semi-conscious in one of the toilets. He was completely out of his head and started to get very abusive. The ship contacted his regiment and the instructions were quite specific – get him to the nearest point of land and tell him to make his own way back to the desert camp. Ordinarily I would have attempted to fly him back to his base camp but his abusive attitude was really pissing everybody off. The engineers had to pull the helicopter out of the hangar and prepare it for flight, an exercise that involved a lot of work at the end of a long, tiring day touring the desert, and this chap certainly was not offering them any thanks. We threw him in the back, with Nick the burly six foot, sixteen stone Chelsea supporter looking over him to make sure that he didn't get too boisterous and interfere with the safe conduct of the flight. As we landed in a car park on the outskirts of the city the squaddie looked confused; he obviously did not recognise anything.

"Right, out you get." I called out over the intercom as Nick opened the rear door and unstrapped the squaddie.

"S'werz the base camp?" His slurred speech made him difficult to understand.

"About thirty miles across the desert in that direction." Nick pointed out to the west.

"You fucking pig bastards, you can't leave me here." The realisation of the situation was starting to sober him up.

"How the fuck am I supposed to get back?"

"They didn't tell us that, now get the fuck out of my helicopter." Like I say, Nick took no shit. He bundled the squaddie out of the back of the helicopter. When he was clear of the rotor blades I lifted the helicopter

The welcome sight of mail and stores arriving.

A game of deck hockey during an afternoon off. Officers v. Royal Marines. A bloodthirsty game in which the Officers emerged the unlikely winners.

into a hover, waved a cynical goodbye and returned to the ship. The sight of the forlorn squaddie alone in the middle of nowhere with the light fading made me feel very sorry for him. I certainly would not have liked to have been in his position. We never heard any more so can only assume that he did eventually make it safely back to his desert home.

Throughout this month we had no idea what the future held for the ship. We had been told in January that we would be sailing for seven months and that we were going to the Gulf. Now that the conflict was over, we had no idea how long the authorities intended us to stay in the region. At the end of March we received the news that we had all been waiting for: the ship was to set sail for the Far East to participate in Operation Starfish, a bi-annual military exercise, held in and around Singapore and Malaysia. The countries that would be participating would be many and varied but that was unimportant to us: we were leaving the Gulf.

My final memory of Operation Desert Storm came as we left the Gulf. The ship stopped at Jebel Ali to restock some fresh food and vegetables before the journey across the Indian Ocean towards Singapore. On sailing it was noticed that one of the sailors was missing. A thorough search of the ship revealed nothing more than a Dear John letter from his girlfriend. We all assumed the worst and the search switched from the ship to the sea. We launched the helicopter and spent the next four hours

Turning day into night. The fires continue to rage...

...blocking out the light. A picture taken at 3 o'clock in the afternoon.

Allied vehicles wait to return home.

Flights over the battlefield revealed some interesting sights…

…especially the results of the precision bombing.

searching the track that the ship had sailed from Jebel Ali. Another two Navy helicopters joined the search but all to no avail. After a further three hours' searching we were joined by another two ships and a command decision was made. *Manchester* would continue en route leaving the remainder of the ships to continue the search. That night *Manchester* transited the Straits of Hormuz on our way out of the Gulf.

"Wake up Dickie, we have got to go flying." It was four o'clock in the morning and Nick was knocking on my cabin door.

"Do be serious, I have only been asleep for four hours. The war's over now you know."

"They have found the sailor. We have got to go and pick him up."

The news lifted me and I jumped out of bed. The possibility that one of the ship's company had been lost had put a damper on the 'leaving the Gulf' celebrations. The ship's company had gelled into an effective and happy team. The thought that one of the team might have taken his own life had affected everybody. I dressed, collected a met picture and joined the Captain and Nick in the operations room.

"Morning Pilot." The Captain greeted me with a big grin. The sense of relief on his part must have been enormous. I doubted whether he had slept at all that night.

"Some of the RFA guys found the missing sailor pissed in a bar. He must have jumped ship when we were alongside. They have him onboard *Sir Galahad*. She is alongside in Jebel Ali. Can you and Nick fly in and pick him up?"

Returning from a day in the desert with some new toys.

*Have tank, will travel
– over car.*

*In formation with the
Big Boys.*

Nick answered for both of us. "Consider it done Sir, we will be airborne as soon as possible."

On the way out of the door we concocted a plan. Ordinarily Nick would sit down with the charts and work out a route, whilst I filed a flight plan and organised diplomatic clearance to fly in another countries' airspace. I assumed today would be no exception, Nick however had other ideas.

"Don't worry about that Dickie. We'll just sneak in low level across the UAE and pick him up. The longer it takes, the further away the ship will be. Let's get going."

A few minutes later we were on our way. I wanted to call one of the air traffic agencies to let them know what we intended to do. Again Nick stopped me.

"Forget that Dickie, no bastard knows we are here. Lets not bother." I felt uneasy about it but continued without talking to anybody. Unfortunately people did know we were there and they were bothered about it. We had been seen on the air traffic radar screen. Nobody knew who we were or where we were going. They launched two Mirage fighters to intercept us. Before we knew it we had an international incident on our hands. By the time we landed on the *Sir Galahad* the whole world had erupted into chaos. Apparently, although we had never seen the fighters, they had intercepted us and were just waiting for authority to engage this unknown military helicopter making its way towards Dubai. To make matters worse, the sailor who we picked up was looking really smug and seemed to have no remorse whatsoever about the amount of

And sails past a reminder of what has passed.

Red Nose Day as the 'Mighty Manch' leaves the Gulf...

heartache he had caused. We were held on deck for a very long time whilst signals flashed between Dubai and London as to why the Royal Navy was making unauthorised flights into other countries' airspace. We later learned that the Captain had received a severe reprimand over the whole incident. He never passed the bollocking down, but took it on his shoulders and continued as normal. It made me feel extremely guilty as the whole cock-up was our fault. In the entire time that I flew with Nick this was the only serious error of judgement that he made.

As soon as we left the Gulf the whole deployment changed. The Captain's view was simple. Each and every member of the ship's company had done everything that was asked of him – now it was time to have some fun. Whilst all matters concerning safety were, as always, taken extremely seriously, anything that did not really matter was given a damn good ignoring. The monthly Captain's rounds which involved the unnecessary cleaning of the whole ship and hundreds of wasted man hours, were forgotten. Morale onboard was running extremely high and it was a great place to be. There was real *esprit de corps*. Spirits were lifted further when we discovered that the ship was programmed for a two week maintenance period alongside in Penang. This enabled wives and girlfriends to fly out and visit if they so desired. As soon as the news was announced I wrote to Jill telling her to book the time off work. Now I really had something to look forward to.

The exercise itself was preceded by a meeting of all the participating units in Singapore. This meant four days alongside and a big party. As

for the exercise itself, as a ship we took it less seriously than most, although it did involve a lot of flying and did teach me a lesson which I vowed at the time never to forget. Nick and I had been crewed up for over a year now. We were a highly efficient and battle-proven team and our confidence was running extremely high. During the course of the previous four months I had been called upon to fly the aircraft to the very edge of its flight envelope in situations that were both hostile and demanding. I felt that I had a feel for the aircraft that only the most experienced pilots would have acquired. I would execute aerobatic manoeuvres that helicopters were not really designed to perform. After every sortie I would rejoin the ship by a fly-by, passing down the side of

Arriving in Singapore...   the ship with the rotors only feet away from the superstructure and then pulling up steeply into a 'wingover' before landing on the back of the ship. The game was to try and scare the Officer of the Watch – the duty officer in charge of driving the ship – by flying as close to the bridge as possible. I would often get a bollocking for flying too close and scaring people. Eventually people stopped reprimanding me: it was obvious that I was ignoring them.

During the course of the exercise we worked extensively with a Malaysian ship. As the exercise drew to an end, the ships parted company and we set sail for Penang to meet the wives and girlfriends. After the final sortie I decided to give the Malaysian ship a fly-past by way of saying goodbye. I had supreme confidence in my ability and wanted to make this fly-past as impressive as possible. I dived towards the ship and accelerated to maximum speed. Passing down the side of the vessel at almost 200 miles an hour, with the blades just inches away from the deck, this must have looked impressive. Then somebody opened an ammunition locker on the deck, throwing a six by four foot steel door vertically into the path of the rotor disk. It was too late, there was no time to react, even if I could steer away from the ship, at this height and speed I would only fly into the water. We were doomed.

To this day I still do not know how the rotor blades missed the door. Whilst my brain was processing the information I must have instinctively moved the cyclic, lifting the disk just enough to miss the steel door by

an immeasurable amount. As quickly as I had moved the control I had
to centralise it again to prevent the blades impacting the water on the
other side. As I climbed away from the ship I could feel the blood draining from my face as I literally went white with fear. I looked across at
Nick. He never said a word but it was the first time that I had seen him
looking really scared. Neither of us ever mentioned the incident again. I
did not stop fly-by's but I certainly left a good healthy twenty feet
between the helicopter and the side of the ship for all future attempts. I
had been warned at the outset of my flying career that the danger points
in an aviators flying career are at 10, 100 and 1,000 hours. At 10 you
make your first solo. If anything goes wrong with the aircraft on that trip
you probably will not have the necessary skills to deal with it. At 100
hours you have enough experience to attempt stupid manoeuvres without the expertise necessary to conduct them safely. At 1,000 hours you
have such supreme confidence in flying your machine that it is easy to
forget the basics. I had around 900 hours at the time and had definitely
forgotten the basics, my confidence way above my ability. The message
was made more poignant in that I was so close to seeing Jill again, a
moment I had been cherishing in my imagination. I had come closer to
dying, all because I wanted to look punchy.

For the ten days alongside I was in heaven. I had been extremely nervous about meeting Jill. Over the course of the previous four months we
had opened our hearts to one another, but letters are no substitute for
time spent together. I had been looking forward so much to seeing her

*...and enjoying a beer
with Richard and
Hugh.*

again but wondered how we would react together. A lot had happened in that time. She must have gone through her own hell, never knowing whether I would return, constantly watching the television news, praying that they would not announce that a naval helicopter had been shot down. Would we need time to readjust to being in each other's company? Had the previous four months changed me? In the end all of the questions were answered the moment I saw her. I cried and gave her the biggest hug in the world. We enjoyed a marvellous ten days that went far too quickly.

Then it was back to sea for the remaining three months of the deployment. We completed more exercises around Singapore and Thailand before being retasked back to the Gulf for another month. Now we returned under British control as part of the Armilla Patrol, the UK's longstanding commitment to policing the Gulf. This was the task we had been expecting to fulfil before Saddam invaded Kuwait. Although we were surrounded by constant reminders of the recent conflict (the darkened skies, the ongoing operation to clear mines, both at sea and on land, the busy toing and froing of ships and aircraft carrying relief supplies) now our role was non-offensive, as we had originally envisaged, and we no longer regularly flew with live weapons. Following this we returned to the UK. For me the entire seven month deployment had been a unique experience.

CHAPTER TWELVE

The New Beginning

To love and friendship, the most fickle of all feelings.

In the middle of July HMS *Manchester* returned to the UK. We had spent nearly seven months away and, for me, the journey ended where I had joined the ship, just off the coast of Dorset. Nick and I flew the helicopter back to Portland where the squadron boss and Commanding Officer, waiting on the apron, welcomed us back to the UK. I shook their hands, smiled for the camera and quickly left. We were the last of the Lynx crews who had seen action in the Gulf to return to the UK, and I got the distinct feeling that people were making the effort to greet us as they thought they ought to rather than as they wanted to. Quite frankly, at that time, I would have preferred that they had not bothered. Seeing Jill, waiting on the squadron balcony, I wanted to be with her as soon as possible. Seven months is a long time to be away, but Jill had been a tower of strength with her constant letter writing and I desperately wanted to be with her.

The ship returned to Portland harbour to clear Customs later that afternoon and I drove in with Jill to collect the rest of my things.

"*Manchester* is going into refit when she gets back into Portsmouth tomorrow, so the flight is being disbanded."

"They're not going to send you straight back to sea on another ship are they?" The horror in her voice indicated that it had been a very long seven months for Jill. Sitting at home watching the continual TV coverage, and not knowing if someone is dead or alive, must be a stressful way to spend your time. Those of us onboard had had only ourselves to worry about and as a helicopter crew we had been, more or less, in direct control of how much danger we put ourselves in. We had also had the luxury of being able to weigh up the situation and take calculated risks to achieve the aim. Our world had consisted entirely of the waters encompassed by the Persian Gulf and, for the duration of the conflict, we had reigned supreme. Jill, on the other hand, had been sitting at home and knowing nothing of this other than the minute by minute coverage on the media. I held her hand by way of comfort and smiled.

"No they're not sending me straight back to sea. The flight is being reformed as *Marlborough* flight, and she won't be doing much until after Christmas. By that time I will have left."

"How do you know?" She was curious, knowing that postings were not normally organised so far in advance.

"I've been offered the opportunity to train as a Sea Harrier pilot again. The course starts next January."

I looked across at her. She obviously remembered the wind-swept hill on the Yorkshire Moors, three years previously, when she had comforted me after my initial attempt failed.

"You're going to accept aren't you?" She knew this would mean moving and spending even more time at sea.

"I really don't know." And I didn't.

Nick left the team to take up an alternative flying position and was replaced by another Observer. About a third of the maintainers came to the end of their posting during the next couple of months and soon the character and make-up of the flight had changed completely.

After three weeks' summer leave I returned to the squadron to continue work. Since I had left nothing had changed and, for all, the vast majority of our time was spent on shitty secondary duties. Pilots still fought over who was going to do the boring check test flight on Friday afternoon, when everybody wanted to go to the Officers' Club for a few beers. Returning to the UK so long after the conflict was pleasant in many ways, the most important one being that it had long since been forgotten by most people. This meant that I could just slot back into life as I had done before and enjoy the pleasures of my new house with Jill without too many inquisitive questions.

As far as the flying was concerned, for some reason which I could not define, I started to find it increasingly tedious. At first I put this down to the fact that I had spent the majority of the last few months operating the aircraft on the very limits of its flight capabilities and considered that returning to more mundane flying was unfulfilling. I soon dismissed this as, on reflection, I considered flying into a confined area, or onto a moving deck in the middle of the night, was just as demanding during peace time operations as any other. I wondered if it went far deeper than that, for although I had never lost any sleep over going to war and killing people – in fact I had found that the trip on the whole had been an enjoyable and enlightening experience – I was not sure whether I wanted to go and do it all again. Now, each time we launched for a simulated attack on the enemy, I took it less seriously than before and, therefore, did not get as much out of it. Flying had been more enjoyable before the realisation that the helicopter was a weapon of war and now I needed a new challenge. I accepted the offer to return to sea harriers.

This decision was not made without a great deal of thought as it meant committing myself to another eight years in the Navy and I was not sure whether I wanted to do that. As much as I had enjoyed myself, the intention had never been to commit myself to a full naval career. As a nineteen year old I had not considered it and now, six years later, I had neither seen nor experienced anything which had changed my mind. I saw the Navy as an organisation where the more astute took advantage of the well-regarded training, enjoyed the short-term career popperunities, and then left for jobs offering better prospects, greater challenges and fatter salaries. Apart from the occasional committed high-flyers,

Christmas Ball 1991.
Back safe and well.

those who remained were all too often mediocre company men who lacked the vision of those who had left. However at this stage my flying ambitions were more important than career considerations. I spoke at length with Jill about this. She appreciated that, deep down, I had always regretted throwing away the opportunity to fly jets. Although she knew it would mean even more time spent away, she gave me the encouragement that I needed. Both Rob and Simon had remained close friends and I discussed the matter with them individually. Simon had already made the decision to leave the Navy again as he continued to find the lifestyle – working and socialising – in the same close-knit community – a little stifling and certainly not a mind-broadening environment. He advised me to go with my heart and take up the challenge, although he warned me that realistically I must do it knowing that I would be committing myself to at least another fourteen years in the Navy. The economist in him pointed out that by the time I had finished the return of service on the Harrier course, I would be too close to receiving my pension to consider leaving until I had reached the age of thirty-eight. Rob, as a frustrated pilot, could not believe that I was debating the issue at all. I had convinced him to take his Private Pilot's Licence and he found that through his light aircraft flying he enjoyed being in control as much as being the tactician. He would have loved to have been offered the opportunity to transfer and train as a Navy pilot. Naturally he advised me to go for what was considered the top flying job.

And so in the January of 1992, it was back to the classroom again as I re-entered the flying training pipeline. The first part of the course was a period flying Hunters – a vintage jet that entered service in the 1950s and is considered one of Britain's most successful aircraft. Sitting in the cockpit it had that feel of the old Chipmunk, with big dials and levers scattered randomly around in some kind of ergonomic nightmare, but this aircraft was infinitely more capable. In its day it outperformed anything else that was in service on either side of the Iron Curtain. Capable of climbing to over 40,000 feet, it would go supersonic in a shallow dive and would race 250 feet above the ground at speeds approaching 500mph. It was a hot ship in anybody's book.

The first part of the course went extremely well. I felt that I was getting to grips with this new form of aviation. My instructor was an Air Force pilot on exchange to the Navy. A mild mannered and placid individual, he created a superb atmosphere in the cockpit, an atmosphere in which I learned an awful lot.

The high point of the course was the my first solo in a performance jet. Performing aerobatics over the Somerset countryside in a jet that holds a distinguished place in the aviation history books was a privilege indeed. The low point was when Brian, my instructor, left, and I fell under the auspices of the squadron boss. Quite simply he was the kind of narrow-minded, ignorant, arrogant individual that Simon so despised and that had caused him to leave the Navy, twice. He was very much old school. He believed that fighter pilots should be the world's punchiest people and chew glass for breakfast. He would not lower himself to talk to anybody else unless they had flown jets. During my first trip with him I realised that things were not going to run smoothly.

We were programmed to carry out a low level sortie over the Scottish Highlands. Climbing initially to high level we transited north before descending to low level in Scotland. Throughout the high level part of the sortie he did not speak, only grunted.

"Descending low level now. Can you check it's all clear out of the window on your side, Sir?"

In the two-seat, training version of the Hunter you sat side-by-side and were reliant on the instructor to keep a good look out of the cockpit on his side. The seating position did not allow the student to see past him.

"Er," was his considered reply. I was not sure whether that meant it was clear or whether he had not heard me properly.

"Sir, is it clear to the right and below the aircraft?"

"Mmm." You complete tosser, I thought to myself.

"I'm sorry Sir, I still can't hear you. Is it clear on your side?" There was a certain amount of aggression in my voice now. Having survived a war I had no intention of flying into another aircraft during a training sortie because some fat, arrogant git thought he knew better.

"YES!" he barked back at me through the intercom. By this time I was way past my predicted 'top of descent' point that would have ensured that I started the low level part of the sortie exactly where I had planned. Now I was high on the descent profile the whole way down and the workload began to increase as I tried to recalculate mentally where the aircraft was going to end up when it reached 250 feet. It is essential to know where you are starting the low level phase of the sortie from. Moving at 500mph surrounded by mountains obscuring your view, it is very easy to get lost quickly.

The sortie was average in the end. I thought I could have achieved a lot more had I not been so unsettled: the cockpit during that sortie was not a place of positive karma. However things got worse when we arrived back in the circuit to land the aircraft. As I completed the circuit and rolled the aircraft onto the final approach, I was extremely happy that we would soon be on the ground and I would no longer have to share the same miniscule cockpit with a man that I was beginning to despise.

"Power." he suddenly grunted. I looked across at him. He always flew with his dark visor down such that you could not see the expression on his face. Looking at the instruments I confirmed that the aircraft was at the correct height and speed as we approached the runway. I was confused, Did he want me to apply power or close the throttle?

"POWER!" This time he roared. I remained perplexed. Seconds later he slammed the throttle lever closed.

"I SAID FUCKING POWER!" He forced the throttle closed with such vigour that my hand resting on the lever was thrown back and my elbow smashed into the back of the ejector seat, leaving me grounded for the next week unable to get full range of movement in my arm. I received no explanation, no apology and, unforgivably, no debrief. My feet were now firmly on the ground again, both physically and metaphorically, and I began to doubt the validity of my decision to retrain. But this incident was not the only one which left me feeling that I had made a mistake.

When I first started the Lynx course at Portland I had purchased a share in a light aircraft based at a small farm strip in Dorset. The aircraft was the prettiest little aeroplane I had ever seen and from the

I buy my Jodel and go flying at weekends.

moment I first set my eyes upon her I fell in love. Jill would always tease me that if I loved her as much as my aeroplane that she would know that I really loved her. Although there were four of us in the syndicate that owned the aircraft, I conducted the lion's share of the flying in it and, if the weather was good at the weekends or in the evenings, I would be airborne boring holes in the skies. On my return from the Gulf, Jill and I spent virtually the whole three weeks of my summer leave flying around the country visiting friends in this wonderful little aeroplane. I found flying for pleasure, just purely and simply for the joy of being airborne, so much more rewarding than thundering around the skies as a weapon of war. The Wright brothers could never have intended their invention to be used for such sinister purposes. During my time flying the Hunter I became involved in air racing, volunteering to fly a single-seat racing aeroplane for a chap I met at an airfield who could not find anyone else mad enough to fly it for him. I loved the air racing and weekends were now spent around other people who found a thrill in simply being in the air just like myself. The atmosphere at these events was reminiscent of the early days at Topcliffe.

The straw that broke the camel's back came when I was told to stop flying light aircraft at weekends. The boss hated light aircraft and light aircraft pilots. He believed that at best they were a nuisance, at worst they were extremely dangerous in that they got in the way of military low flying jets. This was the kind of narrow-minded, self-centred, opinionated view that had angered Simon to the point of resignation and was beginning to detract from my quality of life as a service pilot. I was banned from flying light aircraft for the duration of the course on the grounds that the landing techniques were so different it would only serve to confuse me. I took great exception to being told what I could and could not do in my spare time. The end was in sight.

The course was drawing to a close and the next step would be to return to the Air Force system to fly Hawks. Although I felt reasonably comfortable flying the jet solo I would dread flying with the boss and wasn't reaching the required standard. Knowing that I was on the point of being chopped, I resigned from the course: I did not want to give the man that I held in such low esteem the pleasure of informing me that I had not made the grade. At the same time I applied for voluntary redundancy and started a correspondence course to gain my Commercial Pilot's Licence.

Returning to Portland having failed the fast-jet course on two separate occasions, I accepted the fact that I was not cut out to be a fighter pilot. Whilst I waited for the decision on whether I would be made redundant, I was posted to the training squadron to fly with student observers completing their operational flying training. A few months later I learned that I had not been selected for redundancy. I laughed. It was the ultimate rejection: I had even failed redundancy. Remarkably, even though I made it public knowledge that I was going to reapply for redundancy the following year, I was selected to train as a helicopter instructor. The competition for places on the course was fierce. Only the better pilots were selected to re-enter the system as trainers. Not only were you guaranteed numerous shore jobs but, in addition, being an instructor was regarded as a fairly prestigious position. I was flattered and surprised that I had been selected. I believed that this was an avenue I would enjoy and be reasonably competent at.

The training lasted four months and was thoroughly enjoyable. A tri-service course, working and socialising with helicopter pilots from the Air Force and Army was enlightening, rewarding and, if nothing else, a good excuse for a four month piss-up with fellow helicopter pilots. Flying the Gazelle again was also immensely enjoyable. At the end of the course as I was posted back to the training squadron at Portland to instruct on the Lynx.

During the summer leave period of 1993, shortly after rejoining the squadron as an instructor, I was invited to spend three weeks flying the Navy Chipmunks in central France. Each summer a series of activities are organised for the cadets at Dartmouth, the idea being to broaden their horizons whilst the College is closed for the summer leave period. These included such diverse activities as sailing to the Channel Islands on the Dartmouth-based yachts, canoeing in the Lake District, hang-gliding in Wales and, of course, the summer flying camp in France. The six aircraft would detach to central France, where the weather is guaranteed to be fine, accompanied by thirty, non aviation specialist cadets. Two of the 'old timer' permanent instructors would lead the camp, assisted by four instructors taken from the front-line squadrons. The cadets would fly with the instructors, giving them an insight into aviation and, provided they reached the required standard, a chance to fly solo. Although it

Flying the Chipmunks in France...

meant giving up my summer leave, I jumped at the opportunity to participate and spent three weeks in absolute heaven.

We camped on the airfield next to the aircraft. The routine was fairly intensive for the instructors: up early for a bite of breakfast before preparing the aircraft and briefing the students for flight; flying between 0800 and 1030, returning to the field to change students after the first hour; an early lunch before flying again between 1130 and 1400. By this time the temperature would be well into the thirties and sitting in the cockpit, dressed in flying overalls, the heat would start to become unbearable. On landing, the aircraft would be cleaned and refuelled for the following day's flight, all the work being completed by mid-afternoon. The entire party would then meander down to the local river and cool off, discussing the finer points of flapless circuits or practised forced landings.

Some of the cadets were extremely keen to be given the opportunity to fly solo. With these students I would spend the hour in the circuit watching them overcontrol and fight with the aircraft, mimicking my learning process a few years early. Others were not bothered about flying solo and just wanted to have some fun. In this case I would arrange to meet one of the other aircraft and we would spend the hour chasing each other around the sky or practising formation aerobatics. Flying four hours a day, every day, my own Chipmunk flying skills were becoming honed and I found a new confidence with the aeroplane. I particularly enjoyed the aerobatics and progressed from the basic manoeuvres that I had been taught through training to more advanced competition style manoeuvres. At the end of three weeks I had decided that I wanted to fly aerobatics competitively. On return to the UK, I sold my share in my beloved Jodel and over the following months looked for a share in a serious competitive aerobatic aircraft.

Returning from summer leave I discovered once again that I had not been selected for redundancy. This time it came as no surprise. The Navy had invested considerable amounts of money in putting me through the instructors' course and were not likely to let me go without some return on it. It was rather ironic that I had volunteered twice and yet was asked to stay, whilst people all around me were being told that they were being made redundant against their will. Officers who had committed themselves to the Service for the duration of their working careers, officers who did not possess the cynicism that I had developed, were told they were out of a job. Not surprisingly morale was low. As much as I was enjoying my new career as an instructor, I felt claustrophobic in the depressed atmosphere of discontent. I thought seriously about PVR-'ing[1]. The only drawback was that I was required to give eighteen months notice, and as the market for civilian pilots was already in decline there was no guarantee that I would find a flying job outside the Service.

As I pondered what to do, I found the aircraft I had been looking for; a two seat, open cockpit, aerobatic bi-plane called a Stolp Starduster Two. I convinced one of the pilots I had been on the summer camp with that we ought to buy it together, borrowed an obscene amount of money from the bank, and purchased my dream machine. Less than six

The Starduster on the ground...

weeks after we had acquired the aircraft, I took a friend of mine for a   *...and in the air...*
flight in my new toy.

The date was 3 October 1993. It was a Sunday and a glorious autumnal afternoon. I had flown the aircraft to the local flying club to refuel and on return to the strip met Hugh tinkering with his aircraft. Hugh and his brother Will owned the farm on which we kept the aircraft. Hugh was a very keen private pilot and during the years that I had used his strip, we had forged a friendship based on mutual respect. He too had owned a succession of different aircraft which he had rebuilt over the years and we often swapped rides in each other's aeroplanes. Hugh would spend hours at his farm, tinkering around with aeroplanes. His passion for aviation was deep-routed and in him I found a kindred spirit. When I met the brothers on the afternoon in question, following the usual good natured banter, we decided it was time that I took them for a flight. After a quick trip with Will, running through a few basic aerobatic manoeuvres, I returned to the airstrip and swapped passengers. Hugh jumped into the front cockpit, I started the 260hp engine and accelerated down the grass strip. Even with two people onboard and almost a full load of fuel she climbed quickly, the big engine pulling us easily into the air. At 500 feet I levelled the aircraft and turned downwind. What occurred over the next ten seconds happened very quickly and, although initially I had no memory of it, over the years I have pieced together the sequence of events in my own mind.

The aircraft flipped onto its back so suddenly that I did not realise that it had assumed an inverted attitude. My first indication that something was wrong was being aware that the nose of the aircraft had dropped. My instinctive reaction was to pull back on the stick to correct

...and back on the ground again. The end of a life and a naval career.

the problem. I stopped when I realised that the aircraft was in fact upside down. It should have been flying straight and level but it wasn't and I couldn't work out what was going on. I tried to process the data and match my mental confusion to the reality I was seeing. Now the aircraft was spinning towards the ground – this was something I recognised. I automatically went into the spin recovery drill: close the throttle, ascertain direction of spin, apply full opposite rudder and stick fully forward. I looked out of the front of the cockpit to check if the spinning had ceased. At that moment I realised that the aircraft was far too low to execute a safe recovery, the ground was rushing towards us so very quickly. Strangely enough I was not scared: certain death was inevitable and there was nothing I could do to change it. With our fate sealed there was no panic, no fear, almost a sense of relief. If you are going to die young, then as a pilot this is as good a way as any, the way of dying that every aviator secretly dreams of. I have no recollection of the actual impact.

I think that I may remember lying on a table with people fussing around me, maybe I was being X-rayed, I'm not really sure, but the next positive memory I have is lying on the ward in the middle of the night looking at the pipes feeding into the backs of my hands and wondering what had happened. My injuries were such that I was immobile in bed, I could not focus properly and I recognised nothing. I wanted to yell out but my mouth did not work. The feeling of confusion was total. Gradually, over the next few days, as my strength built, I began to recognise people. I remember looking at my parents by the bedside and feeling relieved that I wasn't alone. Slowly things became clearer. I was aware that I was badly injured but I had no idea where I was or what had happened. As always, Jill was there to support me. It was probably three or four days after the accident that I had my first coherent conversation. What had happened? Why didn't my legs and arms work? Where was I? She explained about the accident.

"Was I alone?" Surely I must have been. Jill could not have been flying with me, she looked as beautiful as ever.

"No, Hugh was in the aircraft with you." She replied with a degree of caution that even in my drugged state set the alarm bells ringing.

"Where is he, I need to speak to him?"

She did not need to reply, her look said it all. It is very hard to portray in the written word exactly how I felt at that moment. No adjective can describe the feeling of complete despair. High on pain-killers I probably could not have thought the situation through and rationalised it even if I had wanted to. The fact was that I had crashed an aeroplane and killed a friend. I was responsible for the death of another and that is very difficult to come to terms with. I was convinced that the accident was my fault. I assumed that I had stalled the aircraft as I climbed away from the runway, a fundamental error for which there is no defence. At that stage I believed that I would never pilot an aircraft again. I felt like a murderer.

These thoughts played on my mind night and day, a mental torment that I could not get rid of. My own injuries, although extensive, seemed irrelevant to me. It is a period of my life that I have contemplated time and time again and yet no amount of rhetoric can describe it. I do not ever want to go back there again.

One week after the accident I was interviewed by a member of the Aircraft Accident Investigation Branch (AAIB). I tried desperately to place all of the shattered pieces of memory back into some kind of cohesive order. The Inspector questioned me further.

"Is that all you remember?" he inquired, I lay back and closed my eyes, desperately seeking another glimmer of memory but my mind would not allow me, protecting me from my own worst nightmare. At the end of the interview he looked me in the eye and spoke gently.

" We think we have found a mechanical failure that would explain the accident."

The relief was unbelievable, followed a second later by immense guilt. No matter how the accident occurred, Hugh and I would never go flying together again. The mechanical failure which the Inspector spoke about was a nut and bolt assembly which held one of the top wings in place. It appeared that the nut had not been fitted properly allowing the bolt to slowly migrate forward until, on the day of the fateful flight, it vibrated out, allowing the wing to flap up, throwing the aircraft into a spin towards the ground. My feeling of despair at my own ineptitude turned into anger that an aircraft that had been passed fit to fly had been allowed to carry such a dangerous fault.

I was in and out of various hospitals for the next six months. Slowly the broken bones and torn skin mended. Remarkably, considering the seriousness of the accident, I had sustained very few permanent injuries.

I broke my ankle, dislocated my knee, broke my back at the base of the spine, broke both wrists, splintered my left elbow and had my face partly ripped off and sewn back on. A left eye that refuses to work properly is the only injury which really troubles me now: the human body is remarkable indeed. I recall the first time that I was allowed out of bed. As I hobbled towards the toilet clutching my sticks, I looked through an archway into the next ward and saw a man with a head the size of a pumpkin and a face covered in lacerations hobbling in the same direction as me. I had one of those, 'there's always someone worse off than you' feelings that the brain interjects every now and again to make you feel better. It was not until the hobble back to my bed, when I saw the same chap again, walking in the opposite direction, that I realised I was looking into a large mirror. For a second I was shocked, then I started to laugh to myself. I looked a right ugly bastard.

Immediately after the accident I was convinced that I would never fly again. As the news that the crash had been caused by a mechanical failure and not pilot error was confirmed, it began to change my outlook. This was mainly due to the help and support of both my family and Hugh's, who offered endless encouragement. The desire to fly again was beginning to return, and being a helicopter pilot by profession, I assumed it best to take my first confidence building flight in a helicopter. It didn't work. The pilot, my friend with whom I had bought the Starduster, believed that the best way to restore my faith in flying was to put the Gazelle through its paces. After a mildly mistimed wingover which led to a frantic last minute pull-out I relived the ground rush that I was beginning to remember so vividly. I felt very frightened, and wondered whether I would be scared of flying for the rest of my life. Rather ironically, just as I was beginning to overcome my fears and was convincing myself that perhaps I did want to continue flying as a career, the doctor broke the news that the damage to my eye was extensive. It meant that the decision as to whether I should remain in the Navy was likely to be made for me not by me.

I returned to naval duties in March 1994, some six months after the accident. Obviously I could not fly and so I became a simulator instructor. The Navy had not yet informed me that I was going to be discharged, but it did not take a genius to work out that the end of my naval career was imminent; my Medical Review Board was scheduled for December.

The value of true friendship became apparent during this period of my convalescence. It also partly illustrated why I was disillusioned with the service environment. Some people masquerading as true and loyal Navy friends turned out to be just work colleagues who soon distanced themselves from me. Others offered help above and beyond that which could be expected from the closest of friends. Whilst I tried to maintain my jovial attitude, it was not an easy period in my life. I was in a dilemma: I loved aviation but was uncertain about going flying. Even if I could overcome my anxieties there was no guarantee that with my damaged eye I would ever be allowed to pilot an aircraft again. At home, I was a bear with a permanently sore head, and became unbearable to live with.

After a particularly vociferous argument with Jill, I left the house. I needed to get away and think things through, to reflect and take stock of my life. In April, during Easter leave, on a whim, I took a flight to Zimbabwe and made the pilgrimage that I had wanted to do for some time. On my return three weeks later I discovered to my horror that Jill had reached breaking point. She had moved all of my belongings out and no longer wanted to be involved with me. My life had reached a new low that I had never even realised existed.

It did take time, but I began to pick up the proverbial pieces. After a month trying to come to terms with a life without Jill, and trying to win her back, I returned to Africa and spent the next five months working on a large game park in Zimbabwe. It was a wonderful way of putting things back into perspective and forced me to approach life in a more pragmatic manner. By late in the year I realised that I still wanted to pursue a career as a pilot, if at all possible, and so returned to the UK. It was now almost a year after the accident and although I was still officially in the Navy I had done less than a month's work for them in that time. I obtained a referral to Moorfields Eye Hospital hoping that the military doctors' prognosis, that the vision in my eye would slowly deteriorate until I was completely blind, was incorrect. Against my wildest expectations the civilian doctors believed that the damage to the eye was in fact repairable, if only in part. The vision would never be perfect, but they believed that it could be improved. However in December I was medically discharged as predicted: there was no call for one-eyed pilots in the Navy. The good news was that the Civil Aviation Authority allowed me to fly again as a private pilot. With time on my hands I used my last Navy pay-cheque to complete my twin-engine rating, something I had always longed to do, and the security of two engines seemed to put my mind at ease. It was just over a year after the accident and I had convinced myself that I was overcoming my fears. I enjoyed the course and after the stipulated seven flying hours, held my new twin engine rating in my hand. However I still managed to find a number of excuses for not flying on my own. With hindsight I realise that I was still scared of flying, but was not admitting it to myself.

The doctors started work on my eye and for the next year I was in and out of hospital again on a fairly regular basis. During this time I remained unemployed. Determined that I would return to aviation as a professional pilot, I was reluctant to do anything else; the hospital appointments made it almost impossible anyway. Strangely enough I enjoyed the year more than I could ever have imagined and I met people outside my Navy circle of friends which was extremely healthy. Although I was not earning an income and was living on social security pay-outs, having the time to enjoy life without the pressure of work commitments, was for me very beneficial. Not long after my return from Africa I had learned that my ex-girlfriend Jill and (consequently ex-friend) Rob were living together as a couple. How long this had been going on for I neither knew nor wanted to know, but I would be lying if I did not admit that I felt upset and betrayed. They were married a year later. On the day that they were mar-

Back into the air again. My beautiful Chipmunk.

ried I threw myself out of an aeroplane at 13,500 feet having taken up sky-diving as my new hobby.

In the end it was my pride which unexpectedly forced me into overcoming my fear of flying. It was not long after completing my twin engine rating a phone call from a naval friend set me thinking. "Dickie there's a share available in the Chipmunk syndicate. Are you interested?" I had previously expressed an interest in buying into this civilian owned Chipmunk, but that had been before the accident. Not wanting to lose face I decided to go and look at the aircraft.

She was beautiful, sitting on the grass strip, just begging me to fly her. I strapped into the front whilst one of the owners, an experienced airline pilot, completed the walkround. I took off; with another pilot in the back, I felt relaxed and at ease on the controls. It was like returning home and rekindled memories of the pre-accident summer in France. I had to have a share in this aircraft even though a part of me was still horrified at the prospect of flying it solo. With no job I could not justify spending the money, but it did not matter. I invested my remaining savings in it.

A month later, having been put through my paces to ensure that I was fit to fly it on my own, I drove to the strip. This was going to be my first solo flight post-accident. It was a beautiful day, a few puffy cumuli dancing slowly around the piercing blue sky and less than five knots breezing gently across the strip. I was scared. I gazed at the windsock, wishing it would tell me that the crosswind was out of limits so that I wouldn't have to go flying. But it was a perfect flying day and my pride told me that I had to go.

I agonised over the walkround, checking every last rivet and then sat in the aircraft. My hands were sweating through my leather flying gloves, I could hear the sound of my deep, anxious breathing on the intercom. I began to taxi the aircraft out, but panic set in. I was overcome by an all-consuming desire to run from the cockpit. The solitude hit me like a punch in the face. I felt so alone. I felt as though I could not be trusted.

I sat in the cockpit with the engine running for a few minutes, battling with my emotions. I know that I've got to do this, I repeatedly told myself. I could have taxied back and taken some more instruction but I knew that I was capable of flying the aircraft solo. I realised that if I went back now I would possibly never fly solo again: I couldn't back down. In the knowledge that this was something I had to do, I opened the throttle and started to roll down the strip. As the tail came up I could see a group of friends standing next to the hangar. Oh how I wished I was standing there and not sitting here. And then I was airborne. I kept the wings level and climbed straight ahead. I felt that if I touched the controls the aircraft would topple onto its back and spin into the ground. I was on a mental knife edge. At 1,000 feet and still climbing straight ahead, it suddenly occurred to me how ridiculous this was. I looked over my right shoulder and started the turn. The aircraft didn't roll over onto its back, just a gentle turn to the right as it had always done. I had done it, I was flying on my own again.

For the next flight I took off with all the confidence that a man with 1,600 hours should have and just revelled in the pleasure of being in the air: the sheer joy of looking down at the green fields from the top of a lazy barrel roll; the pleasure of holding the aircraft in the perfect vertical just before the pedal goes in for the stall turn; the excitement of looking back for the horizon as you enter the loop. Flying is in my blood, all those that suffer from the same complaint will know what I mean. It drives us to spend all our money on flying, it causes us to look to the sky every time we hear an aircraft go over, it makes us stop by the side of the road and look if we happen to pass a grass strip. I had regained the desire to fly but with no associated fear and that made me extremely happy. I took up sky-diving just for a laugh.

All stories must have a happy ending. The repair work on my eye continued until eventually I was allowed to return to aviation on a professional basis, this time as an airline pilot. Sitting on the flight deck of a modern airliner at 39,000 feet is a very different form of aviation from flying a helicopter at 50 feet over the sea at night but I continue to indulge in my true passion of flying light aircraft and I now own a share in an Auster.

So what of the Gulf War? Not surprisingly, because my life had changed so much, I very rarely thought about my time spent in the Navy and in particular the period covering the Gulf War. Perhaps my diaries would still be lost in the bottom of my wardrobe but for that chance encounter on the way back from an eye hospital. As I stood up and started to gather my belongings from the overhead storage rack I heard my name being bellowed across the railway carriage. I looked around, my eyes scanning the crowded compartment.

"Dickie Boswell," the voice bellowed again. "It *is* you. Last time I saw you, we were having a dogfight at 12,000 feet over Kuwait."

Then I recognised David, HMS *Gloucester's* pilot during the Gulf War, and for a second I was back in the Navy, back in the cockpit of a Lynx helicopter, back in the skies over Kuwait where all of my senses were finely honed and life was a big adventure, back to the bizarre environment where I cared not about anything that was outside my immediate vicinity. The sound of his voice took me back in a way that sitting down and writing this book never quite did. I had never really known David particularly well except that we were both Lynx helicopter pilots involved in the sinking of most of the Iraqi Navy during the Gulf War. The last time we had met had indeed been over Kuwait City shortly after the cessation of hostilities. We were engaged in a mock dogfight, something that we had done on numerous previous occasions. Being the more experienced pilot he had always managed to get the better of me but on this occasion I had used every trick in the book and successfully brought my guns to bear on the tail of his aircraft. Had he been the enemy I would have scored my first air to air kill. I remembered the moment well, the final confirmation of my coming of age as a combat helicopter pilot.

"You do remember that, don't you Dickie?"

For a moment I stood speechless, lost in my memories, experiencing again the feeling of camaraderie, the feeling of being alive, the feeling of bizarre contentment at having survived a war. It was perhaps the first and only time that I had missed the Navy, missed the bar-room banter, missed the thrill of flying one of the most capable helicopters in the world. In that split second I realised for the first time that the Gulf War and my involvement in it was important to me.

"Of course I do. I kicked your arse."

Index